Ghosts across Kentucky

D0710224

Ghosts across Kentucky

William Lynwood Montell

THE UNIVERSITY PRESS OF KENTUCKY

Publication of this volume was made possible in part by a grant
from the National Endowment for the Humanities.

Copyright © 2000 by The University Press of Kentucky

Scholarly publisher for the Commonwealth,
serving Bellarmine University, Berea College, Centre College of Kentucky,
Eastern Kentucky University, The Filson Historical Society, Georgetown College,
Kentucky Historical Society, Kentucky State University, Morehead State University,
Murray State University, Northern Kentucky University, Transylvania University,
University of Kentucky, University of Louisville, and Western Kentucky University.
All rights reserved.

Editorial and Sales Offices: The University Press of Kentucky
663 South Limestone Street, Lexington, Kentucky 40508-4008
www.kentuckypress.com

11 10 09   9 8 7 6

Library of Congress Cataloging-in-Publication Data

Montell, William Lynwood, 1931–
    Ghosts across Kentucky / William Lynwood Montell.
        p. cm.
    ISBN-10: 0-8131-9007-X (pbk. : alk. paper)
        1. Ghosts—Kentucky. I. Title.

    BF1472.U6 M66 2000
    133.1'09769—dc21   00-032058
    ISBN-13: 978-0-8131-9007-5

This book is printed on acid-free recycled paper meeting the requirements of the
American National Standard for Permanence of Paper for Printed Library Materials.
∞ ✹

Manufactured in the United States of America

Member of the Association of
American University Presses

Dedicated to all my family members
who told me ghost and ancestral stories as a child;
to my wife, Linda; to my daughter Monisa;
my son Brad; and five grandsons,
all of whom know the old family stories.

Contents

Illustrations

Acknowledgments

I began gathering the stories contained in this book during the early months of 1998 and continued on a regular basis through August 1999. The compilation of this collection of folk narratives about ghosts was greatly aided by the assistance of numerous persons. Were it not for friends, students, and other individuals who collected or wrote newspaper articles about these supernatural accounts across the years, this book would not have been possible. Thus my debt is heavy to many contributors, some of whom will be identified in the following paragraphs. All others are recognized as storytellers or collectors of these accounts in the notes to each of the stories contained on the final pages of this very special book.

First of all, thanks to Roberta Simpson Brown, Judy Bryson, Berry Craig and Norman Goldstein of the Associated Press, Mary Ann Gentry, Frankie Hager, Stan W. Lemaster, Sara McNulty, Charles Mitchell, and Margaret Owens for granting permission to publish ghost accounts from some of their previous books or articles, all of which are identified in the notes.

Newspapers from which some of the stories were gleaned include the *College Heights Herald* (Western Kentucky University), *Columbia Daily Statesman, Green River Sprite, Knox Countian, Lebanon Enterprise, Lexington Herald-Leader, Louisville Evening Post, Madisonville Messenger, Murray State News, Nelson County Record, Owensboro Messenger-Inquirer, Ohio County News, Paducah Sun, Richmond Register,* and *Kentucky Standard.* Thanks also to Max Heath, director of Landmark Enterprises, who supplied me with numerous names of newspapers and editors, as well as telephone numbers.

Libraries and archives whose staff archivists proved so very helpful include the Southern Appalachian Archives, Hutchins Library, Berea College; Mt. Saint Joseph Archives, Maple Mount; Ohio County High School Library; Pogue Library, Murray State University; Special Collections and Archives, Margaret I. King Library North, University of Kentucky; Department of Library and Special Collections, Folklife Archive, Western Kentucky University.

Finally, my heartfelt thanks go out to student collectors at Western Kentucky University from 1969 to 1999, who acquired these supernatural accounts from peers, parents, grandparents, and older neighbors; also to Linda Anderson, Sister Emma C. Busam, Shirley Caudill, Elbert Cundiff, Dr. Ron Dobler, Dr. Terry Hall, Kay Harbison, Dixie Hibbs, Patricia Hodges, Dr. Loyal Jones, Becky Leavy, Mabel Martin, Dr. Robert Rennick, Sue Lynn Stone, James H. Young, and to certain teachers and students in Albany, Burkesville, Campbellsville, Franklin, Madisonville, and Wallins Creek. Without the contributions of stories from these persons and others listed in the previous paragraphs and in the notes to each of the stories, this book would not have been possible.

Thanks to all of you.

Introduction

Across the centuries, people have passed along from one generation to the next their cherished heirlooms, such as beliefs, traditions, and historically significant family and community stories. Sitting around fires or under a shade tree at night, older men and women told stories to entertain, also to explain the unexplainable. Children have always looked to parents, and especially grandparents, for insights into the mysteries of the world about them. Adults told stories about the things they had witnessed or experienced. They often embellished them with their own interpretation of the events described, perhaps even simply to make a good story better.

Kentucky was settled by people with a myriad of social and cultural backgrounds. They were mostly Americans by birth, but of various nationalities and races, being chiefly of English, Scottish, Irish, Scots-Irish, French, German, and African descent. Many of these early ancestors, who moved across the mountains onto the western frontier, preferred the soon-to-be comforts of towns and villages, while others became primarily backwoods people by choice. They fondly accepted the wild freedom of the frontier rural landscape. "A lonely house in the middle of a great farm was their ideal, and they attained it even before it could be done with safety," according to geologist Nathan S. Shaler.[1] All of these groups brought with them the folk heritage of their social and cultural class, as well as fond memories of their places of geographical origin. Folk beliefs and narratives of all varieties, told and retold in any given area, reflect the ethnic makeup of the people who live there. Thus it is that the wealth of the stories and beliefs brought to an area by immigrants are translated, and sometimes modified, as they are passed along from generation to generation.

All across the state, Kentuckians have produced a great body of supernatural beliefs, stories, and historical legends. From pioneer times down to the present, Kentucky has always been rich in ghost legends or personal accounts of ghostly visitations. Traditional stories that tell of ghostly sightings and felt presences of spirits and other supernatural creatures still persist as a vestige of the past, as they help to describe life and times of a bygone era.

Ghost stories often provide Kentuckians at home or elsewhere with meaningful historical ties with their ancestors and with the old family home place. Through family and community beliefs and stories, people are introduced to the names and actions of dead family members whom they never knew personally. Thus, they become acquainted with the ancestral dead as well as the living. At least that's the way it was in times past. Such stories, even those with ghostly themes and elements, are bonding agents. They provide meaningful continuity between past and present generations.

Although numerous present-day Kentuckians live in urban areas, most of them have rural roots. Before and during the Great Depression years of the late 1920s and 1930s, more than one-half of the state's inhabitants lived on farms, in coal mining settlements, in logging and sawmilling camps, or at river landings. An additional 20 percent lived in the county seat towns. Back then, these small population centers were nothing more than agglomerated extensions of the rural culture that surrounded them. Traditional ties with the land were thus keenly felt and tenaciously embraced by people of all ages.

Up through the 1930s, it was common practice for farming and mining families to go to town on Saturdays to sell or barter farm produce and handcrafted items and to purchase staples and groceries. People also participated in special calendrical events and attended movies at the local theater, typically at a price of ten to fifteen cents per person.

Much of the folklore of that pre–World War II era stemmed from pioneer days of the eighteenth and nineteenth centuries when times were not so fast. It was common for people down through the 1930s—community residents and extended family members alike—to come together at the drop of a hat to break the monotony created by isolation and the lack of adequate transportation. With automobiles in short supply, electricity as a still unknown luxury, and very few battery-powered radios scattered throughout the community, people gathered in the evening around the fireplace or on the porch at home or at a neighbor's house to make music and to share beliefs and stories.

Back then, it was common practice for a particular member of the family to assume the role as storyteller and tell "those old scary tales" until the youngsters were often afraid to go to bed at night. In 1976, a resident of Urbana, Illinois, who had grown up in a logging camp in Henderson County, Kentucky, shared the following description of family ghost-telling sessions:

People such as this Cumberland County couple often participated in storytelling sessions, even after television came into vogue. (Photograph by David Sutherland, 1972)

We lived in this little shack-like house there on the Ohio River when I was a little fellow. It had cracks between the planks in the floor. When my dad would tell them old scary stories of a night, I would sit there, just scared to death. Every now and then, I would look down at the floor, afraid that something would reach up through one of them cracks in the floor and grab me by the leg!

Well, after he had told so many of them old tales, we'd all be scared to death. So me and my brothers would hop up out of our chairs and head for the bed. We'd jump into bed, pull the quilts over our heads and stay there that way 'til the next morning. I mean, we was too afraid to get out of bed![2]

Before the days of World War II, belief in ghostly visitations was prevalent throughout much of Kentucky. Powell countian Herbert G. Profitt, member of President Roosevelt's Federal Writers Project (FWP) during the Great Depression years, made the following comments about ghosts back in the 1930s:

Ghosts and haints are believed in and feared by many people. Cemeteries, deserted houses, and places of accidental death are favorite rendezvous for these weird and eerie creatures. Ghosts are never seen in daylight, but in passing a cemetery or other similar place at night, you may find yourself confronted by a headless body, or bodiless head. One may hear strange, ghastly, unearthly, hair-raising sounds that let you know that ghosts are around.

It may easily be supposed that these notions are the survival of ancient beliefs that say the spirits of the dead continue to hover around the mortal body [of the deceased.][3]

Another member of the FWP, John I. Sturgill of Floyd County, offered the following commentary:

Spirits and ghosts walk at night. There is danger in the dark. The night has a thousand eyes, the day but one. Instinct causes people to be afraid at night. Ghosts are seen when there really isn't anything. Many people argue that "seeing is believing," and they will not depart from that belief. . . .

The night is unlucky. All honest folk should be in bed at night. Robbers make their break from 1:00 to 1:30 a.m., and ghosts begin walking just at midnight. Human life is at its lowest ebb from 3:00 a.m. to 6:00 a.m. More deaths occur then; more babies are born then than at any other time, and ghosts remain until dawn drives them away.[4]

Still another essay written by a member of the FWP in the 1930s, this one by R.L. Nesbitt of Casey County, stated that people in that county were once staunch believers in the reality of ghosts. In Nesbitt's words:

In the past, almost every community had one or more haunted or hainted houses, which were either avoided altogether [by people] or approached, if at all, with fear and trembling. . . .

More often than not, these so-called haunted houses had been the scene of some well known tragedy, or at least some sudden or mysterious death of some former occupant. The spirits of people who had been murdered or grossly mistreated during this life were believed either to abide permanently in their former earthly homes, or to return to them at intervals to wreak vengeance on their former prosecutors, if not indeed upon the entire human race. . . .

So firmly was the belief in ghosts or "haints" fixed in the minds of both white and black [people] that vivid imaginations often brought people to believe, or at least aver that they actually had seen some apparition or ghostly figure. . . .[5]

During and after the 1940s, technology became such a factor in people's lives that the old ways were rejected, especially by the newer, postwar generation. The change brought by technology is apparent everywhere today, more than fifty years later. But although technological advances, accompanied by a relative prosperity, did cover the Commonwealth after World War II, it is still possible to find people who cling to beliefs in omens of death and tell about visitations by supernatural beings. It is not at all uncommon to hear traditional stories claiming that the ancestral dead return to visit the places to which they were emotionally tied during their sojourn here on earth. And some contemporary Kentuckians have their own personal accounts of the return of parents, spouses, and children as ghost or spirit entities. That's what this present work is all about.

As stated in *Ghosts along the Cumberland*, "The overwhelming popularity of stories then and now about the return of the dead as ghosts continues to stagger the imagination. Two reasons for their popularity are as follows. First, most tellers and listeners continue to believe in the contents of the narratives, and many of them are told as a personal experience. Even today, numerous adults, teenagers, and children alike, willingly and thankfully share their preternatural experiences with friends and family members who will listen to their accounts in counselor-like fashion. Persons who experience spirit-like visitations will not share these events with those who look with scorn at such claims. Secondly, ghost stories serve as an unconscious form of generational bonding. The most natural setting for a story recounting a supernatural situation was the home, especially the home of grandparents who seemed to derive a great degree of satisfaction from telling the old family legends to their grandchildren. Such stories are always told for the truth."[6]

Today, some parents intentionally tell family stories to their children so that the latter will be introduced to and know the names of certain progenitors whom they never knew. And since numerous persons claim to have had spirit visitations from a deceased grandparent, parent, spouse, or child, accounts of these visits are often repeated to family members as a means of informing them about a dead family member.[7]

People's beliefs and stories about death and dying, whether religious or traditional, tell a lot about who these narrators are, where they came from, how they deal with religious beliefs, and cope with the unknowns in their lives. These stories are not merely fictions that people dreamed up. Instead, they are accounts based on experience, trust, and tradition.[8]

The question as to what ghosts are needs to be addressed at this time. Without arguing for or against the reality of ghosts, I shall attempt to address the question, "What are so-called ghosts?"

A ghost is a disembodied spirit, generally assumed to be that of a person now deceased. Thus it is that numerous people approach the supernatural realm fully confident that ghosts do indeed exist in the present. People feel that ghosts or apparitions are truly human-like beings that are seen, felt, or heard by the beholder(s). A ghost is thus a kind of duplicate, spectral or otherwise, of a deceased human being.

Some presumed authorities define ghosts/apparitions as telepathic hallucinations that are commonly experienced in the mind of the beholder. Whatever is seen or heard by these people is not really there; it is merely a figment of the imagination. Such ghostly entities are thus created in the minds of individuals outside the range of normal consciousness.

Suffice it to say, many people do believe in ghosts. Numerous stories in *Ghosts along the Cumberland* were told as personal experiences of encounters with the supernatural. In the entire book, only three persons who told ghost legends actually denied belief in the creatures they described. All other stories in the book were told by persons who either believed in supernatural creatures and manifestations or told them as factual family episodes experienced by the person or persons described in the account.

Any incongruity between total belief and hesitant belief was explained away by the folk rationale verbalized by a Monroe County female informant in 1961: "Lordee, honey, things just ain't the same now as they were back in those days. Even if we don't see things today, I believe they did see them in olden times."[9] That same person went on to describe four or five encounters with supernatural creatures that she had personally experienced in her younger years.

Ghost stories are typically told by individuals who firmly believe they encountered, through sound, sight, or feeling, the disembodied spirit of a deceased person or animal, which, by some means unknown to them, has materialized or manifested itself. The deceased person may be a friend, family member, or distant relative, thus making it hard to question the validity of such stories when they are told about someone who is loved and respected.

All persons should adopt an open mind and foster an understanding, tolerant attitude toward those individuals who believe they have personally encountered a ghost or other unexplained phenomenon. There are many mysteries and occurrences that cannot be explained away by scientific means, even in today's advanced world of technology. Today, people are less willing to admit belief in paranormal or supernatural phenomena, regardless of who the storyteller is, due to fear of being judged or intimidated by disbelievers.

While some ghosts in movies and on television these days are sinister and frightening, most are not. Nonetheless, the evil stereotype persists. It is apparently felt by some people that ghosts ought to be frightening. This feeling may indicate a deep-seated uneasiness about anything that stands between the living and the unknown realm of the dead.

Ghosts, as described in most narrative accounts, are generally not hostile and actually appear to be indifferent to the living. Some are even timid and rather easily deterred. Most ghosts do their thing in a very unpretentious manner and appear to be little desirous of being seen. They have a role to perform. If it can be accomplished without contact with living beings, ghosts are quite content to go on alone.

The present work, *Ghosts across Kentucky*, is a book aimed at the general reader who is interested in stories that depict the past as well as the present. Altogether, this volume displays a splendid example of the love that Kentuckians across the years have exhibited for oral traditional stories, whether historical in nature, scary, or simply humorous.

The ancient and recent past aside, many of the accounts of the supernatural in this collection represent folk conversations or monologues about personal experiences with apparitions, portents, or other unexplainable occurrences. Such conversations are stamped with the personality of the speaker. Their authentic tone is striking.[10]

Some but not many of the stories in *Ghosts across Kentucky* were intended to scare, entertain, or frighten listeners, or to hold them in suspense. However, most of these narratives were told or written by individuals who firmly believed that they, their parents, or friends encountered through sound, sight, or feeling, the disembodied spirit of a deceased person or animal for reasons unknown to them. It is difficult to question the validity of these stories when they are told by someone who is known, loved, and respected by family and community members.

While some of the stories herein are based on hard, cruel circumstances under which someone died or was killed, such as slavery times or bad working conditions, Kentucky ghosts as a whole do not come back to seek vengeance. Most of them return to visit the old home place occupied by them at the time of their death. Others wish to see, warn, console, save, or instruct living friends and relatives; to remain at the site where they died; to engage in normal pursuits; or to re-enact their own deaths. Finally, there are numerous ghost stories that tell of the restless or unsatisfied dead. Such ghosts often exhibit a mutilated form, likely representing the dissatisfied souls that were forced to lead a painful existence in the land of the dead with some part of the body missing. This latter category includes numerous accounts of headless ghosts or ghosts with some other part of the body missing.

Unlike universal folk narratives such as myths and fairy tales, most of which are set in an indefinite time frame and geographical location, orally communicated ghost tales and other supernatural narratives are geared to a precise time or place, generally both. Too, they are filled with historical data leading up to the appearance of the ghostly being. Ghost stories typically describe the building, vehicle, or spot on the landscape where the ghostly visitation occurs; call real names of people who were involved in the ghostly visitation; describe economic, social, and playtime activities that were in vogue at the time the ghost appeared. It is not uncommon for such stories to provide social, cultural, and economic information about ancestors and ancestral times, as well as contemporary times—information that never gets recorded on the formal pages of history or public records.

Just when and where do ghosts appear? Are they recognizable by the living who see them, or does their other appearance, such as lights and noises, mystify their identity? Are they female or male? Old or young? What physical spots on the landscape are associated with their visitation? In what portions of the house are they most likely to be seen, felt, or heard?

An inventory of the ghost stories contained in this book reveals that only one of twelve ghosts are seen or heard during daylight hours. All others are evidence to the claim that ghosts return only at night or in situations in which darkness dominates. The weather, stormy or clear, is not a major factor in accounting for ghostly appearances. While rain occurs in a dozen stories, only two or three accounts state that it was dark and dreary, windy, warm and humid, foggy, or that it was lightning and thundering. Three of the accounts took place during moonlit nights.

Heading the list as to where the hauntings occurred are, in order of frequency, houses, cemeteries, roadways, mountains, hills, bridges, wooded areas, trees, creeks, fields, tunnels, front yards, and back yards. The first five tend to dominate the scenes where ghostly manifestations are seen or heard. Regardless of the location, approximately one-half of all ghosts that are seen make their periodic appearance just long enough to be viewed by living persons, then disappear without making an effort to communicate with those who see them. Their sudden departure thus leaves it up to the person(s) who saw them to figure out why they came back.

The gender of ghosts is fairly evenly divided, although women, whether young or old or of unspecified age, win the race in this regard. While twenty-three of the female ghosts were not identified as to age, forty-two were categorized as young, and only ten were described as "old" or "older."

Female ghosts are typically misty-like figures that are usually dressed in white gowns or robes, and sometimes regular dresses. One story contains the description of an Indian woman's ghost wearing a black dress. Not more than a half-dozen stories make mention of the clothing worn by male ghosts. One of them is about a man wearing farming clothes.

Twenty-eight of the male ghosts were unidentified as to age, while twenty of them were placed in the "older" category, and fifteen were said to be young males. In six instances, gender and age were not specified. I found it quite interesting that the ghost of a mother holding her baby was reported in one story, and a father and baby were featured in yet another account. Tiny babies were the ghosts in two other stories as well.

Animal ghosts are included herein as a separate category. While few in number, these include dogs, horses, birds, cats/kittens, rabbits, sheep, hogs, and foxes. Living animals that saw or witnessed ghostly occurrences and acted in a frightened manner include horses, dogs, and cats. Numerous ghost narratives passed along from one generation to the next, from medieval times to the present, claim that these three animals are especially sensitive to the presence of supernatural manifestations.

While most ghosts are reportedly the identifiable spirits of dead female and male entities, many stories tell of the return of the dead as ghostly lights and sounds. These lights are primarily flashing lights, lights going off and on, ghostly balls of fire, and lights seen in or through windows.

Of all the sounds associated with ghosts, the most common are those that feature screaming/yelling/crying, moaning and groaning, ghostly footsteps, shaking/quivering houses, windows and doors that open and close of their own accord, rattling chains, and heavy breathing.

Some of the stories included in this book were and still are told only for amusement. Like Americans everywhere, especially those in the South, Kentuckians like and appreciate "those old scary tales" with a funny or "gotcha!" ending. However, for the most part, such "boo" stories are told by and for peers.

The "true" stories that describe what "actually happened" are stories told and retold across the years by family and community members. In the words of Alabama native, Ray B. Browne, "Such tales of actual happenings are retold numerous times, and listened to with rapt attention, even though at times they are far from exciting or amusing."[11]

The stories in this volume were collected in various ways, primarily by students, professors, local historians, and journalists. Some of the stories were tape-recorded and translated verbatim. Others were jotted down on notepads by the interviewer(s) as they sat and listened to the narrators tell stories. These accounts, whether tape-recorded or recorded with paper and pen, were typically submitted to college professors, who subsequently deposited them in a local campus archive or library.

Regarding the assignment of titles to these ghost stories in preparing them for publication in this book, I typically used the original title provided by the person who recorded and submitted them, if that person affixed a title. Ordinarily, they did not. Likewise, storytellers themselves virtually never give titles to their stories. They simply introduce the story by commenting that they are about to tell the listener a tale that talks about or describes "a haint that was seen many times by my grandparents," or with other similar beginning statements. I am the one who typically provided titles for the stories in this book. They are designed to assist the reader in knowing a wee bit about the story's contents before reading it.

In conclusion, Kentuckians are fortunate indeed in having such a treasure trove of older supernatural narratives that typically describe life and times the way they were prior to the 1960s. This is what folklore is all about. Folklore is not the falsehood of history. Instead, it is that part of history that seldom gets recorded in formal records and history books. Oral tradition preserves these accounts.

Regrettably, these old folk stories are likely to die out when the present elder generations are gone from our midst. These accounts are not being passed along to the younger generations, as the latter are typically engrossed with television, video games, and the Internet, and thus feel that they do not have time to sit around and listen to family members tell stories that have survived across the years.

Whether the ghostly part of the story is true or false is not what is important. These narrative accounts often contain historical information about people's personalities, characteristics, and personal appearances, as well as descriptions of old houses, roadways, cemeteries, cropping practices, social occasions, and other topics that are generally not recorded in formal historical records. Family stories of all varieties need to be recorded now. Next year may be too late.

Notes

1. Shaler is quoted by Thomas Crittenden Cherry, *Kentucky: The Pioneer State of the West* (Boston: D.C. Heath, 1935), 31.

2. Curtis (first name unkown), Urbana, Illinois, telephone interview by the author, 1976.

3. Kentucky State Library, Frankfort.

4. John I. Sturgill, ibid.

5. R.L. Nesbitt, ibid.

6. William Lynwood Montell, *Ghosts along the Cumberland* (Knoxville: Univ. of Tennessee Press, 1975), 87.

7. William Lynwood Montell and Trudy R. Balcom, *Ghost and Witch Tales from the 1930s* (Nashville: Express Media, 1997), 3–4.

8. Lynwood Montell, gen. ed., *Mysterious Tales from the Barrens* (Glasgow: Jett Press, 1994), v.

9. Darlene Botts Carter, Rock Bridge, Monroe County, interview, 1961.

10. Jack and Olivia Solomon, *Ghosts and Goosebumps: Ghost Stories, Tall Tales, and Superstitions from Alabama* (University: Univ. of Alabama Press, 1981), 9.

11. Ray B. Browne, *A Night with the Hants and Other Alabama Folk Experiences* (Bowling Green, Ohio: Bowling Green Univ. Popular Press, 1976), xvii.

Chapter 1

Graveyard Ghosts

1. "A Little Girl's Spirit Is Put to Rest"

This friend of mine, Kay, grew up here in Bowling Green. After she got married, they continued to live here but moved out on the Old Morgantown Road after they had this little baby girl. The house that they moved into there on the Morgantown Road was an old three-story structure that was surrounded by a big lot. And, boy, you talk about a spooky place, that was it! I mean odd things took place there in this old house, such as doors slamming, lights flashing, and weird noises like the sounds made by spooks. Lots of times, things there in the house that were part of their personal belongings would turn up missing.

The old house that they lived in had an upstairs, and for some reason Kay's family always felt as if something strange lived up there. You know, something like a ghostly being. Well, one day their little girl was in school, and she drew a picture of the house that had her and her parents looking out three of the windows. She also sketched an old man looking out of one of the upstairs windows, and told her teacher that this old man lived there in the house with them. Apparently she had seen him in the house. Wow, what the little girl must have felt if she did see him, knowing that he wasn't supposed to be there.

The old house also had a basement. And one day, while cleaning the basement, Kay's husband found a door that had been bolted shut. He pulled on it and he tugged on it, but it would not open. He finally got a pry bar and forced the door open. And guess what? He found a skeleton in behind that old door. It scared the dickens out of him, as he figured that the bones were those of someone who had been murdered and hidden there in the basement behind this door.

One day while they were cleaning up the backside of the lot surrounding the house, Kay and her husband found an old family cemetery with a dozen or so gravestones that had been totally engulfed with tall weeds and bushes. You couldn't even see these old gravestones from the house. They were just in a patch of weeds and bushes. Kay and her husband and little girl began cleaning up around the stones. While mowing around the stones, they noticed that one of them had fallen over and was laying there flat on the ground. They picked the stone up and saw that it had a little girl's name on it, a little thing that had died when she was just six years old. Kay's husband sat the stone up and fixed it so that it would not fall over again. After he did this, all of the strange things that they had heard, felt, and seen in and around the old house stopped completely. It was as if whatever had been bothering them had been put to rest. They figured that it was the spirit of the little girl. The little girl was now at rest in her grave.

A lot of people around here have always said that if anything about a dead person's grave is bothered, that person's spirit will be seen or felt at or near the place where the body was buried.

Oh-h-h-h-h, that makes me shudder just to think that such a thing could happen and that I might be the person to witness the eerie things that will take place if it does.

2. "The Ghost of a Man in a Graveyard Holding a Baby"

Before my husband and I got married, we used to go together to church a lot. In the summer of 1972, before we got married that October, we were sitting at a Sunday night service at the Free Union Separate Baptist Church in Adair County. That was the family's church. The two of us were sitting together, toward the back of the church, on the left-hand side. That was the side nearest the church graveyard, but we didn't think a thing about the graveyard while we were sitting there.

The singing was still going on, and because it was summer, it was still fairly light outside. The light soon began to fade, but we could still see all the way to the back of the graveyard. I glanced out across the cemetery, then looked back toward the front of the church again, there where the preacher was located. Then in a few seconds I glanced outside again, but this time there was a man standing out there in the middle of the grave-

Cedar trees located in the middle of a field typically provide passers-by with notice that an old family graveyard is located here. Stories about many of these old burial grounds tell of the return of the dead as ghosts. (Photograph by the author)

yard. There was no way the preacher would have had time to walk out there in the middle of the old graveyard and be standing there in the midst of all them graves. But, anyway, there was this man standing out there. I could see him as I looked out the window.

He was an older-looking man, probably in his fifties, with white hair. He had on a navy blue suit. And he was standing there holding a baby across his shoulder. The baby was wrapped in a pink blanket. You know, the way you have to hold their heads and necks steady when they're tiny. Well, he was just standing there holding that baby and looking down at the ground. I didn't know who the man was, so I finally just looked away. And when I looked back, by golly he was gone. Just that fast! And he couldn't have had time to walk away, but he was gone.

It was beginning to scare me. Was it a ghost of some kind, I wondered? I never said anything about it to my husband-to-be. I didn't want him to think that I was nuts. A ghost! Heaven forbid!

I never forgot what I saw there in that old graveyard that night, but I never told a soul about it. However, about four years later a bunch of us were sitting around at my sister-in-law's house telling ghost stories. My husband piped up and said, "Well, I don't want you all to think that I'm crazy, but let me tell you about the ghost that I saw about four years ago over here at this church in Adair County. It was in an old cemetery there by this church."

And believe it or not, he goes on to tell about this man and baby, exactly the same thing that I had seen that night. He had seen the same thing that I had, but he didn't tell me because he didn't want me to think that he was nuts. That's exactly the way that I felt about not telling him.

He had gone a little farther with the story, however. See, he had counted the number of cemetery grave rows over and how many rows back the man was standing, and went out there to look the next week. The grave that was there was that of a fifty-four-year-old man, whose wife was still alive. And right next to this man's grave was the little grave of a stillborn baby girl who had the last name that he did.

It just might be that what we both saw was a ghost of the father holding his little baby daughter on his shoulder.

3. "The Pale Lady in the Graveyard"

This happened in the fall of 1986. Jon Hunt, who was my best friend, and I were riding around town here in Morgantown one night. And Rhowda Mitchell, Meike McPherson, and Rhowda's male cousin flagged us down. They wanted Jon and me to go with them to Mt. Vernon Cemetery and look for ghosts. It is said that they are seen and heard in abundance at this old cemetery. Anyway, Jon and I thought it would be a good chance to scare the girls and that guy to death, so we accepted their invitation to go with them.

Mt. Vernon Cemetery is out toward the Fifth District Elementary School. There is a sign on the side of the road going toward the Fifth District that tells exactly where the graveyard is. Anyway, the five of us drove out there in Rhowda's car, which was a Cadillac. As we approached the old graveyard, the lights of the car could only show us the tops of the trees surrounding the graveyard. See, the graveyard is on a slope going downhill, and there is a ridge at the top of the hill where the cars must stop. Because of this, a person can't use headlights on a car to see anything in this cemetery.

When we got there, we got out of the car and started walking toward the cemetery. It is told around through here that if a person goes to the center of Mt. Vernon Cemetery and touches the big oak tree there, they will see a spirit. Meike and I went into the graveyard first, followed by Rhowda and Jon. The other guy was so dad-blamed scared that he stayed in the car—afraid to get out and face the possibility of seeing or encountering a ghost. As Meike and I proceeded to walk forward into the old cemetery, the big oak tree started to come into sight. We were sort of scared ourselves, but didn't let on as we had planned the ordeal to scare the girls. Jon would slip away from the group and hide, waiting to scare the girls while I made up something scary to tell the girls so as to get them to run toward Jon. That way, he could yell, "Boo," at them and scare them to death as he reached out his arms to grab them.

Anyway, Meike and I got closer to the tree, and I could see Jon sneaking off around the corner of the graveyard to get ready for the scheme. As he was sneaking off, Meike and I were getting closer and closer to the big oak tree. A few minutes later, Rhowda got really scared and began running toward the car. She wanted to hide and get away from it all. While she ran for the car, Jon ran after her just to scare her all the more. During the chase, Jon tripped over a wire and was lying hurt on the ground.

While all this was happening to Jon and Rhowda, Meike and I kept getting closer to the tree. I thought this would be my best chance to scare her, so all of a sudden I stopped walking and started pointing in behind the big tree and saying things like "Oh, God, what's that?" or "Look out, it'll get you!"

All of a sudden, Meike started screaming. I thought that I had scared her too badly, and I told her that we should leave, but she wouldn't move. She kept looking behind the tree and screaming. I looked to see what she was screaming at and immediately saw that it was a real ghost. It was a white glowing misty-like figure of a person standing there. And, boy, that was all I needed to see! I grabbed Meike, picked her up, and made a beeline for the car. And while I was running to the car with her, I saw my friend Jon lying on the ground. Well, I put Meike down and helped him up. Then we all headed for the car, and as we got into the car, Meike kept screaming.

As we pulled out of the graveyard, Meike kept screaming and yelling, telling us that we had to go back to the graveyard. When we got at the Kwik Pick, a store there in Morgantown, we finally got her calmed down enough to tell us what she had seen. She told us that she had seen a pale lady dressed in a long-sleeved dress with a hooded robe, and the pale lady had her arms crossed like she was holding a baby.

After telling this to everyone at the store, hardly anyone believed her. In desperation, she came over to me and asked, "Didn't you see it?"

I told her that I had seen something but that I wasn't sure what it was.

The only explanation that I could give to her for what we had seen was that maybe it was the reflection of some sort of light on a tall tombstone.

Finally everybody calmed down and we all went home for the night. The next day, Jon and I went to the graveyard to look for any clues that might tell us what had happened the night before. As we approached the tree, my theory of light reflection was destroyed, as there were no tall tombstones at all. We told the rest of our group the news of our graveyard investigation, and we immediately agreed that it must have been a real ghost that Meike and I both saw.

We never went to the graveyard again as a group, but Jon and I did go back a few times. We never did see anything like I saw that night when me and Meike saw what appeared to be the Pale Lady.

4. "The Rose Lady in the Graveyard"

Monroe County does love its ghost stories. A place especially involved with such goings-on and things that go bump in the night is a place called Little Sulphur Creek. That's out on the river road, not far from Tompkinsville. I am still amused by all the stories my ancestors, who originated in that part of the county, told when I was a little boy. A lot of my people are buried over there.

One of the most romantic, yet peculiar, stories was about the Rose Lady and her little girl. That's one of the few accounted-for stories that's come down to family members across the years. Here's the way my people always told it.

A gentleman was plowing his field one day—a field I've walked across many a time—plowing his cornfield to be exact. Up above this cornfield on a hill is an old cemetery, one of the oldest in this county. One of the dated gravestones goes back well beyond the Civil War. Most all of the graves go back to the nineteenth century. In fact, the last burial there was in 1912. That was my great-great-grandmother Brown.

As the story goes, this gentleman was plowing his field of corn. He happened to look up toward the graveyard, when all of a sudden he saw a lady and a small girl standing there in the cemetery. They were standing by one of the old, old tomb rocks. The woman was quite beautiful, and the reason she was called the Rose Lady was that the dress she was wearing was the color of roses. And so was the little girl's dress. Their ghostly apparitions took the old gentleman by surprise. In fact, he was so surprised that he hesitated to plow his field anymore until he was able to calm himself down and investigate what he had seen standing there by the old gravestone.

Well, he was known as a level-headed man, so after he had paused for a few minutes he began plowing a bit closer to the Rose Lady and the little girl. He watched them as they seemed to sway to and fro as they walked away from the graves. They were either admiring the beautiful scenery or were perhaps looking at the graves of their departed loved ones.

Now the peculiar fact is this. That was in the 1910s when this all took place, but the lady was dressed definitely in a hooped skirt of the Civil War period. And so was the little girl, whose ghostly spirit was there with her, appropriately dressed in pantalettes and a short skirt, but it was a hooped skirt.

Well, the gentleman kept plowing closer. He drove his mules a little closer, then a little closer, and a little closer. Finally, he became frightened; the ghost-like figures appeared to be getting more real as he got closer to them. In fact, he was thinking about calling out to this lady to see if she would answer him. Instead, he mustered the courage to walk right up to the Rose Lady and her daughter. As he got closer, man did he ever feel stupid. He could see how wrong he had been by thinking that he was seeing a woman and her daughter. Truth of the matter is, instead of being a Rose Lady and her daughter, there was nothing but a rose bush entangled with another rose bush which had been gently swaying in the wind.

That particular story has lived on for more than fifty years. Yet some people there on Little Sulphur Creek claim that the rose bush has long since been dead, yet the Rose Lady can still be seen at certain times during the year.

This same cemetery that is so enhanced with family history sometimes invokes terror to anyone who walks by. It is said that they see ghostly specters hopping and scampering around. These are the ghosts of others that have been laid to rest there for more than seventy years.

5. "The Ghost of Della Barnes"

There is a cemetery in Paducah, over here in west Kentucky, that is haunted by Della Barnes. Tradition has it that Della was murdered in 1800, way back in pioneer times. The legend of Della Barnes claims that if a brave soul goes into the cemetery where Della was buried on Halloween night and looks at the statue over Della's grave, her blood will be running down the hand of the statue. Now, to me, that's scary. Supposedly, when Della was murdered, her murderer cut off her hand. That thus explains the bloody hand on the statue.

The legend goes on to say that if you look at the statue, and especially at the blood from the arm oozing down the body, you will be cursed. Kids around here go to the cemetery and play pranks on one another, trying to scare the daylight out of each other, but I don't know of any cases where the curse was actually put into effect.

I don't know why, but the statue has been stolen from Della Barnes' grave there in the old cemetery.

6. "The Misty-like Figure in the Graveyard"

I heard this story years ago from an old man who believed and told more scary stories than Carter had little liver pills. He was an old fellow from over here in Todd County, and boy could he ever tell those old tales.

The one that I still recall him telling was about this little country church and old graveyard that were located close to where he lived at the time. It seems that a couple of years earlier, there had been a revival at the church. Well, these two men who were mortal enemies had gotten into a terrible fight, and one of them stabbed the other in the stomach with a great big old long, very sharp knife. The man died and was buried there in the old cemetery by the church.

The fellow that told me this, Eugene Cox, said that one night he had been visiting a sick neighbor. To get home, he had to ride by the graveyard late at night. It was a very dark and dreary night. As Mr. Cox came near the church and cemetery, his horse started acting funny and bucking up, and couldn't be managed at all. Said there was no way to control it. I've always been told that horses could tell if a spirit or ghost was anywhere around. Mr. Cox said that he finally got the horse under control, stopped, and got off to try to figure out what was wrong.

Just about the time he got off of his horse, said he saw a pale object rising from the corner of the old graveyard where the murdered man had been buried. And would you believe it, the misty-like figure was headed toward him! He said that whatever it was looked like a sheet and that it flapped at him real fast. Said that his horse went berserk, plumb wild, until the ghost began floating away from them, down across the graveyard, then disappeared. His horse just stood there and watched as the ghost went away. Then the horse just eased out of there and walked slowly down the road on the way back to the barn.

7. "Ghostly Sounds and Lights in Bonanza"

The night Uncle Jarb Caudill died, some strange things began to happen up around Bonanza, here in Floyd County. Folks began hearing weird sounds coming from the graveyard, like moaning and groaning and yelling, stuff you've never heard before. Man, they said it was something awful. That graveyard lay on a hill just in behind Jarb's house. Aunt Lou used to swear by her good black stockings that the window panes rattled in her house every time that the strange ghostly sounds were heard. I guess the house heard them, too. Some of the menfolks would take rifles and go out looking for whatever was making such a racket. Well, one time when they heard the weird sounds it was dead dark. They grabbed their guns, and they picked up some lanterns to have light to walk by.

They first went to the graveyard, but whatever it was that made the sounds was gone. But there was big gaping holes in some of the graves. Then they heard the noise over on the other side of the mountain and set out to go get it. They ran and ran but could never catch up with the awful noise that they heard. It was first on one side of the mountain, then on the other, screaming in a loud, shrill voice. Some of the men claimed that they saw something that looked like a huge, white dog, but when they would get close to it, it would disappear. It was the general belief that it was Uncle Jarb's ghost that came back to haunt the community.

On the other hand, some people claimed that on dark nights you could see a white glow coming from the vicinity of the graveyard, and a couple of times dogs have been found dead in the hills. Some even claim that at times the ghost comes down to Uncle Jarb's old house, because strange lights have been seen in the windows. Several times, men have set out to hunt the creature that haunts the graveyard, but never have any luck in finding it, as it continues to evade them. Of late years, when people see the glow on the hill, they just ignore it or say it's the moon's reflection. I don't know what it was. I'm just telling what was told to me, but I do believe that they heard things and saw something every now and then.

8. "A Woman in White Standing by a Graveside"

There was this young fellow in the Morris Chapel Community here in Adair County. He was known as a "sot," or to say it another way, he was an alcoholic. He was also quite a ladies' man, riding horseback or muleback for several miles to attend all social gatherings, or calling on some beautiful girl. And he was known for his strength and courage as well.

One time on a moonlight light he rode his horse some distance, going through this graveyard. As he approached the graveyard, he saw a lady dressed in white standing at the head of a grave. She was also practically in the road or path that he was traveling on. For him to turn and go back would be cowardly, so with all his might he decided to go right past her. All of a sudden, his horse spied the woman standing there, and, boy, did it ever start bucking up and down. It took him a while to calm the horse down, but the fellow finally got through that old cemetery.

Needless to say, he didn't go back through that graveyard on his way home. He had to go ten miles farther the other way home, but that didn't bother him one little bit. I guess he was a scaredy-cat.

This fellow never knew if the ghost was real or not, or whether it was just an illusion that resulted from too much whiskey. But don't forget, his horse saw the ghost woman, too.

9. "Ghosts of a Rabbit and a Man in a Mountain Cemetery"

My grandfather said that when he'd pass this cemetery near Mud Creek while on his way home from his day's work at Boldman, just across the Pike County line, a thing that looked to him something like a rabbit would run out in front of him. And it happened over and over so many times that he finally got scared, so he started taking a pistol with him.

He shot at this thing several times and said it looked as if the fire from the bullet would go right into the fur of this animal. It looked like a rabbit, but he couldn't be sure that it was. It followed him, even after he'd shot it several times. Never did stop following him down the road.

Even after people started to drive cars through there, they also saw something in that same graveyard. They claim that whatever it was looked as if it was a man in long underwear. He just comes out, maybe from a grave, and goes across the road in front of the cars.

As for me, I've been through there but I've never seen him.

10. "That Was a Ghost!"

My granddaddy, Dr. Billy Richardson, was afraid of ghosts. He said that there was one place that he'd always try to miss whenever he was out on horseback making house calls. It was a cemetery. He said that every time he'd go by that cemetery, he was scared to death, but he had to pass by there in order to get to these houses when people needed him as a doctor.

He said that he'd go around one way, then go around another way. He tried every way to get around that old graveyard, but said that every time he'd cross by this cemetery, a ghost or spirit would always come out of a grave. It was never the same grave, but it was always a grave in that cemetery that this thing would come out of and come right toward him.

He said that he had always got away from whatever it was, but one time he said that he thought that it was going to catch him. He said that he started his horse to running, and that horse was running so hard that it would hit limbs and everything as it ran. He finally got away from it, but he exclaimed, "Now that was a ghost!" Said, "That ghost got after me every time that I went down through there."

11. "Ghost of an Indian"

Sam Smith's great-uncle Arch Smith and Ike Barksdale, who was a black fellow worker with Arch, they were driving a team of big mules that were pulling a road wagon down Kettle Creek here in southeastern Monroe County. I mean, this is beautiful country now, and it was back then.

Anyway, they were going down Kettle Creek in this wagon, and it was after dark. As they were passing by this Indian graveyard, located on Harm Wells' farm, a white, ghostly figure appeared suddenly. They both saw it, and they both said, "Howdy do, sir."

There was no answer, but whatever this ghost thing was kept right alongside them as they traveled on down the creek. They were in the wagon, and it was walking along beside them. But, all of a sudden, it jumped up onto the wagon and stood on the back end of it. Uncle Arch spoke again, "Howdy do, sir."

Still, no response. By this time, Uncle Arch and Ike were really getting concerned. Well, Uncle Arch decided to be "Big Pete." He told Ike to give him the whip, said, "I'll find out why he doesn't want to speak to us."

Ike gave Arch the whip, and Arch lashed out at the white figure standing there in the back of the wagon. Whatever the thing was just stepped off the wagon and disappeared. Soon it appeared again right next to the wagon. Both of them spoke to it again, "Howdy do, sir."

Again, there was no response. So after the third time of getting nowhere with this white ghost-like figure, they both became frightened for their very lives. Uncle Arch told Ike to give the mules the lines, that is, speed them up. Well, they almost ran these mules to death, since it was close to four miles that they made them run at full speed.

Uncle Arch and Ike are both dead now, but they both told this story for fact as long as they lived. Harm Wells is also dead, but he told my husband, Sam Smith, that he, too, many times had seen something after dark near the Indian graveyard there on his farm.

12. "The Red Glowing Eyeball"

My father has had several scary incidents to happen to him across the years. He swears all of them to be true, and I've never caught him in a lie.

Around the year 1966, he and Judd Watson were driving around in a '61 four-door brown Chevrolet. They were on Jacob Well Road in Hart County, and they kept seeing lights on the ground shining through the trees. About the time they got to Concorde Church and graveyard, which are up on a hill, he saw this light that looked like, in his own words, "a big red eyeball."

The light moved around the church, and they took out after it in their car. After it passed by the church, the eyeball turned left and went up the hill. Then it turned left again and went down to the cemetery where it centered right above a couple of tombstones. They both decided to investigate, and as soon as they opened their car doors, the eyeball just disappeared like "someone turned off a switch."

The two men were petrified, and they left there in a hurry. In fact, when my father told me this ghost story, he admitted to still being unsettled by the event.

13. "The Ghost of a Woman in a Grave House"

Along about 1920, I was hauling staves in Magoffin County for a stave mill company. Me and about 15–20 other fellows was doing this. We would wagon the staves out, and it took us about two days to make the trip to the railroad station. I lived about half way on the road, so it took about one day to go each way.

One morning we all went to the stave mill and got a load and we was coming down Lick Branch there in Magoffin County on the Middle Fork River. So we was all coming around the face of the hill. There was wagons in front of me and wagons in back of me, some twenty-five yards away from me each way. The wind was a-blowing and it was in the spring of the year. The wind was blowing straight across from where we was coming around the hill. They was a bottom and creek, and across the bottom and the creek was this graveyard. Looked to be about twenty-five or thirty graves.

Two of these graves had little houses over them. One was checked off with narrow white strips and had been painted, and the other one looked to have been sealed solid; both covered. The one that seemed to be solid, the door on it came open and stood back wide open, plumb back.

The wind was blowing but the door stood still, and there was a large woman, fleshy-like, about 175 [pounds], dressed in black. She was at the back end of the little house, but she kept coming forward and then stood in the door. She was dressed in black with a black ribbon tied around her waist in a big bow, and the end of the ribbon went down to near the bottom of her dresstail.

This little ribbon was blowing back and forwards, and she stood there something like twenty-five minutes. I kept my eye on her, didn't take my eye off to amount to anything. Directly, she begin to disappear. She was going to the back of the little house, disappearing. She disappeared right in the back of the building. When she got out of sight, the door went to [closed].

. . . I never did see that anymore, but still hauled staves past there in later months.

14. "Haunted House on Straight Creek"

A man by the name of Grant Pop Woolum and his wife lived in a house that was haunted. At nights, they could hear some two or three persons singing. They would light their lamps to go and see, but could not hear or see anything. They would come on back to the house and the singing would begin again in the nearby graveyard.

Finally, an old man on a walking cane walked into one room and got in the bed. And from that, he got out of the bed and walked into the loft. The loft seemed to be tearing all to pieces [as he did this]. They closed up the doors, and the women from the graveyard came down and set on the doorsteps. The others walked into the house with the door locked and stayed until daylight. Then the women walked back to the graveyard.

They would sing about twice a week at the graveyard like someone dead—sounded just like ghosts.

One night, one of the [ghost] girls on the outside got up and went upstairs and went to bed until daylight.

Mr. Woolum and his wife got so scared that they got their neighbors to come in the next night to hear [these women] singing at the graveyard. The neighbors went to the graveyard but couldn't find no tracks there in the graveyard.

The Woolums finally sold their home and left.

Cemeteries with houses erected over burial sites provide cozy settings for the return of the dead as ghostly beings. (Photograph by the author)

15. "Hant Tale"

The first cemetery in Warsaw, Kentucky, was located behind the house of Will Roberts. After many years, the graveyard was covered by a brick factory. From these bricks, the courthouse was built which stands today. Since the bricks were made of soil from this old graveyard, many people say that the courthouse contains the bones of our ancestors in Warsaw.

At night, when the courthouse is closed people have said they hear voices calling. For this reason, many people are afraid to go in it at night.

16. "Ghosts in Antioch Church and Cemetery"

My father-in-law, a retired coal miner, was also the caretaker of the grounds at Antioch Cemetery in Muhlenberg County. The old church building and the cemetery were all that was left in an area that was bought out by a coal company to be used for strip mining.

On a warm summer day, my father-in-law was getting the lawn mower from the trunk of his car when he began to hear singing within the church house. He said that it was beautiful music, just as wonderful as if it were being sung by angels.

When the singing stopped, he heard the familiar voice of the deceased church minister speaking. He approached the building to see what was taking place. Instead of going in, he just peered through the window, but there was silence. Mystified, he resumed his work at cleaning the old cemetery.

On another occasion, both my mother-in-law and father-in-law were at the cemetery. He was mowing and she was tending to some of their relatives' graves. Suddenly, my father-in-law saw a man walking down the road. The man then turned toward him, and my father-in-law recognized him as his wife's father, who had died several years earlier. The man continued walking until he reached a tree, then he suddenly disappeared.

All of this happened very quickly, and there were no witnesses. Even my mother-in-law didn't see her father. They could never understand what that was all about.

17. "Night Hand"

In 1917, one cold and stormy night, my uncle had ridden his horse to visit relatives. Rain, wind, terrible lightning almost swayed the old pine trees to the ground. The storm didn't get any better, so about midnight my uncle decided to return home. He didn't want his parents to worry about him.

He mounted his horse and started down a dark, muddy, and narrow road that passed directly by the old family cemetery. He almost passed the old graveyard when something or somebody grabbed the horse's bridle. The horse became frightened, reared, snorted and stopped dead still.

My uncle turned back up the hill and got another running start. The same thing happened again.

He tried one more time, though he and the horse were both trembling. Then a hand reached out. The horse lunged. My uncle hung on with a death grip. He finally had to go several miles out of the way to reach his home.

The next day, he heard dirt was moved from a grave and tattered clothing was strewn about the old cemetery.

18. "Another Version of the Della Barnes Ghost"

Whether her death was accidental or not, some say the ghost of twenty-three-year-old Della Barnes walks through Paducah's Oak Grove Cemetery on restless nights.

Della, the daughter of famed councilman George F. Barnes, reportedly died in 1897 from an overdose of morphine. But since her death and an erection of her likeness at her grave, haunting rumors have abounded.

Some say she committed suicide at the end of an unhappy love affair and still wanders the graveyard searching for the unrequited love of her life.

Others contend that Della was married and tricked her husband, "a bruiser of a man," into stabbing her to death.

She loved roses and always wore a bouquet of them on her dress. One day Della hid a knife in the flowers, and when her husband embraced her, she was stabbed in the heart.

Only her skirt and part of her left hand remains, but when her figure was still intact [on the gravestone], curious visitors swore they saw Della's right hand, which held a bouquet of flowers, curled into a gnarled claw with outstretched blade slicing the night air.

19. "Senora's Ghost in Smithland"

Some see her by the river, others see her in the cemetery, but most tales agree that Senora is forlorn because her husband left her, and she is angry because another occupies her grave.

The Smithland Cemetery on Cemetery Road off U.S. 60 in Livingston County is home to the grave of the lovelorn bride of Ned Buntline, the father of the dime novel.

Buntline and Cuban bride Senora Sebrina of Havana stopped off for a stay at the Gower House in 1845. After he came a hair too close to a feverish lynch mob outside the hotel, Buntline fled for Nashville, leaving his bride behind.

Senora was remembered as a cultured, high-bred lady of distinction, tall and stately, with long, black hair and dark eyes, who waited wearily many months for her husband's return. After she died of a broken heart, she was buried on Cemetery Hill, which overlooks the Cumberland and Ohio rivers.

Two years later, two grave diggers were preparing for a funeral on the sloping hill in the cemetery when they dug into an unmarked grave. In it was the well-preserved body of a woman with long, black hair and clothing and jewelry like Senora's.

With the funeral procession closing in, they had no time to dig a new grave, so they allowed the burial to take place there in Senora's grave. This disturbed Senora so much that her spirit is still seen there from time to time.

20. "Anna Beauchamp's Ghost"

The first ghost story that I remember hearing as a child was about the ghost of Anna Beauchamp. However, before I go any farther with the story, here's what is written on the bronze marker about the Beauchamp tragedy:

"Jereboam Beauchamp and wife Anna buried here in same coffin at own request. To avenge her alleged seduction by Col. Solomon Sharp, Beauchamp murdered him at Sharp's Frankfort home, 1825. Beauchamp and Anna were held in Frankfort jail. She was released but joined her husband in his cell, refusing to be separated even by force. He was sentenced to hang.

"On execution day, they attempted suicide by stabbing themselves. Her wound was fatal, but he lived to be hanged that day, the first legal hanging in Kentucky, 1826. . . ."

My mother always told me when I was a child that Anna Beauchamp sometimes roamed Taylorsville Hill, which is where she and her husband are buried in Maple Grove Cemetery. Mom told me that Anna's ghost always wore a bonnet and that she had on a long dress, the kind that formal Southern ladies wore back in the early years of the nineteenth century.

Anna's ghost is typically seen walking along the side of the road near the old cemetery.

21. "Human Bones under the House"

When she was a young child, this lady in Jeffersontown lived in a house with her aunt and uncle. This house they lived in had formerly been a house for elderly poor people. Her sister lived there, too. Anyway, she and her sister could hear a piano playing during the night, and they could also hear pages in the Bible flopping back and forth on a table out in the hallway.

Some years later, the house burned. Their uncle decided to rebuild there on the same spot. While digging around the basement foundation, the workers found some human bones. It just may be that some of the poor people who lived there at one time were buried there. I guess these residents were dissatisfied, thus causing their spirits to return.

22. "Raven Hill Cemetery"

My girlfriend told me all about this old cemetery in the Grapevine section between Madisonville and Earlington. I had never heard any of it in my twenty years of living nearby, but several people in Madisonville seem to know quite a bit about it.

The cemetery itself is on an old gravel road that isn't used much. Four of us drove by one night so that I would know its location, but nobody seemed to be anxious to stop.

Nancy and her sister and some other people went out there one day last year to look around. They went back again that same night. They found one open grave which is supposed to be haunted by a blue light that follows people around after dark. Nancy says that they saw the light, but since they had already heard about it, it could have been a case of imagination.

The story goes that the occupant of the grave escaped and is now looking for somebody to take his place in that grave. It is said that he will pull or push anybody who comes near the grave after dark to try to get them to tumble in.

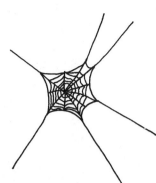

Chapter 2

Disappearing Ghosts

1. "The Old Woman without a Face"

One evening, my four friends and I were sitting around talking. Earlier that evening we had been playing various card and dice games, which was somewhat of a tradition among us, and we had grown tired. A fellow in the group mentioned that he was anxious about an upcoming trip to some woods in the neighborhood. Another guy in the group commented that he would never hunt in those woods again. When he said this, he could easily detect the entire group's curiosity, so he proceeded to tell us the story of the woman without a face.

He told us how he and his dad had heard other hunters talk about the woman that haunted the woods in that area, and how she had reportedly lost her face to some type of cancer. He said that the hunters who claimed to have seen her said that she had never attempted to harm them, but that her appearance had always frightened them. It has become somewhat of a tradition in this community to go to the woods to hunt and to see if the woman with no face would appear. My friend and his dad chose to ignore the warnings that were always given to them by fellow hunters, so they went hunting in the woods anyway. Here's what happened to them.

My friend and his dad had been waiting in the deer stand about an hour. It was just before dawn, and my friend suddenly saw a figure of what appeared to be a woman coming toward their stand. He turned to look at his dad, and he, too, was staring in the direction of the approaching figure. It seemed like hours, but it was actually only a few minutes until the figure was standing directly below the deer stand looking up at the two of them.

The figure was in fact a woman, and my friend and his dad both claim that she had no face. The woman did not speak to them or try to harm them in any way. Instead, she simply turned from them and walked away as quickly as she had approached. So the father and son abruptly ended their hunting trip, and they both vowed never to go back in those woods again.

I found my friend's story to be frightening and intriguing at the same time. One reason for my interest in this legend is because it reportedly occurs close to my home. However, it is of greater interest to me because of the historical area in which the woman makes her appearances.

The patch of woods that this old woman supposedly haunts is the exact same spot where the Chalybeate Springs Hotel was once located. This old hotel was one of the few places, with the exception of another family with a big house, where people who were traveling could spend the night. Oral tradition in the Chalybeate Springs community claims that Andrew Jackson spent the night in the Chalybeate Springs Hotel. The only thing that remains of the old hotel today is the well house that provided the hotel with mineral water. The reason that I find the historical location of this legend so very interesting is that none of the hunters have ever connected the old woman to the hotel. And, yet, that appears to be the exact explanation.

Many years ago the Chalybeate Springs Hotel was the center of the entire Chalybeate community. The old hotel was a source of employment, trade, and even entertainment for members of the community. The entire community flourished because of the revenue brought into the community by the hotel.

A local family owned the hotel, and they always gave back to the community with the profit they earned from the hotel. When the old man who owned the hotel died, his wife had to run the establishment alone. Both of her sons had gone north to attend college. However, not long after the woman took over, she became very ill. She sent word to both of her sons and asked them if they would come home to take care of her and the hotel. Her sons never responded to her request, and the woman died of cancer right there in the hotel. It was said that the cancer had completely eaten away her face.

After she died, her sons sold the old hotel and the land it was on, and they both continued to live up north. It is still said that the old lady never got over the fact that her sons would not leave school and come home to take care of her; thus, she died brokenhearted. Therefore, she still wanders in the woods where the Chalybeate Springs Hotel was once located, in hopes of finding her sons. Often she mistakes hunters for her sons, and when she approaches them and sees that she is mistaken, she quickly departs.

I suppose that the old woman with no face will continue to roam the woods in search of her sons; thus, hunters in the community will continue to be a little extra cautious when they hunt in the woods where the old hotel once stood.

Whether or not the old woman without a face continues to exist, she provides basis for a great story and creates a meaningful tradition for the residents of Chalybeate Springs, one of Edmonson County's most historic places.

2. "A Visit by the Ghost of Daniel Boone"

The incident I am about to relate happened in the summer of 1858, at a well-known country house in the vicinity of Lexington, Kentucky.

I was sitting one evening in what was called the octagon parlor with two or three school girls and their hostess, my eldest daughter. The day had been intensely hot, and the close, sultry afternoon was followed toward evening by a heavy rain. As I set talking with the young people it suddenly occurred to me that my husband was alone in his library, and I concluded to go and sit a while with him.

The library was in one of the wings of the house, and to reach it I went through a small reception room, into what was called the library hall. The door of the library stood open, and as I crossed the threshold I stopped in amazement. My husband, who had been writing, had just turned his chair toward a visitor—a most remarkable one in appearance. Seeing me enter and knowing what my surprise must be, he said, "It is someone who has taken shelter from the storm."

I then walked in and stood by the table, gazing with wonder and astonishment upon a man, evidently in the prime of a very vigorous manhood, dressed in the backwoodsman's style of over a century ago—buckskin hunting shirt, leggings, etc. He was sitting in a large leather-covered chair by the library window, which opened to the floor and out upon a paved terrace, where the rain was falling in torrents. On the opposite side of the window a long rifle was leaning.

My husband asked one or two questions of his strange guest, to which he replied in monosyllables, and then after a visit of about two minutes, he suddenly arose from his chair and walked over to his rifle. There he turned around and paused, probably for the purpose of putting on his cap, and I found myself face to face with him. In the few seconds that we thus stood he was absolutely photographed upon my memory.

He was tall and finely formed, and I think could be called athletic. He was as straight as an arrow, and there was an easy graceful swing of the body as he walked across the floor. His complexion was evidently bronzed by exposure; his eyes were very dark, or so they appeared to me, and his well-shaped head, high from the ears to the crown, was set gracefully upon his shoulders.

This strange visitor, even while my eyes were fixed upon him, did not seem conscious of my presence, although we stood face to face, and without a word, he took up his rifle and walked out into the storm, from whence he had come. As he did so, I said in a low voice to my husband, "Daniel Boone's ghost." And so this strange apparition has always been called by members of my family.

As he [Boone] walked into the library he said, "It is a rainy evening." And yet, coming in out of the pouring, drenching rain, he brought no traces of the rain with him. There were no streamlets of water falling from the fringe of his hunting shirt; no water ran from his rifle upon the carpet.

My husband made repeated inquiries in Lexington and in the country roundabout, but no one was found who had heard of such a person as our mysterious visitor.

Was it the spirit of some pioneer whose camp had been located on the spot where the library is built? Or was it the spirit of the great pioneer Daniel Boone, as he was in the strength of his manhood, come back to visit his old haunts?

3. "The Ghost of Panther Creek"

Back when we lived in Daviess County, we were surrounded by Panther Creek. My parents went over one night to visit a new neighbor who had just moved into the Panther Creek area. They came home in the night very much excited over what they had seen on the way home. They were so excited that they told me over and over. I have never seen them so excited.

To get home, they walked up this narrow lane, with a slat and wire fence on either side. A fruit orchard was on the right side, a field for cultivation on the right. They said that all at once Mama saw an object moving right along with them, staying exactly the same distance away from them. So Mom stepped it up a little and got in front of Dad.

He said, "Wait a minute, Sarah, there's something following us, and I can't see what the son-of-a-gun looks like, or what it is doing. Let me get a stick of wood and I'll find out."

Well, he drew closer to the fence, and the ghostly thing backed away a little. Dad asked, "Did you see anything?"

"Yes," Mom said, "and I have for quite some time. Let it alone; don't bother it."

But Dad got a stick of stove wood and threw it real hard, and it seemed to have gone right through this thing, whatever it was. It didn't make a single sound, though, nor did it flinch or stop in its movement as they walked. It also stayed the same distance away from them. Well, they were somewhat scared by now, and they speeded up a bit. It went right along with them until they came to the horse-lot gate on one side of the lane, and over in the orchard side was the hen house. It was there that it disappeared. They said that it looked like a great big gunny sack, or even a great big grass sack, tied with a foot and a half drop-over from the top. It was two and a half feet above the ground, but it had no legs. It was tagging along at whatever speed they made.

They were indeed excited. The next day when Mama told the lady who owned the house as well as the hen house where the thing disappeared, the lady said to Mom, "Mrs. Garrett, I have prayed and prayed that somebody else might see it. It has been seen many times before, and exactly just like you described. And it was right there by the hen house where it always disappears."

People continued to talk about this ghost-like thing for years afterwards, but they could never figure out what it was they had seen. And as another fellow there in the Panther Creek community once said, "Thank goodness, at least it never did leap at anybody and yell, 'Boo!' or 'I gotcha!'"

4. "Barn Ghosts Scare Campers"

One night me and several of my friends went out on a camping trip. It was cold and dark in the night, so we found this old barn that we might camp in. It was a big old barn and was pretty well preserved. But, best of all, it kept out the cold wind and weather. We went ahead and built a campfire and began to roast some hotdogs. We were just sitting there having a great time, when all of a sudden the fire kinda just flicked up high and low, then went out completely. It was weird; we didn't know whether it was the wind that put the fire out or what.

We were sitting there, and I had my back towards the door; so did another guy. Cold chills started running up and down my back. So this guy poked me in the side and asked, "Do you believe in ghosts?"

I said, "Naw, I don't."

He said, "Well, just look over your shoulder; you'll change your mind."

And so I looked over my shoulder, and up at the door to the barn stood a white maze, white mist, taking human-like shape. And we all jumped up. There was only this one door to the old barn. So there we were, all five of us trapped in the old barn with this white thing standing at the door. We couldn't figure out what it was, and it was making moaning noises. Then it came closer and closer to us, and we were all backed up against the wall. Since I was in the front of everybody else, I tried to climb over the wall to get out of there.

This white, misty thing kept getting closer and closer, and finally I got so terrified that I just ran, ran straight at it. Well, I must have run through it, for the next thing I knew, I was outside the door. But there that thing was, too. It had gone outside with me!

Then, all of a sudden, we began to see several of these white things around us. We just stood there while they kept circling around us, getting closer and closer. The wind started blowing and the night was getting darker, and, boy, were we ever scared. Scared to death, nearly!

All of us were standing there in a circle with our backs against each other. Still, these things kept getting closer and closer to us. They weren't really walking, nor were they really flying. They just sort of hovered about a foot or so off the ground. When we thought they couldn't get any closer, one of them spirits kinda mumbled something, and all of them quickly disappeared in the night. And, boy, we were so relieved that they were gone and we were still all right, that nothing bad had happened to any of us.

5. "Grandfather's Ghost"

At the age of sixteen I went through a series of emotional setbacks. Within the course of two months, my parents separated, both of my grandparents on my mother's side died, and I was in a car wreck that sent me to the hospital for two weeks.

I was at my grandmother's bedside when she died and was able to tell her goodbye. My grandfather, with whom I was very close, died while I was in the hospital. He was on his way to the hospital to bring me some clean robes, but he died just as he started to come. From what I was told, he died from a heart attack in our driveway. I was not there to tell him goodbye.

Two weeks after Grandfather's death, and five days after my release from the hospital, I saw him again. I had just come home from cheerleading practice, and it was around 7:00 p.m. when I felt someone in the car behind me. I turned around and there, sitting in the car that he always loved, and died in, was my grandfather. He smiled at me, then waved goodbye. After that, he disappeared. I never saw him again.

6. "Farmer's Road Ghost"

Many times while I was still in high school, I heard this story about a ghost that could be seen along this country road near Bardstown in Nelson County. I never believed it until I saw the ghost for myself last summer.

The legend goes that a farmer was crossing this road and was hit by a car. He died on the spot.

Well, last summer I was driving back from Bardstown late one evening on this particular road. As I rounded a curve, I saw a man in denim-colored coveralls and a straw hat standing there in the road. I was going pretty fast, so I slammed on the brakes to the car. But I was still positive that I would hit him. I closed my eyes and waited for the impact, but it never happened.

The car stopped, and I got out to look around, but nobody was on or near the road. I went back to the car and got a flashlight out of the glove compartment. Using the flashlight, I looked on both sides of the road, but still couldn't find anything. I even looked for footprints in the dirt on the side of the road, but didn't find any. I know without a doubt that if that had been a real person, I would have hit and probably killed him.

Now then, I, too, tell people about the ghost of the old man on this backcountry road.

7. "The Ghost at the Window"

The house I live in over in Mayfield is very old and quite large. In fact, it was built in the late 1800s during a time when hospitals were almost un-heard of. A man supposedly had his appendix taken out at that time, in the room which is presently my bedroom. The man died, so they say.

One evening back in 1974, some friends and I were playing in the living room on a very dark, dreary, rainy night. We stopped our games for a minute to see how hard it was raining. When we looked outside, we saw the dark figure of a man looking in through the window at us. All three of us saw the same thing. We knew it was a man. It scared us, so we turned our heads away from it. When we looked back at the figure, it wasn't there. It had vanished. We never saw it again, thus never knew what or who it was.

But it sure scared the daylights out of us when we looked out the window and saw it.

8. "The House That Wasn't"

One night there were about twenty to twenty-five of us just sitting around there in Glasgow. We were all bored stiff, so someone said, "Let's all go out in the country."

Naturally, since some of the guys were drinking, they wanted to get out of Glasgow. I know Barren County pretty well, but I don't know where we went to that night. All I know is, we were in a big grassy field up on a high hill. There was a cemetery nearby and a small clump of trees. We all got out of our cars and started walking around up there on the hill. There were some trees over on another hill, and about ten of us were looking over that way when someone noticed what appeared to be a house.

It took a minute or so, but it looked as if the moon was shining right down into those trees and onto a little wooden house. Somebody suggested that we walk over there and look things over.

We thought it pretty weird because there wasn't really any road to get to the place. As we got closer, it looked like the trees were in a big circle around the house. But as we got to the edge of the trees, the house was gone. I know it was there, for everyone saw it and not everyone was drinking. I don't know where it went or what happened. All I know is, it truly was there, and we all saw it.

9. "Was It the Ghost of a Woman, or That of a Dog?"

The balmy, late summer evening of 1947 held no fears for a group of Owensboro teenagers on their way to a party. They were laughing and joking as they approached the Old Wilson's Ferry Landing, just west of the city.

Suddenly, their laughter ceased, and they froze in their tracks as the apparition of a tall woman in white clothes rose up before them. And were they ever scared! Frank Bollinger, one of the boys, collapsed. His friends had to drag him a half-mile up the lane. They stopped at the farm of Mr. and Mrs. Elmo McKay, who were able to revive Frank with cold towels applied to his head.

News of the eerie phenomenon spread like wildfire, as it had been too weird, yet too real to have been faked. The curiosity of two brothers, Harold and Harry Sapp, who were auto mechanics, was aroused. So they decided to check things out by visiting the old ferry landing.

As they approached the lonely site, once the busiest section in that region, Harold glanced back over his shoulder. A luminous, feminine figure attired in a flowing, long-sleeved white gown stood there in the middle of the road. Whatever it was did not move. Harold saw a white, misty shawl covering her head, but he wasn't able to see her face. The figure did not utter a sound. Harold looked away to speak to his brother, and when he looked again he saw only a white dog that disappeared behind a clump of trees. He noticed that the dog seemed to glide rather than walk, as its legs were not visible.

Harry Sapp also saw the dog and claimed that it was about three-feet long and glowed as though it were covered with phosphorus.

This story continued to spread throughout Owensboro, and a young milkman, Shirley McLimore, sixteen, decided that he, too, would like to see this changing ghost. With a number of older friends, he went to Wilson's Ferry. This is what McLimore told a reporter:

"It was all in white and it took about eight steps, not on water, but in the air. It walked like an old woman. It never moved its arms. Then it turned into a white dog that floated away a few feet over the surface. I watched until the weeds hid it. Man, I was scared . . . ."

As a result of the publicity, a great many people went to see the ghost; also the local constable and men from the sheriff's office investigated. However, on these nights, the ghost failed to put in an appearance. . . .

10. "Ghost of Man Disappears"

One bright, moonlit night in early springtime, my husband and I, along with an elderly neighbor, were sitting in our living room next to an open door. We saw a man coming toward the house. He had on a hat and coat, with the coat collar turned up high around his neck. He was also carrying a lighted lantern.

We gave him time to come in, but when he got close to the porch he just walked on by without turning his head to look at us. Well, we got up and went outside to see where he had gone. We looked and looked and looked, but could find no trace of him. But the strange part was that there was no place that he could possibly hide and put out his lantern in such a short time.

None of us believed in ghosts then, and still don't, but what we saw that night simply cannot be explained. We all saw it and we have always described what we saw the same way. That sure was weird.

11. "The Weird Shadow"

My cousin and I were sitting on a boathouse on Kentucky Lake, watching the sunset. It was beautiful as it shined across that body of water. The two of us had been talking about girls, about school, and about other teenager topics. It was almost dark, and we could see camping lights coming on all around the lake. We were both juniors in high school and had not ever given much thought to the supernatural.

We turned to look at a camper behind us and saw a shadow on the wall against the boathouse. This shadow was bent over like an old man and was carrying a long stick that touched the ground. We yelled to whatever it was to come on out, but the shadow did not move, just ignored us. We went over to see what was creating the shadow, but it was gone by the time we got there.

We spent the next few hours trying to find the source of the shadow, but there were no clues. There was hardly any light that could have caused the shadow, so, believe it or not, we assumed that it was a ghost. When we told our parents about it, they just laughed at us. But my cousin and I were sure that we had seen something weird, something like a ghost, yet no one believed us.

12. "The Ghost That Listened to Gospel Singers"

Out in the Jett neighborhood, which is about three miles from Frankfort on the Lexington-Versailles Road, there is an old legend that was told to be absolutely true. About two miles out, there is a swamp, which is owned by the Popular Dairy. This swamp is the home of a very interesting ghost.

Allen Cromwell, Thomas Rodmand, and Robert Jones, all three prominent young men from this section of the county, were returning home one Sunday evening from church. And as all three of the boys were good singers and really loved to sing, they were driving along this highway in an old-fashioned rock-a-way [wagon], singing one of their favorite old hymns. Without any warning or noise of any kind, there suddenly appeared a horse and a rider by the side of the horse they were driving. This other horse was about three feet taller than the one they were driving, and there was a man riding this horse. He had on white flowing robes.

The boys were not frightened, as they well knew the story of the ghost that inhabited this section of the road. Just as long as the boys kept singing, the other rider rode right alongside the horse they were driving. When they reached the top of the hill, the song ended. And without any notice of any kind, the ghostly horse and rider just floated off into space.

The people who lived in that section have never been able to explain what or who that was, or whatever became of the ghost. This story was told by Allen Cromwell's sister, who stated that he came straight home from church that night and told them about the ghost.

13. "The Phantom Road Wagon"

This happened to me and my granddad when we were living there in Guston, Meade County. This was back in 1988 or '89. I had a dog there, and her name was Browni. And she was a good dog, very protective of me and Granddad both. We had a hammock that Granddad built, stretched between two trees.

Granddad had gone to visit another family member, and that left just me and Browni at home. Well, this was during the summer, and I was sitting in a chaise lounge under a tree. It was somewhere between six and seven o'clock–dusk.

We had a fence going around the front yard that me and Granddad made. It had a front gate going out towards Highway 428, the blacktop road in front of the house. I was laying there in that chaise lounge, and my dog Browni was laying there beside me. I heard a sound that sounded like someone yelling up in the direction where my Aunt Garnett and Uncle Wesley lived.

Browni heard it, too. We heard this yelling, but I couldn't figure out what it was. I got up out of the chaise lounge and walked toward the front gate. I was leaning there on the front gate, listening to where this yelling was coming from. I looked up the road and saw what looked like a blue glow up there on the horizon. I kept looking, and Browni was looking at it, too. It got bigger and bigger, then materialized into a horse pulling a road wagon with a man in it. I mean he was beating that horse for everything that was in it, yelling at this horse, "Yi, yi."

They were coming down the road, and it seemed like this horse was running its level best, but it wasn't really going that fast. Seemed like it was kinda moving in slow motion. Well, it came on down past the house, but the man never did look at me. It got real cold when that man and horse and wagon passed by the front gate. Browni didn't bark or anything, just watched them. And I watched them, and there was dust coming up from the horse's

Elbert Cundiff and his dog, Brownie, sensed a phantom wagon running on the road passing in front of the Cundiff cottage (right) in Guston, Kentucky. (Photograph provided by Elbert Cundiff)

hoofs on this blacktop, but there wasn't any sound. They went on down past the house, then made a turn and went up through the field and disappeared. They went right through the fence there beside the road.

My dog gave a "yelp," and she ran and went underneath the floor of the house and stayed underneath there for three or four days, wouldn't come out. I couldn't explain what it was, so I talked to Michael Paul Henson, a friend of mine in Indiana. He's written some ghost books. He said he had an old map at home and looked on it when he got back. He said that back in the 1800s, there was a dirt road going along just a little bit further than where 428 is now. Down below our house, on the other side of the road, it made a turn. There was a curve there. Apparently this man on this wagon went around this curve and had a wreck and died. Or maybe somebody was chasing him and they killed him.

When that took place, this man had whiskers, and he had a hat on, and was dressed in black. It was a road wagon he was in, but the wooden

Above, The road passing in front of the Cundiff cottage in Guston, Kentucky. *Below,* The Cundiff cottage. (Photographs provided by Elbert Cundiff)

wheels didn't make any sound on the blacktop. And when they made that turn and went up into the field, the man and his wagon just disappeared.

14. "Ghost Wagons along the Old Trace Road"

The Old Trace Road passed right behind the house in which I grew up here in Monroe County. The deep ruts and wide tracks were easy to see, even in the middle of a pasture. It was the first road to access this part of the state. The buffalo created the original trail, stretching from the river to the uplands. The Cherokee people used the trail, too. But the huge deep ruts were created by the early wagon trains which passed through the area in the late 1700s and early 1800s. Most people in my community didn't pay much attention to the old tracks.

The Old Trace Road had been abandoned as a roadway for many years, even when I was a boy. New roads had long since taken its place. But even now, when the ruts of the old road are becoming harder to find, the history of the road and the pioneers who traveled it has not been lost. The mysterious, ghostly images of the wagon trains and the people who journeyed west with them are still seen by some people living along or near the Old Trace Road.

The first person who claimed to have seen the wagon trains was a boy by the name of Zeke Bray. He was born around the turn of the century to a couple who lived on a section of the Old Trace Road.

This old historic road ran in front of the Bray place and then down to the Ramsteads,' their nearest neighbor. From there a new section of road began and the Old Trace Road curved off behind the Ramsteads' barn and out into the pasture and woods. One summer day when Zeke was about twelve years old he was fixing the barnyard fence. He thought he could hear someone shouting over his hammering, so he stopped and looked up.

He could hardly believe his eyes when he saw a wagon train coming down the Old Trace Road where it passed behind the barn! He knew they weren't supposed to be there. But they were, wagons that appeared just as they would have looked in pioneer days. And the sounds! He could hear whips cracking, babies crying, and people shouting. He saw the women and children riding in the big wagons. The men walked alongside. He even saw the cloud of dust behind the wagons.

It was strange enough to see a wagon train pass, but then Zeke noticed something else. "There is something strange about this wagon train," he thought to himself. "There's covered wagons there all right. There are all sorts of people, and babies crying, too. But there are no oxen or mules or horses. Nothing is pulling those wagons!" The wagons seemed to move forward on their own power.

Zeke watched the movement of the strange wagon train a few minutes longer until the image and the sounds began to fade. Then everything was gone. He dropped his hammer and ran to the garden patch and told his mother what he had seen. He knew that she would believe him.

"We must wait and see," she told him. "It must surely be a sign from God."

Not too many years later the "horseless carriage," or automobile, became common. Zeke took this as proof of his vision and went on to become a preacher. He told the story of the ghost wagon train many times in his sermons.

Zeke Bray was not the only person who saw the ghost wagons, although he was the only person who became a preacher on account of it. Just twenty years ago a fellow by the name of Jack Miller, who lives not far from the old Ramstead place told me another tale about the wagon train.

It was on a warm, sticky, summer night, and he had all the windows open to catch the breeze. The moon was high, and it was pretty bright in his bedroom. He was just about to doze off when he heard a funny sound. It was kind of quiet and far-off at first. Sounded like voices, the voices of many people, even babies crying. Miller's nearest neighbors live about a quarter of a mile off, so he was pretty sure it wasn't them. Slowly the sound got louder, he said, until he sat up in bed and looked out the window to see where it was coming from. Miller rubbed his eyes, because he couldn't believe it, but there was a wagon train coming through the cornfield. It was headed right for his house! There were people riding on the wagons and walking beside them. There were whips popping, and the creaking of the enormous wooden wagon wheels. But strangest of all, there were no oxen or mules or anything pulling the wagons. He said he was sure, because he got a good look at the wagons when they appeared right in his bedroom! They came on through as if his house weren't there at all.

Jack did not tell this story to just anyone. He told it to me only after I asked him if he had ever followed the path of the Old Trace Road, which I knew was near his house. Jack did a little exploring of his own after he saw the wagon train, and he found out that his house was built right on top of the old road.

Just last year I heard yet another tale about the wagons. The fellow who told it to me lives in Metcalfe, the next county over, but still on the path of the Old Trace Road. This fellow, whose name is Cassidy, is very honest and truthful. If he said it was snowing in July, I'd run and grab my boots. He didn't know that I had heard of the ghost-like wagons before. He said, "You know, there is something strange about my house."

"Is it built on the Old Trace Road?" I asked him.

He looked at me in a surprised manner, then asked, "How did you know that?"

"Go ahead and tell me what you have seen in your house," I urged him.

A bit hesitant, Cassidy dropped his head and responded, "There's been covered wagons passing right through my house, and people riding on them. This has happened several times now."

So the ghost wagon train continues to travel on. These ghosts appear, sometimes with animals pulling the wagons, sometimes without them. Why this happens is a mystery no one can solve. Perhaps the deep, old ruts of the trail contain not only the dust of history, but the hopes and dreams and passions of people who cannot die, or at least appear to be living forever.

15. "The Ghost of a Woman in Black"

Down at my old house in Greensburg there was a time when a ghost appeared in the presence of my brother and his friend. That was back in 1968 or '69 when both of the boys were about five years old. They were outside playing in the backyard when they both saw this ghost-like old woman at exactly the same time. This old lady was dressed in a black robe and was walking on the front porch. It scared both of them, so they ran to get their mothers. They weren't gone but a few seconds, but by the time the four of them got back to the porch, the woman was gone.

Nobody knows what or who it was that the boys saw, but to this very day they both swear that they saw this old woman, or a woman's ghost, there on the porch.

I guess that a lot of other people have heard that something strange was seen here, for lots of teenagers have driven by the old house just looking for something ghostly.

16. "A Ghost Chased by Campers"

Mark and I were camping in my backyard about 150 feet away from the house on a little hill. We had set up a five-man tent and drank a six-pack of Miller beer, then we decided to go to sleep. Mark woke me up saying that someone was outside the tent.

Well, I'm very grumpy if someone wakes me up, so I told him to shut up and go to sleep. So I dozed off again, and again Mark woke me up a few minutes later saying that someone was on the outside of the tent. So I got up and unzipped the tent and we both went outside.

Whatever it was, was on the other side of the tent, so we walked around to the other side. I guess we surprised it for all we saw were two glowing white sneakers. It ran toward this dry creek bed, and we both could only see these white sneakers as it ran. And the faster that we ran, the faster it ran. Finally, it jumped into the leaves in that old creek bed. Well, I picked up this big stick and yelled, "You'd better come out of there."

We were only four feet from the point where it jumped into the creek bed, but we heard or saw nothing just then. I had my stick ready to clobber whatever it was, and all of a sudden it was on the other side of the creek, and it ran farther and farther away from my house. Mark and I split up so that one of us could catch it by the big creek that begins at the far edge of my yard.

When we met up there, neither of us heard or saw anything. We didn't hear the water splash, but we knew that to get away from us it would have to run across the creek. By that time, we were both so scared that we ran back to the tent, pulled up the supports, and dragged the tent back to my house. We threw that tent in the downstairs room where we slept that night. Weren't about to have anything else to do with that ghostly whatever it was.

17. "The Horse with No Track"

When my father was a little boy, he and his father and mother were sitting in the house talking, like people used to do back then. They heard something, then looked out the window and saw a man on a white horse riding down across the yard.

It was raining that day, so my grandfather went out into the yard to look for the man and find out what he wanted, or what he was doing there. But when he got out there, he found no one. Nor did he find any horse tracks in the mud that the horse was sure to have made had a real horse and rider passed by. All three of us saw whatever that was, but there was no man or horse out there. This mystery was never solved. Must have been a ghost passing by.

18. "Uncle Lattimore's Ghost"

There's a man by the name of Lattimore. Uncle Bill Zeke said he didn't believe in no such things as a hant. You know, people back then called them, you know, hants. Said he didn't believe they was nobody could come back. And said one day he was working over at Short's Chappell. And this was so! And said he went down on the creek one evening, and come in. Said it was almost dark.

They'd buried Uncle Bill Lattimore that evening. This was so! Uncle Bill Zeke said he looked and seen Uncle Bill Lattimore coming down the hill, and they just buried him that evening. And it was almost dark. And said he was aiming to speak to him. Said he was coming up the hill, and he looked up. He just bowed his head down, stepping over in a little gully. And said when he looked up he was aiming to speak to him. And said Uncle Lattimore just went right around behind the tree and he disappeared. He never did see him no more.

19. "The Phantom Car of Keysburg"

When I was a small boy, we lived on Keysburg Road here in Logan County at the end of an old muddy driveway. We lived in this big white house that had a big yard and lots of trees. At nighttime around ten o'clock we always heard a car coming down the road. It sounded like it was coming to our house, so all of us would always get up and look to see who it was that was coming so late. Well, lo and behold, every time we looked there was always nothing to be seen.

Well, one night my brother and I thought we would get smart and slip out and hide to see if we could see anything. So around 9:30 we went out and hid behind some bushes and waited. Well, around ten o'clock, we saw a car coming down the mud road toward our house. When it got to the old tree stump in our yard, the car disappeared. My brother and I got so scared that we took off running toward the house just as hard as we could go. Well, we ran so hard and so fast that we both thought we'd die by the time we got there.

When we got inside the house, our mama looked at us and said, "You boys look like you've see a ghost or something. What is the matter with you?"

We wouldn't say anything to her, and we never did tell her what happened. But I'll tell you right now, we never again went out to see who was coming down the road at night. No sir!

20. "The Woman Visitor in the Old House"

When I was just a young boy, I went to stay with my Aunt Elmer, and she told me about the ghost of a woman in her house. The house that she lived in was on the Keysburg Road. It was just a regular old white house with a regular size yard. The yard had a few trees in it.

Aunt Elmer said that one morning she got up to make biscuits, and was over at the table doing so, when all of a sudden a woman with a white dress on came through the screen door and went over to her stove and just stood there for a few minutes like she was cooking. Then she turned and went back out through the door. In a few minutes she came back into the kitchen. This time she was wearing a brown dress. She did the same thing as before, then went back out the door again. My aunt said that she never seen the woman again.

In this same house, my aunt said that a person couldn't sleep with the lights off, because if you did have the lights off you would feel something laying on top of you. It gave a smothering feeling. When they'd turn the light on to see what it was, there was nothing there to be seen.

An actual account of this is that one night my uncle and aunt went to bed in that room. My uncle told my aunt to get off him because she was smothering him. Well, she told him that she wasn't on him.

He said, "Yes, you are, too."

She said, "I am not on you."

Well, they got up and turned on the light to see what it was, but when they did they saw nothing. So, from then on, they slept with the light on throughout the night.

21. "The Ghost in Junkyard"

One night I was coming home after seeing this girl whom I am dating here in Franklin. She lived across town from me. That's a long way, as I had to walk to see her. I was quite young at the time. I was living on Breckenridge Street, so by the time I got home it would be around 1:30 to 2:00 a.m.

There used to be an old junkyard on the left side of the street. However, now there's nothing there now but an empty lot. One night when I got to the junkyard, I saw a man walk out of the entrance to the junkyard, walk over to the road, and then wander into the yard right next to the junkyard. He walked maybe ten yards into the yard and then he was gone. Simply disappeared.

It shook me up pretty bad. But I went on down the street and went into our house. The next morning I told my mother what I had seen. It wasn't very strange to her at all. She told me that she had seen him, too, and then she told me a little about him.

It seems that this man was in a fight there in the junkyard, and he was stabbed and cut up pretty bad. Then he stumbled out of the junkyard trying to get some help, but died there in the yard where his ghost is now seen just before it disappears again.

22. "Tammy's Ghost Seen by Fellow Employees"

For several years prior to my retiring, Muhlenberg Community Hospital had a history of certain personnel seeing the apparition of a past employee there in the hospital. These sightings always occurred prior to the death of a patient who was known by all the employees. The apparition that we saw belonged to an employee who had died suddenly and quite unexpectedly. Her given name was Tammy, and she was a nurse in the Long-Term Care Unit of the hospital.

Tammy was known to have a preexisting heart condition. She often came to work quite ill and would then have to leave and return the next day. She always called in when she had to miss her shift due to illness. One day, when she failed to get to work, the nursing supervisor sent someone to Tammy's home to check on her. They found her body, thus indicating that she had died in her sleep, alone, with no one to aid her. About a month passed, then the sightings of Tammy began at the hospital.

She was frequently seen in the area between O.R. and Intensive Care, always when a patient was in the process of dying. One sighting was so clear to the viewer that facial details were observed. Tammy was always wearing her uniform that she had worn to work prior to her death. Her presence was never threatening. Instead, it gave a sense of peace and caring.

On a few occasions, she was present in the elevator with me and the night nursing supervisor. It was as if she were present to comfort the hospital personnel as much as the dying patient.

Not long after she was seen, Tammy would disappear. Even those persons who never actually saw her could always sense her presence. Many employees would not let you talk about the sightings and would panic when they felt any sense of difference in the surroundings.

The night nursing supervisor and I would often talk about Tammy as if she were there with us. We knew that she would soon appear because we were keeping vigil with a dying patient.

I don't know if anyone has seen her apparition since the night supervisor and I both retired. And, by the way, the night supervisor has since died.

23. "The Ghost and Granny Newman"

Grandmother Newman had been on a trip with several friends back in the thirties, and it was in the early evening when they got back–not quite light, not quite dark. They let my grandmother out across the street from her home on West Main Street, here in Frankfort, and she stood by the car talking to her friends about the trip. Suddenly an extremely large woman came up from behind her, in full view of the five people in the car. She seemed to press herself against my grandmother, almost engulfing her. The strange thing was that she seemed completely unaware of this woman, even as her friends stared in horrified fascination at the evil expression on the large woman's face.

After talking for a while, my grandmother said goodbye and walked away from the car. The occupants of the car were horrified to see that the woman was following her across the street, but granny stopped and waved again, apparently unaware of her "ghost." Then everyone began to come alive, and finally an older man in the car jumped out and went across the street. Strangely, there was no woman there when he got to my grand-mother. This was strange because the man later claimed that he kept eye contact with this evil "ghost" until he was just a few feet away. My grand-mother was fine, and being a practical woman, she never acknowledged the existence of that ghost.

The five others in the car have told this story often, and none of them deny that the ghost was actually there. Some of them think that it is sig-nificant that this strange thing occurred just one block from the cemetery.

24. "The Riding Ghost"

Once there was an old man by the name of Trigger Toe Noah. He always said that he was as mean as a snake in the grass. He used to come over to Trace Fork of Licking [River] to visit. This was where he spent his childhood.

One night, Trigger Toe left his wife at home to keep house and to do the chores. He rode away on his old mule, Dory. Long in the night, his wife heard him coming home riding as fast as he could ride. She jumped up and ran to the door to see what was wrong. Just at that moment, he hollered to his wife, "Come here, Nancy, and put this woman off from behind me."

So Nancy went out to the gate to help her husband. As she approached the gate, a woman in white jumped down from behind Trigger Toe and ran around the house.

Old Trigger Toe yelled out at her, "Hey, come back here. You've spent this much of the night with me, why not spend the rest of it? I've not been able to get rid of you all night."

25. "The Disappearing Ghost"

One night on an old country road below Corbin an old woman was riding a horse home from a day of shopping in Corbin. She was crossing a small hill in the road, and right on the other side she saw a man standing directly in front of her. His body and head glowed like a light in the night. She didn't know whether to turn and run, or just stand still. However, she didn't have any choice, for the horse become so frightened that it leaped and threw her to the ground.

This man said, "I'm sorry if I have scared your horse, madam." Then he disappeared right in front of her eyes. She walked on home, not knowing whether to tell of her experience or not, for she was afraid her family would think that she was losing her mind.

26. "A True Ghost Story"

In 1921 I taught at Bethel School in Madison County. While teaching there, I boarded with a widow woman whose name was Broadus. One afternoon, when I came home from school, Mrs. Broadus said, "I want to go over to a nearby school tonight, and I want you to go with me if you ain't afraid."

I told her that I wasn't afraid to go with her. Then she told me that there had been some "things" seen down at the bridge. So she decided that we would go across the hill before dark because it was nearer; then we would come back down the pike that night.

We started to the school before dark and went the nearest way. She was driving a white mare hitched to an open buggy.

After the school program was over, we hurried out to the buggy in order to get a head start so we could keep with the crowd and wouldn't have to go across the bridge alone.

We had traveled about two miles without seeing anyone. Suddenly we saw the outline of a buggy going along in front of us. The ponies were pulling the buggy, and the best we could tell there were two people in the buggy. The moon was shining bright, and we could see the wheels on the buggy turning.

Mrs. Broadus said, "I believe I will whip this mare up a bit so we can get closer to that buggy, because we are getting close to that bridge."

She whipped the mare, and we went much faster, but the buggy always stayed just the same distance in front of us. We got to the place where we could see the bridge, which had a top on it. The bridge made a shadow on the road in front of us. Just as the buggy got to the shadow of the bridge, the buggy disappeared. There wasn't anyplace it could have possibly gone.

Mrs. Broadus and I were speechless. We were at the house before we made a sound. Mrs. Broadus asked, "Did you see that?"

"Yes, I did," I answered.

I still don't believe in ghosts, but I saw that.

27. "The Shady Lady in Franklin"

In the back of my house here in Franklin is a huge, open field. I have to go across that field in order to get to my friends who live on Breckenridge Street.

I'd been going across this field for quite some time and nothing ever seemed strange or out of the way. Then, one day in early spring, I was going across the field and I saw this lady who was just wandering back and forth in the field. The closer that I got to her, the more unusual that I thought she was. For one thing, the clothes she had on were old but not torn anywhere. The strangest thing was that she was so pale. She was black, or would have been. Now, she was more or less gray.

Another odd thing is that she never looked up to acknowledge that I was even there. I stopped to look at her for a few seconds and then moved on. At the moment, I just thought it was someone that had gotten drunk and wandered into the field by mistake.

I went on over to my friend's house, and we went back to take a look at this person in the field. When we got there she was gone. We just assumed that she had wandered out of the field the same way she had wandered in.

A few weeks later, I saw her again. No one seems to see my shady lady except me and my brother. She never looks up. She paces across one section of the field and then she disappears. No one seems to have any clue as to who she could have been. There is no account of anyone being killed or any other violence that has taken place in this field.

28. "The Ghost of a Girl Chasing a Ball"

Out here on Falls Road, where Leamon Perry's old country store used to be, there is supposed to be a ghost running across the road. I've never seen it, but other people say it is the truth. I've asked several people about this story, and they all told it the same way.

It seems that at a certain time of the year you can sometimes see a little girl chasing a ball across the road at night. One person even told me that they knew of somebody who was driving down the road and had a wreck when they saw a little girl running across the road in front of the car. They were just so scared, afraid they would kill her, that they banged up their car when they swerved so as not to hit her. And, believe it or not, when they got out of their car there was not a trace of her anywhere around.

29. "Haunting Experience in the Murray State University Theater"

Fork-lift horns beeping when nobody's around. Elevators that seem to have minds of their own. Mysterious heartbeat sounds in headphones.

Evidence of Vincent Van Ghost?

Maybe, says James I. Schempp, Murray State University's unofficial expert on the campus poltergeist.

Vincent, said to haunt the shadowy world of the University Theater and its environs late at night, is a friendly ghost, to hear Schempp tell it: "He never tries to hurt anybody; he just appears sometimes, as if he's watching us, and then disappears."

Schempp, theater technical director, claims he's seen Vincent twice—the first time about five years ago [1975] during a late-night work session on a stage setting. The house lights had been switched off, and except for the stage, the theater was shrouded in darkness.

"Out of the corner of my eye, I noticed somebody standing and just watching me work. I thought I knew who he was, and so I said, 'Dammit, Jeff, don't just stand there, get to work.'"

But when Schempp turned to face who he thought was a goldbricking student worker, he saw nothing.

"I remember he was wearing a red-checkered shirt and blue jeans," said Schempp, who later caught a glimpse of the same figure lurking at the edge of the stage. "Again, I only saw him out of the corner of my eye, but he was wearing the same thing."

Vincent is supposedly the ghost of a construction worker killed in an accident several years ago when the Price Doyle Fine Arts Building, which houses the theater, was being built. That accounts for the work clothes, according to Schempp.

Others who claim to have seen Vincent report he is headless. Schempp learned of Vincent in the fall of 1971: "I was away in southern Illinois and when I got back to campus, some students told me that late one night they heard the horn beeping on the electric fork lift truck we use on stage."

The truck, Schempp added, was locked inside the scenes shop, and he had the only key: "There was no possible way anybody else could have gotten in there."

Schempp says that Vincent is also said to frequent elevators, again after dark. He remembers riding one elevator that kept stopping on a utility floor where the doors, which cannot be opened without a key, parted automatically. . . .

30. "A Woman's Ghost in a Long Nightgown"

I can personally vouch for the truth of this story that happened back when I was a teenager in Logan County. We were living in an old log house at the time, an old log house that was about 200 years old. I mean that old house had seen a lot of history pass through its big rooms.

About 100 yards away was what remained of an old, early graveyard. It had no markers in it, but when we first moved there, the graveyard had some sandstone rocks that stood around a huge cedar tree. You know, back then, people used to use cedar trees to mark their burial grounds. Anyway, this old tree had been struck by lightning; thus it and the remaining rocks were shattered and destroyed.

I shared a bedroom with a younger brother. One night I awoke to see bending over him a female figure. She was wearing a long nightgown-like garment that seemed to be patterned with tiny blue flowers. She looked fairly young, and I felt a strong sense of caring and concern.

She straightened up and looked at me. Then she began to rise upward toward the ceiling and faded out of sight. She simply disappeared before my eyes. I'm very positive that I was not dreaming. I really saw that, but never did know who it was.

31. "Woman Is Seen, Then Disappears"

This doctor, who was an educator, and his wife moved to Carrollton in the late 1980s and rented a twenty-year-old house on Winslow Street. Often, they heard 1940s music coming from above the kitchen ceiling. They searched the attic several times, but never found anything that might explain the music noises.

One evening, his wife decided to go to bed but he decided to stay up and finish watching a movie on the television set. A bit later, out of the corner of his eye he saw what he thought was his wife cross the hallway and enter a door over on the other side. Thinking that his wife might be sick, he went to the door he had seen her pass through. But no one was there in that room.

His wife was sleeping peacefully in her bedroom, but he didn't wake her up.

Apparently they never told anyone but me about this. They soon bought another house and moved out.

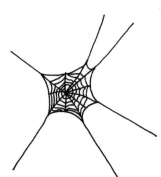

Chapter 3

Ghostly, Unnatural Sounds

1. "The Heartbeat"

There was an experience that happened to me back around 1973. Mom and Dad, Granddad, and I had moved into a house that belongs to Harry Richardson. This house is in Irvington on U.S. 60, real close to the Irvington Drive-in. This house belonged at one time to two brothers, Bob and Emmitt Smith. They lived there in the early 1900s before the addition to the house was built on, when it was only a cabin.

Emmitt Smith's room was upstairs, and Bob's room was downstairs. In the process of their living together, and in the process of the passage of time, Bob met Gladys Spink and fell in love with her and married her. For some reason or another, Gladys didn't like Emmitt at all.

Emmitt had heart problems and was on medication. And he always kept his heart medicine on a table setting right next to his bed. Well, one day, Bob had to go to town. He told Gladys that he had to go to town, and for her to keep an eye on Emmitt. Emmitt was upstairs.

Well, while Bob was gone, she went upstairs when Emmit was asleep. She took his heart medicine and went downstairs and locked the door going up to his room. So, when he woke up, he needed his heart medicine and reached over for it. Of course, it wasn't there. So he came down the steps to see if Gladys knew anything about it, but when he came to the door he couldn't get out. He knocked on it, banged, and tried to get the door open, but couldn't. So he went back up the steps, and when he got back upstairs

The Harry Richardson house in Irvington, Kentucky. (Photograph provided by Elbert Cundiff)

the exertion of going up and down the steps and knocking on the door so much just wore out his heart and he fell across the bed and died. This was on December 5, 1939; Emmitt was sixty-three.

When she didn't hear anything out of him in a few minutes, she went back up there and found him laying across the bed dead.

Well, she positioned him just like he died in his sleep, and put his heart medicine back on the table, went back downstairs, and closed the door but didn't lock it.

When Bob came home, he asked her if she heard anything out of Emmitt. She said, "No, everything has been quiet."

He said, "Well, I'd better go up there and check on him." When he went upstairs to check on his brother, he found him dead. He came downstairs and told her.

She said, "Well, I don't understand that."

He said, "Well, I don't either. His heart medicine was setting right there. So I guess it was just his time."

Well, Bob didn't know it, but his wife was the one who murdered Emmitt. And we didn't know all this when we moved there, didn't know that anything was wrong with the house. The very night that we moved there that day, it got dark and we still hadn't unloaded and unboxed everything, but we had put up our beds.

Well, I had a room, and Mom and Dad had a room. This house had a bathroom in it. Granddad had a room next to the kitchen. I was in my room getting ready for bed around eleven o'clock. I heard something but didn't know what it was. I listened and it started off real faint, sounded like a heartbeat. The more I listened to it, the louder it got. Sounded just exactly like a heartbeat. Well, I thought I don't want to be the only one hearing this, so I went there to get Mom and Dad up. Dad wouldn't wake up, but Mom got up and come in there to listen and she heard it, too.

I asked her, "What does that sound like to you?"

She said, "It sounds like a heartbeat, doesn't it?"

It was shaking the whole house. Sounded just like it was going to explode the whole house. Sounded like it was coming through the ceiling of my room. Then, all at once it just stopped.

I looked at her and she looked at me. We didn't hear it anymore, so she went back to bed, and I did, too.

2. "Noises Made by Murdered Jewish Pack Peddlers"

Up here at the Red Hill Church house in northern Monroe County, it is said that you can hear a lot of different noises. It seems that Aunt Martha Hagan and Evelyn Hagan had been visiting someone one night and they were going home in the dark. Said something followed them plumb on down nearly to their home before it disappeared and was never seen again. They never did know what it was. Anyway, this Donna Dubree and her daughter Eve went to a meeting up there one night, and this is the truth.

Me and my daughter was setting out there in the yard at the church house. There was nobody there but me and her. We seen something white that was bigger than a cat but not as big as a dog coming up the road. Well, my little dog was with me and he wouldn't get anywhere close to it. He went out like he was going to take off but he would never get about it. He came back over to me and sat down.

The reason for this place being haunted is that a Jewish pack peddler was killed there, over there close to the church house. They beat him to death and then stole all his stuff that he had for sale as he went from house to house. After that happened, people said they could hear noises that sounded like chains falling from the trees, and all kinds of other noises as well. Ghostly noises, they said.

Nobody ever looked into the details of his death. But, now, that sort of thing happened a lot back then. Pack peddlers were killed and secretly buried, sometimes underneath houses, as they passed through the country selling their stuff. And truth of the matter is, many of these peddlers would come back as ghosts.

3. "The Beating Heart"

There was a Curry fellow who, back in earlier times, owned Camp Currie near Kentucky Lake. He lived on that land and it is said that he made moonshine whiskey. He had a whiskey still there. One night when he was out making the stuff, some police officers slipped up on him while he was making whiskey. They shot him right there on the spot and blew half of his face off.

Later, Mrs. Curry was cooking some sausage and she looked up and saw her husband looking in at her through the window. It scared her so much that she dropped the pan of sausage, and a fire broke out. She went running outside and then fell on the walkway. The next day, all they found was her heart. What that means or what had happened, I don't know. But today all that is left is the walkway and some steps. If you put your ear down against the walkway you can hear her heart beating.

Mr. Curry is still seen there roaming around on the land.

4. "Noises of Chains"

In Henderson, there is a creepy old cemetery that everyone there calls "Agar's Grave." It is an old graveyard where an old church building with a big red front door stands in front of it.

When I was a teenager, we all played around there. We'd try to be "big shots" and go out there to the old graveyard. Since everyone else had done it across the years, we felt that we had to do it, too.

One night we had gone out there and were walking around the old church when we suddenly heard what sounded like chains rattling real loud inside the church. People had always claimed that if you heard this rattling noise you should kick up your heels and get away from there immediately. If you didn't, Agar would get you, for he had come out of his tomb again.

Well, believe me, when we heard the chains rattling, we ran like mad!

5. "The Rocking Chair That Rocks on Its Own"

One night after the four of us had gone to bed and were asleep, my younger brother went to our parents' room and woke them. And he woke me by talking to them.

He told them that the rocking chair was rocking by itself. The rocking chair was in the living room. It was new. He said that he went to the living room and saw it rocking back and forth. And he said when he walked through the living room, the room felt cold to him.

My mother told him to go back to bed. Said there was no one in the room to make the chair rock by itself. Said it was only the wind doing it.

Well, he went back to bed and left his light on. I was awake, lying there. Everything was real quite. Then I heard the rocking chair rocking back and forth, "Squeak, squeak." It kept on rocking for awhile, then stopped. But soon it started rocking again. I was afraid to move! I laid there for at least two hours, listening to it.

The next morning we had a family discussion about it. Mom tried to tell us that it was the wind. But we disproved her theory when we went to the living room and took our hands and pushed the rocking chair back and forth. As we did so, it didn't make any noise. The chair had to have a weight in it before it would make a squeaking noise.

I don't think that anyone else heard it, but on the nights when I would get home about twelve o'clock, and everyone would be asleep, I would go to bed. Sometimes, just as I laid down, it would start rocking. It would rock for awhile, but finally I would drop off to sleep.

I don't know how many times that I heard it. Mom and Dad always wanted me to wake them up, but I was always too scared. Since that summer, I haven't heard it. But Mom says that now, when she is home by herself, she, too, can hear the chair rocking.

6. "The Drunkard's Warning"

Bill Horsley's dad told this story that was supposed to have happened up in Elliott County. Said there was a fellow there who was what they called "a common drunk." He drank whiskey all the time, and he rode horseback while he was drinking. They said he'd go someplace where they were having church services, ride up in the church yard, pull out a gun and go to shooting. This would always break up the church service.

One night he was drunk, had a gallon of moonshine whiskey with him. He had to ride up this holler that had hills on both sides of it, and it was very dark there. He heard a noise behind him that sounded like chains rattling, or being dragged along the ground, bumping up and down. He looked behind him and didn't see anything that was causing the ghost-like noise. But whatever it was scared both him and his horse. Said the horse was so scared that it began to buck like the dickens, and did for five to ten minutes.

Well, the man was scared, too. He accidentally dropped his gallon of moonshine whiskey and broke the glass jug it was in. When that jug broke, it made the horse feel as if it had been cut loose. So, man, that horse took off running, just flying down the road!

This guy quit drinking after that. He never touched a drop of that stuff from that time on.

7. "Ghostly Footsteps on the Railroad Track"

This place called Whitehouse was the railhead here in Johnson County for many years. It was at first a landing on the Big Sandy; it had big hotels and everything. Then the railroad came and the steamboats stopped running. But, it's a fact that where there's a head of transportation, there's always a lot of crime that takes place. One night, right where the ghost of this woman walks the railroad tracks, ten people were killed. It was a feud. They just shot and killed one another. And this girl was found murdered there, laid across the track, her head on one side and her feet on the other. The train ran over her dead body and cut her right into. That was back in the 1890s.

I never got to hear the ghost that walks down the middle of the railroad tracks over here at Whitehouse, but my son did. He was fishing with some friends and they sent him up to the schoolhouse pump to get some water to make coffee. While he was on his way to the pump, he heard it coming. When he figured out what it was, he just froze there in his tracks. And when whatever it was walked by him, he just dropped the bucket and flew. He ran down the hill just as hard as he could run, and he would never go back up there again.

The Meade boys heard it, too. One night when they heard this strange sound, they said they were going to see what it was and would catch it. So they went down there, and one of them set down on that rail, and the other boy sat on this side, and they just waited for it to come. Suddenly, they heard it coming down the track! It sounded just like a woman in high-heel shoes walking on the rail ties.

They had their feet out, see, set down on the rail, put their feet together so she'd have to walk across them. But they said the steps came right down to where they were, just stopped right there behind them, then walked right on across the track and went right on.

They never did see anything, but both of them heard the sound. And they still say it was there, whatever it was.

I don't know whether what they heard took place because of something that happened there on the track. A lot of different things happened down there across the years, including a lot of murders committed there. Also a young girl was killed. So it could have been her that everybody heard.

8. "Brother's Ghostly Footsteps"

My brother-in-law, Lafe, died a tragic death on January 6, 1932. Also in 1932 my brother George drowned on May 7. At that time, we lived in Boldman, Pike County. When this happened, my brother was only a high school junior, and he had told us that he was coming to visit us.

He had a friend, who was a little bit older than he was, who was a railroad engineer. He told my brother and other friends, "Anytime you want to go for a train ride, I'll take you up. You can ride in the cab with me."

Well, my brother told him that he and Mont Mills, a cousin, were coming up to ride with him. My brother told him, said, "We're going to come up and spend a weekend with you."

About one o'clock on a Saturday morning, about the time this train was to come through, my husband Melvin waked me up as he was getting out of bed. He said, "George is out there a-hollering."

And he hollered just as plain as could be. Called us both by name. Melvin hurried and jerked his pants on, ran out the door, and hollered back, "This way; we're over here. Back this way, George."

Me and Melvin went running out there but there was nobody to be seen. My brother wasn't there. He never did come.

At six o'clock, a neighbor lady came down the holler and told us that George had drowned. He was in the swirl hole at Whitehouse, but couldn't swim, and it was very cold. He shouldn't have been in the water, but these friends of his begged him to get in there with them. Well, of course, Daddy and the whole family ran to be there with him. I stayed with Mom, who was sick in bed.

That night, or when it was almost dark, I decided to go down to O.L. Wiley's below Whitehouse and make a telephone call. He was the only person who had one back then. It was sent through the gas company. I wanted to call my husband and ask him to go report George's death to his own family.

I got to the top of this bank where these footsteps walked along with me. . . . There were several bunches of stickweeds there, so I stepped over those weeds and waited. They were coming all right, and they were the same footsteps. Well, I just stayed hid. Whatever it was never did see me. And when this thing came on up here and turned down the bank, it hit this sand and the footsteps stopped right then. I just stood still.

Finally, I went on and sent the telephone call to Melvin, and he went up Mud Creek to go and tell his folks, who lived over at Harold, about George's drowning.

After Melvin got there, he and Big Yank, we called him, were walking, and they heard this moaning, just like really suffering. Melvin said that when he heard this, he didn't feel good. They turned around to look back as they kept walking, but said that they didn't see anything that was making that noise. This same moan continued to follow them around the bank out there. They were both scared to death. And my husband isn't a fraidy cat! He doesn't believe in things like that, but this thing really got to him.

Whatever it was that was making this moaning noise followed them so far, then it quit. They didn't hear it anymore. But it just might have been my brother, the one that drowned that night.

9. "The Feeling of Death"

A very strange thing happened to me at the age of eleven when I was in the fifth grade here in Warren County. My teacher was Mrs. Fatone. She had us read a book about the Queen of Sheba.

When we finished reading the book, the teacher gave us an assignment that included making fake tombstones. She wanted us to put on the stones that we died either in the 1800s or 1900s, specifying the date that we died.

At first, I thought that would be fun, so I put my death as happening in the 1900s, at age seventeen. But for some reason I did not like that age. A strange feeling began coming over me, so I changed the date of my death to say that I died when I was one year old.

That afternoon when I got home from school, I showed it to my Mom. For some reason, she didn't care for it very much, nor did I. She threw it in the fireplace.

Ever since we drew those tombstones at school, something just didn't feel right even though I changed my age. I had a feeling that death would either happen to me or someone else in the family when I turned seventeen. Well, six years went by. I would think about that every now and then, still somewhat worried. Well, when I reached the age of seventeen, I thought about it a lot. I didn't like the feeling that I had. I told some friends about it, but they thought I was crazy. My boyfriend at that time thought that I was, too.

Well, the year passed by and I was getting closer to my eighteenth birthday. I had a feeling that death would hit me when I turned eighteen.

One night just five days before my birthday, my boyfriend Justin and I were scheduled to go to a ball game. He was in the band. But we decided not to go. Instead, he wanted to go to a movie. I was not feeling very well at the time, but I decided to go anyway.

I had seen my good friend Scott at school that day, but for some reason we did not say anything to each other. We just gave each other a look that sort of said, "See you later."

After Justin and I drove home from the movie, we passed an ambulance and the feeling that I got was not good. I usually didn't get such feelings, but when I got home Mom told me that Scott and his girlfriend Lily had had a car wreck and that things didn't look at all good. That night I went to the hospital with Justin. About three hours after we got there, the doctors came to tell all of us that Scott had passed away, but that Lily was fine.

Later on, strange noises entered the scene. Scott's parents, his grandparents, his sister, and I would hear strange tappings on the window and other places in our houses. We would look around to see who or what it was, but no one was there. All of us just knew that it was Scott's way of letting us know that he was still with us and that everything was okay with him.

10. "Strange Doors and Latches"

In the Lamasco section of Lyon County there are numerous tales of supernatural and beyond-human occurrences. One of these tales concerns a Negro slave who was whipped to death by order of his mistress. The blood clots may still be seen on the floor of the two-story house, which is located about a block off the road from Cadiz to Eddyville. It is not far from the home where Denny Meyhugh and family reside today.

The door at the head of the stairs, opening into the room in which the slave was beaten to death, is said to still bear record of the blood-curdling event, in that every night at the stroke of twelve midnight, it swings open, creaking as though an unseen force is being used, no matter how securely it may be fastened. The present tenants have grown accustomed to

Although not a common practice, some pre–Great Depression era storytellers, such as Granny (Harris) Witty Rasner, attempted to portray ghostly movements and sounds as they told ghost tales and other scary stories. (Photograph provided by Ella Washam)

the nightly procedure and pay no attention to it, except to send chills down the spines of listeners who hear the story.

11. "The Ghost That Followed a Family to Missouri"

When Dew Bruce discovered that the farm he bought in Henderson was haunted, he was surprised. He was even more startled when he found that when his family moved to Missouri, the ghost did, too.

It all began in 1947 when Bruce purchased the W.W. Gower farm, located on the Airline Road, one and a half miles southeast of Henderson. The farm was occupied by the Marvin Blanford family until late September of that year and the Bruces moved into the house in October.

On their second night there, they heard a door opening and footsteps moving throughout the house. But they couldn't see anything making the sounds.

The noises were heard by the Bruces, his sister, and some friends from Missouri. . . . After that, they began to feel that the ghost headquartered in the barn and roamed the house at will. A total of eighteen persons claim to have heard the ghost. As word of the mysterious footsteps spread, there were many skeptical listeners.

A group of Henderson residents went to the farm and challenged the ghost to make some noises. They were promptly converted when the distinctive sounds of footsteps filled the air.

The ghost frequently visited the Bruce residence, always entering and leaving by the same door.

On one occasion, the Bruce's daughter . . . was sleeping on the couch in the living room. She was awakened by the sounds of the back door opening, followed by the familiar footsteps throughout every room in the house.

They assumed the ghost was searching for something, because during one daytime visit, a roll-type desk top was heard to open and close. However, nothing was ever disturbed. If the ghost did go through the papers in the desk, it always left them just as neat as it found them.

Another strange sound the Bruces became accustomed to during their twenty-year stay was the noise of a car driving up and a car door opening. Although they would run to the window each time they heard the car, they were never able to see anything. . . .

In 1967, the farm was purchased by the Kentucky Highway Department for a right of way. Bruce then moved his family to Canalou, Missouri, assuming that the ghost would remain in Henderson. After all, it had been there when he purchased the farm.

However, the family had been in the new surroundings only a few days before the distinctive footsteps were heard. And although he can't explain how the ghost got there, Bruce is absolutely certain that the sounds now heard in Missouri are the same as those previously heard in Kentucky.

Only one thing has changed. The ghost is now visible. Although Bruce never saw the apparition while living in Kentucky, he has seen it twice in his present location.

Described as a beautiful young woman, the ghost appeared by the front door both times, and then slowly faded away.

12. "Ghostly Groans"

Old Uncle Joe Fielders and Dick Downs stopped at my house one day to get out of a big rain. This rain resulted in what we called the Flood of 1919.

In their conversations, they told of a vacant house at the head of Steel Branch that was haunted. According to their story, the family that occupied it at the time moved out of the house. One day, some fellow came along, stopped in, and saw a couple of wooden forks used for a gun rack nailed over a door.

Deciding that he would like to have this gun rack, he got up on a box, took hold of one of the racks and began trying to pull it loose from the wall. As he did, a mighty groan was heard in what we called the loft [upstairs]. He immediately let loose of the rack and got down. When he did, the groaning stopped.

Waiting for a while, because he wanted the racks very badly, he decided to make another try at getting them. He took hold of the racks, but when he did the groaning was heard again and it was so loud this time it almost shook the entire house. He not only jumped down from the box, he ran out of the house without a backward glance. He didn't want anything else to do with that ghost-like noise. Didn't want to hear it anymore.

13. "Phantom High Heel Walker"

This is a story about a high heel walker. It is supposed to take place on rainy Monday nights down in Auxier. Lots of people in the lower end of Auxier have heard the phantom high heel walker. You can actually hear the high heels clicking on the streets when she is walking up and down them.

This is just a guess as to what this is all about, but there was a woman who was killed in a car wreck. She was a nicely dressed woman. Her name was Gladys Music. Some people think that she might be the woman who does the walking. I don't know if anybody has ever actually seen her or not when they hear the footsteps.

I would say that she was killed back in the early 1940s. There's an old house down in Auxier that she lived in when she was killed. It's still standing. Many people have said that this house itself is haunted.

I don't know exactly what has taken place. All I know is what I've heard people say.

14. "The Undying Footsteps"

Several years ago after I had rented a place in this community, imagine my surprise to hear reports on all sides that the place was haunted. It was said that the building's foundations had been built by a certain man who built a filling station, apparently for the purpose of furnishing power for cars. Instead, he had used it for furnishing spirits [whiskey] in the form of good old mountain dew. In the process, he was blown up.

Following this incident, a man in white would appear at the exact place where the building had gone up in smoke. The occupants of the house which stood near related that footsteps were often heard crossing the porch when no visitor could be seen. Not being of a superstitious nature, I paid these tales no mind and went ahead with my plans. Everything went along smoothly for some time, except that one Sunday morning a gentleman came to purchase a bottle of strong drink, because he had done so in the past.

It took quite a bit of talking to persuade him that none was available. Not long afterwards, we were entertaining company and I was in one door and my sister in another, when I heard supposedly someone crossing the porch. Naturally, I rushed to the door. In the meantime, my sister had heard the same footsteps, so we reached the door about the same time. No one was in sight, and we were not quite so sure that there were haunts. But several times in the future, similar incidents happened.

One morning a girl appeared at my back door asking for something to eat. She was on her way to Pikeville by her thumb [hitchhiking]. I invited her inside. While the coffee perked, footsteps moved across the floor of the front room. My first intuition was that she had a companion who would block the front, while she would block the rear.

I rushed to the front, planning to slide a bolt on the inside of the front door to cut off entrance that way, since my only way of escape would be by way of a dining room window which lay between the two doors. However, she evidently had not played any tricks, as there was no one at the front door—just a repetition of the false footsteps.

As time passed, the footsteps did not come so frequently, and I even mustered courage to spend one night alone, although I wouldn't go so far as to say my slumber was of the smoothest. Until this day, I can't explain the why or how of the footsteps.

15. "The Baby's Cry"

In a house on Smoot Creek [Letcher County], a baby's cry was heard by everyone that spent the night there. The cry was heard until the house was torn down and a new house was built on the same site. There is no information as to whether the baby's cry is heard in the new house or not.

Two explanations were given for the cry of the baby. A baby that had died mysteriously was buried just off the back porch. No one knew of the child's death until someone observed the grave while visiting its parents. It was rumored that the mother had left the child with the father for a weekend, and the child had been killed at a drunken party the father had that weekend.

Another explanation was that the cry came from a suitcase of baby's clothes in the attic. They were the clothes of three infants that had died in early childhood. The suitcase was in the corner of the attic, and that was where the cry came from until the suitcase was moved into the middle of the floor during the spring cleaning. Then the cry was heard from the middle of the floor.

This story was verified by many people, and each declare that they had heard it but could offer no definite explanation. But each person said the cry sounded as if the baby was in terrible pain.

16. "Fiddler in a Cave"

A story that has been told for many years in Bardstown concerns a cave that starts at one edge of town and ends at the other, passing under the square. It seems that at one time everyone wondered where it ended, so an old Negro man decided to explore it.

He carried a violin, which he played as he walked along, and a group of friends followed the path of music on top of the ground. The music stopped abruptly at the spot where the courthouse now stands, and the man never came out of the cave.

They say that on certain nights, when there is a full moon, if one puts his ear to the ground in the courthouse yard, he can hear violin music played by the old man's ghost.

17. "The Crying Baby"

It was told that a family of three lived in Aunt Roxie's house before she moved in. This was a husband and wife and their infant baby. The man got mad because his wife went to town without taking the baby with her. So, in anger, he took a pair of scissors and stuck them into the baby's throat. He then placed the baby in a shoe box and buried it alive, next to a fence post.

My cousin and I used to go there and play in the yard after Aunt Roxie moved in. Out there next to the fence we could hear a baby crying. We heard it but never thought too much about it. Sometime later on, they found a baby in that shoe box that was buried next to the fence post where we used to play.

No telling what we would have thought if we had known what those sounds were.

18. "The Ghost That Sat on the Bed"

One night about nine o'clock, I heard someone come across the porch, then into the room, and up the steps. I was sleeping in the front bedroom upstairs. Something walked across the floor and sat down on the bed beside me. I thought it was a neighbor, Wallace Hughes, who usually came over at night.

Well, I felt for someone, but nothing was there. I couldn't feel or see anything. Well, just at that same time, Mother hollered up at me and asked who it was that had come in.

I told her that it wasn't anybody.

She said, "Well, I know it was, because I heard someone come in."

Well, when she said that, I ran downstairs and we got a light and went back up and searched the place over. But we never found anything.

Let me tell you right now, I just let that thing have my bed, because I didn't want it any more after that.

19. "The Three Ornery Boys"

Three young men, Lee, Lynn, and Edgar were in their prime and just spoiling for a good time. So, on a night that was perfect for a coon hunt, they gathered their hounds and took to the woods anticipating a good catch.

On their way, the young men came to the house of a neighbor who was famous for the delicious apples he grew. Knowing the man was elderly and possibly hard of hearing, they raided his cellar and left with a good supply of apples. Then, at the edge of the pasture, they ran across the neighbor's beehives and robbed them of honey.

Deciding that it would be more fun to eat than to hunt, they found a place of privacy, built a roaring fire, passed a bottle of bourbon, and settled down to a game of cards to determine who would get the apples and who would get the honey.

They had just gotten interested in the division of their loot, when they heard a strange noise coming from the direction of the Scott grave-yard.

They sent the coon dogs out to chase whatever it was, but to their surprise, the dogs returned to the fire, tails tucked between their legs. The noise continued as though someone was running a stick across the palings of a fence. First, the noise was above them and then it was immediately below them.

They decided that it was Lynn's brother George trying to scare them. So, having solved the mystery, they continued their game.

But the noise didn't stop, and the dogs began to howl and moan. Finally, whatever was making the noise seemed to have settled in a tree right above them, making the most awful sounds and moans they had ever heard.

Their consciences were hurting them over stealing the apples and honey, and they concluded it was old Satan himself after them. So they broke and ran to Lynn's house, where they remained the rest of the night. . . .

Today, if you travel down that same road on a still, dark night, you can sometimes hear the footsteps of "something" following just behind you.

20. "Ghostly Horse Hoofs"

A lot of good stories are rooted deeply in the countryside of north Logan County, and the poor, hardworking families that make a living from its reluctant soil.

An older cousin of mine told me this story about himself when he was a young man. It seems that he and his aging mother, along about the end of World War I, rented a cabin that had not been lived in for quite some time. It was within their price range, as only a token rental price was asked. My cousin felt that he had found somewhat of a bargain, as the use of a small orchard was included with the house. But it didn't take him long to realize that more came with the house than free apples and peaches.

On the very first night there, when they had barely retired for the night, a thundering sound of horse hooves began to circle the house. Think-ing that some rambunctious friends were trying to play a joke, my cousin thought he would surprise them. He creeped toward the front door, then heard the sounds of running horses turning the corner and heading toward the front door. He flung the door open, then leaped into the front yard shouting so as to frighten the horse. He was amazed to find himself con-fronted by the quiet of a peaceful, country night. There was absolutely noth-ing to be seen and nothing to be heard except the normal sounds of a north Logan night, sounds coming from frogs and crickets and things like that.

They continued to live there for some time. He soon got used to living with a few ghostly horses and unknown sounds. Nothing ever bothered them, but ghostly sounds in and around that old house never did stop being heard.

21. "A Night on Gap Hill"

In 1990, the Port William Historical Society published a hundred-page book of *Memorable Events*. One of the contributors was Barbara Stahl, whose father, Charles Hunter, had lived in Carrollton from 1907 to 1923. His memories of this area were picturesque.

For many years, the Gap Hill Cemetery, located off Highway 227, was used for burials. A few tombstones are still visible, but most graves are unmarked. Barbara tells us:

"My father was dared by some of his friends to spend the night on Gap Hill. It was supposed to be haunted. 'Well, I will if you'll go along, too,' he told his friends.

"That evening, they sat around an old tree stump in which they had built a fire. There was Charlie, his dog, and two friends. Light was fading from the sky; getting dark.

"They were sitting around talking, and when it got dark the dog started whimpering with his tail between his legs. Dad was a little bewildered by his dog's behavior. Then he heard a faint sound circling the hill. As it went around and around, it became louder and louder, like horses' hooves roaring and getting closer.

"Dad looked into the darkness to see what it was, but there was nothing to be seen. Only the sounds to be heard. When he looked back at his friends, they had run away from there. They had run down the hill along with the dog.

"Dad gave no second thought to this. He, too, took off down the hill, and he didn't stop until he ran right through the middle of some blackberry bushes down at the bottom of the hill along the railroad tracks.

"He was so scratched up by the bushes, he was a real mess. He never did find out what it was they heard, and he never again tried to spend the night up on Gap Hill."

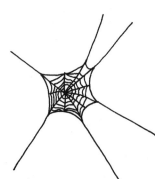

Chapter 4

Headless Ghosts

1. "The Headless Woman of Benton Hollow"

Not more than a half mile from where we're sitting right now is a hollow. It goes by the name Benton Hollow. There's a peculiar legend about this place, a legend called "The Headless Woman of Benton Hollow." It seems to be that on certain nights, a headless woman appears and canters about, always within a certain vicinity and always looking for her head.

I think that this legend originated decades ago, more than likely a hundred years ago. This part of Monroe County was still a little bit wild at that time.

The legend claims that a young couple came through this part of the country on their way to a certain parcel of land which they had probably obtained from the government. Anyway, during their journey, they went through Benton Hollow. As they went through here, an accident occurred for which no reason was ever provided. During the accident, the young bride and groom were both killed. And, in fact, nobody ever knew who did it, or why, or when. They did know the "how" part, however, as the young bride lost her head.

Some local residents found their bodies a few weeks later, quite decayed by that time. The peculiar thing was that the groom, while being quite dead, was still totally intact. But the bride was decapitated. A vigorous search took place all through the vicinity, looking for her lost head. But they never did find any clues to explain this gruesome murder, and nobody knew just what to do about it. They took the two bodies and buried them nearby as quickly as possible.

According to the old legend, on certain nights the young woman, in spirit form, still comes back from her unmarked grave, looking for a suitable head. Many has been the poor traveler who was scared out of his wits when he passed through Benton Hollow. They see the headless woman's ghost, always dressed in a dull, black gown, and always carrying a dull butcher knife.

The people of this neighborhood still believe this story. As for me, I remember when I used to walk to the Old Mt. Herman School, I would walk through Benton Hollow. In the winter time, the days were short, the sun would be getting low, and the hollow would be quite dark. As I went through there, quite hastily, I remember reciting the Twenty-Third Psalm, as it always seemed to comfort me.

That's one legend that will live on and on. Whether the poor lady will ever find her head or not, that's a question that still perplexes people through here.

2. "The Headless Man"

I went down the road one night, here in Clinton County, right down below Lee's Chapel, and I met a man that didn't have a head. I don't know why, but I wasn't really scared. Ordinarily, that would have spooked me out! Anyway, this headless man said "hello" to me, but I just went on down the road, and he, also, kept walking in the other direction.

What happened was, it was really dark, so I just went up to the side of the road I was walking on and, when I looked, I saw somebody coming. But I could never see a hat or anything, and I couldn't see its face. When we met, he didn't have a head; just said "hello," then kept staggering down through there.

I turned around two or three times to see if he was turning around and coming back towards me. But he never did turn around; just kept going on down the road. I never did know who or what that was, but I certainly was not dreaming when I saw it.

3. "Headless Horseman of Humphrey Hollow"

Once upon a time, many years ago, a headless horseman was seen riding down through Humphrey Hollow here in western Metcalfe County. A neighbor of mine, name Kyle Huckelby, said that he was out squirrel hunting when this strange thing happened.

He claimed that he saw a movement off in the distance. So he went over to find out what it was. And, believe me, he found out the hard way just what it was. He said that he chased this thing quite a ways down through the hollow. All of a sudden, he could see that the thing, maybe a human, that he was chasing, had no head on its shoulders. And it was riding a horse. He said that he turned around as quick as he could and began running away from that thing. He knew the minute that he saw it that he had come into contact with the Headless Horseman of Humphrey Hollow, something that had been talked about by the old-timers for years and years.

4. "The Headless Woman"

Down here on Otter Creek, at the foot of this mountain, there are some good farming bottomlands. For some time now, people down there have been seeing a woman with no head walking across there. They say that she's dressed in a white gown.

One of my boys was courting this girl; well, she's his wife now. He was driving this old car of his up through there one Sunday night, and he saw this headless woman's ghost. He got out of his car and took off running across that field, trying to get away from whatever it was that he had seen.

Well, there was a patch of fog floating along the top of that creek. He thought that it was a ghost. He came on home that night and told us about seeing whatever it was. He said that he finally went on over there to investigate what it was that he had seen. It was a body of fog, but said that it looked just exactly like the misty figure of the headless woman that so many other people had talked about seeing.

Now, it just might be that many of the ghosts that people see are really nothing more than white, foggy mist.

5. "The Headless Woman of Kino"

There was this woman here in Kino that had no head. Poor, pitiful, old woman. I saw her in broad open daylight. It was at dinner. I don't know whether she's still standing by herself or not, but she was the last time I saw her. I was rolling a cigarette when I saw her. She had on the longest dress you've ever seen, just as white as snow. I looked at that old thing for a few minutes, then my hair started raising up off my head. She didn't have a head on her shoulders. I ran off and left her.

My own father told me that one time this headless woman got on his horse behind him. Rode up there with him to the old Scott place, then hopped off. He never could see her after that.

However, once we saw her as we rode together in this wagon on our way to church. She crawled up in the wagon with us. She got out of the wagon when we got up there at the Scott place. All total, I've seen her four times myself. I saw her one time when she was picking up and loading some wood on this wagon. I never could see her horse, but I could hear it snorting through its mouth and nose.

I was always scared to death to walk to school by myself, afraid I would see her. It's been about thirty years now since I saw this old headless woman, but years ago, she was seen a lot.

6. "The Woman with No Head"

It was a summer day around 1962 in the small farming community of Kino, located east of Glasgow. Willie Bunch was walking home after spending the night with his friend Fred Duggard. He was carrying a rooster that he had bought from his grandfather for a grand total of twenty-five cents. It was a damp, wet day and getting near lunch time.

Just off the old dirt road that Bunch was walking on, a tree had blown down, and he sat down to roll himself a cigarette. While he was getting his tobacco out of his pocket, he looked up and there about twelve feet away stood a woman with no head.

"I looked at the bottom of her feet to the top of what would have been her head, but I really couldn't see what it was or who it was," Bunch stated.

This woman was dressed all in white. The gown, that Bunch later assumed to be a wedding gown, trailed along far behind the old woman. He watched her for a few minutes, not believing his own eyes, while the old woman picked up some firewood.

While trying to get away from the ghostly woman, he grabbed his rooster by the neck instead of its feet, and choked the poor creature to death. "Why, its neck was two feet long," Bunch said. So he just threw the rooster down when he saw what he had done, and went on home.

Another incident involving the old headless woman occurred to the Bunch family on their way back from church one Sunday. They were all riding in a horse-drawn wagon, and were traveling along on a little dirt road on which Willie Bunch had previously seen the headless being. As they neared the Old Scott Place, as it was called back then, Bunch's grandfather heard a horse galloping and snorting from behind. He turned around but didn't see a horse. All he saw was the old woman with no head crawling into the back of the wagon with them.

Pathways through clusters of trees and along isolated roadways are popular hideaways for spirit presences and headless creatures. (Photograph by the author)

He sat in the back end of the wagon until they got to the Scott farm. There, the headless creature got off, walked toward the farm, and disappeared from sight. Bunch's wife, Louvenia, also saw her that time.

Bunch also claimed that the headless woman was responsible for planting a field full of flowers.

"I guess that field had an acre or more of flowers," Bunch claimed. "They were the prettiest things I ever saw, and I'm being honest," he said.

All total, Bunch saw the old woman with no head four or five times, but he wasn't the only one to ever see her. According to his grandfather, one day the old woman suddenly appeared on the back of his horse. She then dismounted as they neared the Scott farm.

Willie Bunch's eldest son, Lee, also saw the old woman. That was at his grandmother's house where the woman with no head was walking down the stairs. Lee said that he counted every step that she took as she came down the steps and went on out of the house. This time, she was dressed in a long, black dress and was carrying an umbrella, but she still didn't have a head.

That old headless woman was almost always seen in the same area, gathering firewood or going to the Scott farm. Every time that Bunch saw her, it was still daylight and was usually wet outside, as if it had just rained the day before. He heard that someone had cut off a preacher's head in the area.

Bunch didn't know whether or not the preacher had anything to do with the old woman, or if seeing her was just a coincidence. Nonetheless, that was the only reason he could give as to why there was an old woman with no head lurking in the woods around Kino, Barren County.

7. "The Headless Ghost That Joined a Rider on His Horse"

Over at Hagers Gap here in Johnson County, Bee Webb killed a soldier who was hiding out. Well, Bee was coming back home one night through Hagers Gap when a man jumped onto his horse, and I guess the man was so heavy that he almost weighted the horse down to the ground.

Well, Bee looked back there behind him and saw that it was a man, but whoever it was didn't have a head. But just from the way the headless man felt, Bee could tell that it was the same soldier that he had killed. So all that Bee could think was that the man had *him* now. Bee said to him, says, "I guess you've got me now.

Just about that time, the horse reared up and the headless man fell off, so Bee got away.

What happened to Bee is one of the reasons nobody'll cross Hagers Gap by themselves, especially back in the old days. When the steamboats would land up here, everyone would get together before they'd go across the gap. At one time, somebody saw this headless figure driving a wagon through Hagers Gap. Said that the man was hauling a wagon load of heads— human heads—and these heads were all hollering, "Oh, Lordy! Oh, Lordy!"

I don't have any record of who that man was. The story came from my grandfather.

8. "The Trotting Horse"

This story was passed down by my grandfather Jim Wells and his twin brother, Will. It took place right outside a store owned by their father, located about a mile down river from Hagers Gap here in Floyd County. I guess it was about twilight one day, and the boys were outside. A man came riding up on a horse, and believe it or not, the man had no head.

Something else that was strange about him was that he had some wood kindling in his hands. The little boys didn't know what to do. The fact that the man had no head scared them, and the fact that he had some kindling in his hands gave them the idea that he intended to burn the store building down.

The boys ran in the store to get their father. By the time he came out, the rider had swerved the horse away and was taking off down the road. All they could hear was the sound of the horse's hoofs going across the bridge. Then it would turn around and the horse could be heard running back in their direction.

Later on, other people could hear these sounds, too. It has come to be known as the Trotting Horse.

9. "The Headless Woman That Joined Riders on Their Horses"

There's a place here in Wayne County that is located between Dry Valley and Rocky Hill. It's known as Gaylor Gap. A Frenchman came in there in the early days and settled. His profession was making hats. And there was this beautiful young lady with him whom he claimed was his daughter, but no one was ever able to verify this. So as time went on, she mysteriously disappeared. No one knew where she went, nor when. But after that, the local people claimed that Gaylor Gap was haunted.

They said that every night, if you rode through the gap, a lady dressed in white, with no head, would jump on the horse behind you, ride through the gap with you, then disappear. Many people have told me personally that they have seen the headless ghost woman. And all of the older generation around there were totally sold on the truth about that story.

One night when I was teaching at Rocky Hill back in the 1930s, I'd been helping this beginning teacher at the Dry Hollow School with her record book. We didn't get her book finished until well into the night. And there was a little snow on the ground that hadn't melted, but it was frozen enough to be crunchy.

As I was going home to Rocky Hill, and nearing Gaylor Gap, I heard people talking and I thought that probably someone knew that I was out and had planned to scare me. So I picked up a rock in each hand. As I neared the voices, the crunching of the snow alerted them that I was approaching, so they hushed their talking.

As I got closer to them, I recognized the men. However, I didn't speak to them. I was wearing a white scarf, and had a black and white mixed-color tweed coat on. And there was enough light provided by the small amount of snow that they only knew that it was a woman.

When I got to my boarding house, I told this young couple that I boarded with about what had just taken place with these men. Well, we all laughed about it, and I told them that the next day they'd be hearing about the ghost lady going through Gaylor Gap. So from that time on during the rest of the school year, the more they told that story, the bigger it got.

To this day, these men do not know that they didn't see the real headless lady go through Gaylor Gap.

10. "Headless Neighbor"

Back when my father and his brothers were kids, they lived in a small rural community at the top of a hill. Across the road from them lived this Smith couple. The man's name was John and, according to my father, they were considered well-to-do. However, John must have had some sort of problem, because one night he took a shotgun, put it under his chin and blew his head off.

At that time, my Uncle Wilbur was fourteen years old. About that same time, people had reported seeing bizarre things after dark. The Studewells had a garage at the bottom of the hill. Well, one night in the spring of the year, when Uncle Wilbur was walking home, he says he saw something come out of the garage. He swears to this day that he saw John Smith, without a head, come out of the garage.

It scared Uncle Wilbur so badly that he ran all the way up the hill and didn't stop running until he got to the house. Even then, it took him half an hour to calm down enough to tell his family what had frightened him so badly. Said he was scared to death.

11. "Headless Man Ghost Tale"

A lady by the name of Mrs. Hall lived in this community in Bath County. She was very religious and attended church every time there was a church service in her home church. She lived about two miles from the church. The road she traveled over was very spooky. There were trees along the road. Some old houses were close to the road, and about one more mile there were no houses. Nothing but trees along the road at that point.

One night, Mrs. Hall and her daughter went to church. The night was very dark, and they had a light to guide their way. After they had gotten about a mile away from home, Mrs. Hall heard footsteps trudging along the road. As this sound came closer, she could hear queer sounds of a different nature, then she could see the image of a man.

She could see his legs and his body and a white collar, but she couldn't see his head. This man was headless. As she came nearer, the image disappeared and the sounds stopped. Mrs. Hall was so excited that she hardly knew where she was. She went on a little farther, then she turned to go back home.

When they got back to this same spot, there was a strong breeze that almost swept them off their feet. Something then brushed by Mrs. Hall's side and almost took her with it. She was holding her little daughter's hand tight, and something was trying to pull her daughter away from her.

Her daughter began to cry and said that something had her by the hand. Mrs. Hall and daughter began to run and scream as loud as they could. As they neared their home, her husband heard them and ran to meet them. But they were scared so bad that they didn't even know him.

Finally, they realized who he was, and Mrs. Hall told him what had happened. Then he began telling them that some years ago a man had been beheaded at that spot along the road.

They never went to church at night anymore.

12. "The Headless 'Haint'"

Many years ago in Harlan County, there was a church meeting one night. It lasted very late. After church broke, people went their separate ways. It so happened that one lady lived way back in the woods farther than the others.

Everything was very still and quiet as she walked along this winding path. This sort of made her jittery. Her nerves were acting up, so she says to her nerves, "Now nerves, youse quit being so jittery and behave yourself, there's nothing going to get you if I can help it."

She walked a little farther and she heard a funny sound. It sounded as if something was moaning and groaning. This scared her almost out of her wits. She turned and saw this big "haint" without a head. She says to herself, "Land sakes of mercy, what in the world?"

She was scared stiff. She began saying over and over, "Move feet, move. Move feet, move." But they wouldn't go. This "haint" without a head followed her home.

Boy, I'm telling you, she made ninety miles an hour up that mountain. When she reached her shack, she went inside and bolted her door. She never left her shack after that.

The tale of this terrible night was spread through the community the next morning. From then on, people watched for the headless "haint."

Several weeks later, a neighbor found the old woman dead. To this day, nobody knows how she died. Some people thought the "haint" was a warning to her [that she was to die soon].

13. "Ghost of the Coal Mine"

They called him Big John because his name was John and his frame was big. He was a native of Russia and had found his way to the coal mines to work. He lived and bached in a little shack near the mines.

Big John became an expert at explosives and that was his undoing because one day he got careless and blew himself to Kingdom Come. The coal miners heard the explosion and they came running. Big John was dead; his head was blown clean off.

Not long after that, one of the miners was reporting to work early, and he went down into the mine in the cage alone. That is, he thought he was alone. He walked on in and shut the door and there wasn't anybody there. Then he heard somebody breathe and sort of grunt, and he turned around so the light on his cap would shine on whatever it was.

What it was, was terrible. There stood a man without a head on his shoulders. The coal miner could look clean down inside of him. He turned his light downward, and there he saw Big John's head. He was holding it in his arms and the head was smiling and happy, just like it had been during lifetime.

The poor miner didn't know what to do, so he just shut his eyes and put his hand over his mouth to keep from screaming. When the cage he was in landed, the ghost was gone.

14. "Ghost of the Headless Man"

Sam went hunting one night, and while he was out in the woods it started to rain. He knew he couldn't do much hunting in the rain, so he turned around and started back home. On the way, he said he seen a little shed and went inside. There was nothing in there but a dirt floor and another door on the other side.

All at once this other door opened and a man walked in. But, wow, this man had no head. It had been cut off. Sam shot at this headless thing and emptied his gun in the process. Then he run out of the shed and went home.

The next morning, he went back and there was not a shed to be seen anywhere. But he said that there was a tree there that was full of bullet holes where he'd emptied his gun shooting at whatever that headless thing was.

15. "Headless Ghost Sits on Couch"

This is a story about my great-uncle and his young wife. After they had been married for only a year or so, they moved into a new home—a rural tenant house on the borderline between Butler and Logan counties.

Along with their new baby, they moved and settled in their new house. Their first night there, after a hard day of moving and putting into place all the things that a growing family accumulates, they had a late dinner. After they finished eating, they built a roaring fire in the fireplace and settled down on each end of the sofa there in front of the fireplace. They were relaxing and enjoying the peace and quiet of a country night.

They had just begun to wind down their busy day. Their baby was sound asleep on a nearby bed and perhaps their own eyes were growing a bit heavy. Life was good at this point but about to suffer a drastic change, both in their peaceful setting and appreciation of their new home.

To their surprise, an outside door opened and in walked a headless specter. It scared them to death. This headless creature walked across the floor and sat down on the sofa right between the couple.

I mean, it scared them to death. They hopped up and took off down the road, each trying to outrace the other to a relative's house nearby.

Taken into the safety of a different house, someone there finally asked, "Where is the baby?"

Only then did they realize that they had completely forgotten their child. They'd left it there in the room with that headless creature.

Family members volunteered to retrieve the child. The parents were strangely reluctant to return to their house, but when they did, all was well. Upon the bed the baby was safely sleeping. It was totally unaware of the terror and fright that its parents had lived through that night.

Needless to say, they soon moved out of that house, never to return.

Animal Ghosts

1. "Pig Woman of the Woods"

My brother told me this story, which he claimed was a favorite of his scout troop. It's a story about a pig woman of the woods.

Many years ago there was this young lady who lived out in these woods with her parents, who raised hogs that were caught in traps in the woods. We're not talking about the fat, tame pigs that people nowadays raise. We're talking about big wild razorback pigs that were caught in the woods. There aren't any pigs like these left in the woods, or very few at least, but in those days it was said that you couldn't go but a few feet in any direction without bumping into one.

The father of this young lady that this story is about was about six foot, five inches tall, and weighed 300 pounds, all muscle. He would go out and catch these razorbacks in these traps and then carry them back with his bare hands for five or ten miles to his cabin.

One day, he went out to the pen to quiet the hogs down, and they went totally wild and tore him to pieces. Killed him right there on the spot. While he was still screaming, his wife ran out of the cabin with a shotgun, but she couldn't shoot without hitting her husband. So she grabbed the ax from the woodpile and jumped into the pig pen and started hacking at these hogs that were killing her husband. Soon, she was overpowered and torn apart, too.

Now, the daughter, young and pretty as she was, was also a very brilliant lady. So she stayed in the cabin. But it wasn't long until the hogs went totally wild and tore down the fence and came crashing into the cabin. The daughter hid in the clothes closet, but the hogs found her. But instead of killing her, they cut her up pretty bad with their teeth, and took turns rooting her body around the room. They left her in a bloody heap in the floor.

About nine months later, she had her own baby girl. Well, it wasn't really a baby girl. It was half razorback and totally vicious. But the young mother, being insane from the attack, raised the pig girl into a pig-like woman, who was named Pig Woman. Soon thereafter, the young mother died. But Pig Woman lived on in the woods, busily occupied with tearing apart travelers after dark, long after her mother died. Some people say that you can still hear her snorting out there in the woods.

You can believe me or not, but I've heard Pig Woman out there. Just to be safe, I always sleep with a knife nearby and next to a tree that I can climb into easy. From what I've been told, Pig Woman can't climb, and I never eat bacon or ham or sausage in these woods.

2. "The Ghostly White Dog"

My family and I lived in a little house next to the railroad track here in Harlan County. There was a creek between our house and the railroad track. Anyway, late at night, you could go outside in the backyard and look over toward the railroad track and see what looked like a big white dog. It had the reddest eyes you've ever seen, and they would glow real scary-like in the dark. These eyes would follow you anywhere you went in the yard, but this dog could never come across the track. So what these eyes looked like were big, glowing, red coals of fire.

Late one night, my husband and I were walking down the road from our house, and this dog-like thing was following us from a distance. It never got very close, but its eyes would never leave you. Once you got to a certain spot in the road, this dog would just disappear. But you could go on down the road, turn around, come back, and the dog would reappear at the same spot where it had disappeared earlier. It happened like that every single time you were out at night.

One of the strangest things about all of this is that the dog never made a sound. It never barked or whined. It truly never made a single sound as it walked, not even the crunching of leaves. And it never left a paw print, not even in the mud. There were several times that my dad and I went to look for prints in the mud when I was little, but we never found anything.

Several other people can give you a similar account of this same thing happening to them, but no one can tell you exactly what it was or why it was there.

3. "The Mysterious Dog"

When my mother was a small girl, she lived in a rustic country house with her parents and many brothers and sisters. This was truly a large family, and they experienced some weird and interesting things across the years. Mother said that there were a lot of strange things that happened in that house, like someone walking through the rooms when no one was there, and even noises that sounded like someone falling across the bed, even after everyone had been tucked in for the night.

One night, after their nightly prayer and devotions, and the whole family was tucked into bed, a large white dog came walking through the house. My grandma told Grandpa to get up and put that dog out. When he got up to do it, there was no dog to be put out. No dog there. They said that they got eerie feelings when that happened.

Well, it happened again. That white creature walked through the house, through the bedrooms, but no one could find it when they got up to see what it was. Grandfather checked all the doors and windows, and found everything to be locked up tight. There was no dog to be found anywhere. Just what that really was, and what its intentions were, will likely never be known, but my mother claimed that every member of the family did see it. They declared that it looked just like a big white dog.

4. "Ghostly Cat Man"

One day, this old fellow was walking down a country road just outside of Jeffersontown, here in Jefferson County. He heard the painful-like cries and meows of several kittens in a nearby field. This man loved animals very much, so he decided to investigate the cause of the noises. In doing so, he found several mischievous young boys who had dowsed a litter of kittens with real gasoline and were preparing to ignite them with a match. Horrified at what he saw, the old man leaped on top of the kittens to save them, just as one of the boys threw a lit match into the pile of cats. Both the man and the precious little kittens were set on fire and burned to death there in the field. The young tormentors were never brought to justice.

The story about this has it that the old man comes back from the grave to protect animals and torment those persons who do harm to animals. It is said that he appears as a large black cat with red, glowing eyes. In this form, he will appear in the presence of animal tormentors and tease them into chasing him. He will either lead them on a wild goose chase until they become hopelessly lost or cause them to dash out into traffic and be struck by an oncoming car. The ghostly cat man does this because he is seeking retribution for injustice dealt to him by other tormentors of poor, innocent animals.

5. "Ghostly Black Dog"

This is really weird. It's hard to believe, but it did happen. There we were, my friend and I, driving along Jack Hinton Road here in Daviess County, about 1:30 in the morning. Well, that Jack Hinton Road is so blasted dark that people like to drive on it just to see the stars.

Well, that night, my friend David and I were driving fairly fast. We looked up ahead, and there was this utility pole with a light on it. I could see, even from where we were in relation to it, that there was someone standing under the light. Without saying anything, I suddenly got the creeps. As we got closer to the person, David took notice of him and slowed the car down. I wanted him to speed up and move on ahead, but the person wasn't just some podunk pis—g on the light post. Whatever or whoever it was, was wearing a hooded robe and started to point directly toward the center of the car, almost as if he weren't concerned with who was in the car.

We both said at the same time, "What the heck is this all about?" Then David suddenly slammed on the car brakes, and my chest hit the dashboard.

This knocked the wind out of me, but it didn't matter. There was a black dog in the road. It was just sitting there, the headlights reflecting out of its eyes. It didn't look menacing or evil, just had a scary, black appearance. Now here's the weird part. That dog got up and walked over to the side of the road where the figure in the robe was standing. Only, now he, or it, was gone.

We got ourselves together and prepared to get away from there. Then, I saw the dog walk over to a ditch and disappear. That was it. We left there and didn't say a word to each other until we got to David's house. Even then, we didn't feel safe in talking about it. That was too weird to think about, let alone talk about it.

6. "Ghostly Red-Eyed Dog"

My cousin, Eddie Durrett, was walking to his grandmother's house about 10:30 one night. He was walking alone on this road, when suddenly he heard chains being dragged along behind him. At first, he paid no attention to the weird sounds. Then, about every 300 yards, he would stop, and the noise would always stop when he did.

Finally, he became so scared that he got up enough nerve to look back over his shoulder. He saw these two big red eyes staring at him. Wow, was he ever scared spitless!

Whatever it was that had the big red eyes, had an appearance somewhat similar to a dog. But it could not have been a dog, for dogs don't have horns. And whatever it was there behind him had big horns on top of its head, and a chain wrapped around its neck.

For sure, it wasn't a dog. Eddie believed at that time, and still does, that it was something like a ghost, maybe a demon. Anyway, he ran just as hard as he could go, with that thing chasing along right behind him. He finally got to his grandmother's, but luckily he didn't get caught by whatever it was that was after him.

7. "The Ghost Dog in Bardstown"

In my hometown of Bardstown, there is a very old house about one and one-half miles south of town. It was built with slave labor. When I was in high school, a very wealthy old man, who rarely ever came out of the house, lived there. He has since died.

Since the house was built with slave labor, stories have circulated about slaves that had been buried under the foundation. There was also a huge staircase in the front foyer that was said to have had a slave skull embedded in the top of the banister. So the stage was set for an abundance of ghost stories to circulate about the house and surrounding grounds.

One of these stories was about the ghost dog. It supposedly lived with the slaves back when they first built the old house. It is said that the dog's ghost is a restless spirit that roamed the grounds guarding the graves of the unceremoniously buried slaves. Another popular theory was that it was the dog of the overseer and could harm you if you got too close or angered it in some way.

To see this ghost dog, one had to drive out to this old house and down the long private drive. You had to then make the circle at the end of the driveway and go about halfway back down. At that point, your headlights would hit an antiquated storage shed. It was then that the ghost of the dog would appear in the middle of the driveway, directly in the path of your car. It didn't look like a normal, living dog with flesh and fur. Instead, it was white and had a hazy form. Yet, it did have very good definition with the eyes, ears, tail, nose, etc., being very plain to make out. It really was very convincing to see. It truly looked like the spectral appearance of a long dead dog. It would stay there in the road until you drove almost up on it; then, quite suddenly, it would just disappear.

Everyone drove out on Sunday to see it, and it would be the chief topic of conversation on Monday in the Alcove, where we all hung out before school and after lunch. At least one group of our peers drove out there every weekend to see that ghost-like dog. There was always at least two people in the car; no one went alone to see it. Typically, the car was full of people.

As a joke, sometimes those who knew about the "thing" would take a younger person or someone who was not a regular member of the social group out there so as to frighten them. This was also a popular spot for guys to take their dates, because it was very conducive to the performance of the traditional role of the male comforting and protecting the frightened female.

8. "Ghostly Yelps and Howls"

Back in 1890, when I was a young blade of nineteen, I did my courting in a horse-drawn buggy. One Sunday evening after calling on Miss Mattie Barnett of Webertown, I was on my way home to Patesville. As a buggy approached Pullman's corner (now Arrington's corner between Patesville and Fordsville), I spotted a huge, shaggy-haired dog. Even in a sitting position, it appeared to be five-feet tall. It was the largest dog I had ever seen. It didn't move or make a sound.

I quickly pulled off the road and grabbed my shotgun. I was afraid to shoot for fear it belonged to a neighbor. I was also afraid it might attack me as I went past. It didn't look too friendly.

While pondering my dilemma I was suddenly startled by furious barking noises off in the distance. Looking over my shoulder I saw dozens of small dogs running toward me. They were too small to be real, and they came directly at me. Their yelping and barking was deafening. However, instead of attacking me, they charged between me and the big dog. I got off several shots. But they kept running and barking until I couldn't see them anymore. The bullets went right through them.

The big dog disappeared during the furor. I never saw it again. I lost no time in getting home and reporting the incident to my family.

The next morning investigators found plenty of evidence that shots had been fired, but not a trace of the dogs. I continued my courtship with Mattie and we subsequently got married.

I saw the little dogs again and again. It always happened on Sunday night, always at the same spot, and the little dogs were always running and yelping as if their lungs would burst. I put up with a lot of razzing from skeptical neighbors, and for that reason I tried vainly to shoot and wound one of the little creatures, so that I would then have proof of what I had seen. But that was not to be. The little ghost dogs continued to romp and bark with great impunity.

9. "A Family's Fear of a Ghost Dog"

There is an old house over here in Henderson, located next to South Junior High School. Actually, this old house is a mansion. My ex-friend told me last year that, a long time ago, this old lady lived in this mansion, and she had a dog. The dog just followed her everywhere she went, and it just loved her dearly.

Well, one day this old lady died, and the dog couldn't find her anywhere. Every day, the dog would look for her in the same spot, but she was never there. Finally, the dog died, and another family moved into this old house.

Weeks later, this new family heard a dog barking somewhere in the house but they could never find it. They looked and looked. When they went into the room where the old lady had died, sure enough they heard the dog again, but they could never find it.

Another week or so passed. This family had their own dog, and they put water and food for it out in the kitchen, but not until the husband put their dog outside while his wife was cooking dinner. She heard a dog drinking water, but knew it couldn't be their dog, because it was on the outside. But would you believe it, that was the ghost dog that was drinking the water?

It scared her, and it scared her husband when she told him about it. They immediately proceeded to move out of that old mansion, never to came back again. They were truly scared, afraid that they would see that old ghost dog again.

10. "The Ghost Cat That Revealed Hidden Treasure"

Shortly after the Civil War, when tales describing the great military conflicts were told by about everyone in the Hardinsburg area, this terror was often overshadowed by stories of the spirit world. I'm talking about ghosts. The great-great-grandfather of an Owensboro resident decided to spend the night in a haunted house in Hardinsburg. It was a rental house. Following the Civil War, a long series of families had moved in and out of the house in rapid succession. People began to inquire as to the reason for these hasty departures and were told that the house was haunted.

Deciding to find out for himself as to the veracity of the rumors, the hero of this story took with him a lamp and a Bible, reasoning that no self-respecting ghost would ever bother a person reading the holy word.

He had been reading the Bible for only a short time when a large cat appeared and put its paw on the very verse that the old fellow was reading. Somewhat alarmed, he said to the cat, "What in the world do you want?"

The cat replied, "Behind the fireplace are thirty pieces of gold. They'll be yours. Just watch me." With that, the big cat eased over to the fireplace and placed its paw on a certain stone, then disappeared.

When the old gentleman regained his composure, he went to the fireplace, removed the stone and, sure enough, there he found thirty shiny gold coins.

The cat ghost was never seen again, and the house was habitable once more. Many people lived there after that, and all of them kept looking, hoping they, too, would find some pieces of gold.

The Owensboro resident who shared this story stated with a gleam in his eye that his grandmother kept one of the gold coins in her purse to use as proof when she repeated the story.

11. "Yellow Dog Ghost"

A group of men were living in an old barn converted into a house back in the country where an old strip mine was being completely stripped. It was almost a deserted village, with several old houses scattered over a mile radius. Every night these men would come in from work and sit around and drink and play cards. Every so often, they would hear noises upstairs in the loft. One of the men, whose name was Henderson, would scream at the booger up there to come on down and play. Then he would swing from the trap door of the loft and dare whatever it was to step on his hands.

This one night was just like all the others, and after setting up the sash across the barn door, they turned out the lantern so that there was no more light. Suddenly, Henderson began screaming and hollering and begging for help. All the men were frightened, so they hid their heads, except for this one fellow, Brown, who lit the lantern. Well, there on top of Henderson was an enormous yellow dog. It ran off when the light came on, and oddly enough, Henderson got up and ran after it.

The men were terrified, as Henderson had screamed something like, "It's the devil, boys." They immediately packed all their belongings and gear and moved camp about a mile down the road.

The next morning, Henderson wandered back into camp and said, "Well, boys, I'll never be afraid of that again."

The men had left their horses back at the barn, and all of them refused to go back and feed them, except Henderson. He would go back every night at twilight and feed the horses, and then come back to the camp. A few years later, Henderson drowned in a pond. No one ever had courage enough to ask Henderson what that yellow thing was all about.

12. "Princess Roams the Woods"

Quite a few years back, a beautiful German Shepherd dog known as Princess was found to have rabies. The police were called in immediately to do away with the dog.

Upon the arrival of the police, Princess must have sensed her coming doom, for she headed for the large clump of woods located behind her owner's home, the Moores. The chase was immediately commenced, for the police knew it was their job to rid the community of the dangers presented by the rabid dog. After many hours of searching, the dog was finally cornered and the execution begun.

The scene wasn't a very pretty one, for the first bullet only grazed Princess in the front leg. She jumped in a half-crazed and painful series of leaps. Finally, a policeman's bullet found its mark, and the dog was put out of its misery. The community residents thought they were rid of the menace for good now, but they were soon to find out differently.

The story goes that every year on April 17, the anniversary of her death, the ghost of Princess can be seen roaming the woods behind the Moores' home. Proof of this is the strange occurrence which is always said to happen the next day. A neighborhood dog is always found to be mad.

So I guess that Princess does come back, just like they say.

13. "The Silver Fox"

Quite a few years back, three farmers who lived near Gamaliel were going hunting one night. They took their hounds and drove over to their favored spot, which was located on a bluff overlooking Line Creek. The moon was full stage, as they set down to listen to the chase.

At first, there was no sound from the hounds. These hunters just sat there listening to the stillness of the night. Then they heard the sound coming from one of the hounds off in a distance. He was on the trail of a fox. Then the other hounds were heard, and the chase was on.

The hunters began to notice that their hounds were not chasing a fox across the fields and through the woods, but were simply chasing it here and there. The hunters noticed that the fox was headed in their direction. At that very instant, the fox seemed to glide out of the woods, and it was over the creek bluff and across the creek before you could say, "Tadpole." The hounds were right after the fox. They stopped at the creek and swam to the other side and were off on the chase again.

The hunters had never seen a fox like this before, a long silver fox that seemed to glide over things as it ran. About three hours later, the hunters had still never heard from their hounds again. The last time they were heard was when they chased the fox over the bluff. The hunters left for home, not thinking any more about the silver fox.

The hounds never came home and, to this day, no fox hunters around here will go fox hunting when the moon is full, afraid that their hounds will never come home.

14. "Ghost-like Things in the Woods"

I was going home one night, down through the woods path out here. The woods was so very dark, but I went on down through the woods, since I couldn't see what I was doing anyway.

When I got about half way down through the woods, I looked up there in front of me, and there lay something in the road, right in the path that I had to walk along. I couldn't get around this thing in any shape, form, or fashion. Nor could I turn around and go back for that matter. Man, it was dark.

I stood there a little while, thinking about what that thing could be. The hair on my head raised up, and my cap fell off on the ground. So I reached down, hunting for my cap. I looked right down there near my feet; there was something else there. It was a big, white thing, looked like a big sheet or something, right below me. Well, that scared me worse than the other thing had.

I decided that I'd try to go back the way I had come. But about the time that I got turned around, I saw another one behind me, and, boy, I was right in between them. I didn't know what to do. So I decided that I'd find my cap. Well, I just made a big lunge, and I went right across the top of them. But I was so scared by now that I couldn't run. I just froze there.

The Cundiff and Anderson Graveyard in Breckinridge County. (Photograph provided by Elbert Cundiff)

Finally, I did find my cap. I'd put it back on my head, but it would always fall right back off. It fell off on the ground right close to this big white thing. I slipped up close to my cap, to try to get it. When I did that, there wasn't nothing close to me, but I was still just scared to death.

When I got there to my cap and reached down to pick it up, why right down below me there was something white there, something that went, "B-a-a-a-a-h."

It was a sheep. There were three sheep laying there in the woods, and they just about scared me to death.

15. "Funny Ghost Story"

This is a story that Granddad told. It isn't what you call a true ghost story but it was a funny ghost story. Here's the way that he told it:

"I heard that joke about these two Bewley boys that Pop used to tell. My Pop was Orlie Cundiff.

"About eighty or ninety years ago [now about one hundred years], there was two Bewley boys. They was brothers and would do anything in the world for a prank.

"They was going to Guston. Both of them had a girl friend at Guston. So, lots of times they would go together, you know. They'd walk, for back then that's the only way they had to go unless they had a wagon. Wasn't no cars or nothing like that.

"One of them got ready to go to Guston to see his girl friend, and he asked his brother to go with him.

"Naw, I don't want to go," the brother said. He was going to stay at home.

"So, he had a great big old black dog. It had growed up with them and thought the world of both of the boys. So Bewley decided to go on to Guston to see his girl friend. And this other brother stayed at home.

"So he went up there to that Guston Graveyard [now Cundiff and Anderson Graveyard]. Up there by where my sister [Garnett Guy] lives. There was a path that come right down by the graveyard and come on down to his home. He lived about a mile from Guston.

"He took him a sheet along with him, went up there and got in the graveyard and tied it over that dog and made great big ears on that sheet and just wrapped his dog up in it, all but his feet, and left him so he could run.

"So he set there and his brother came back by there. It was about half-moon, about half shining. So he set up there 'til his brother passed the graveyard and then he turned that dog loose. So the dog just took right out down that path behind that boy because he knowed him. The dog just thought he'd follow him on home. He wanted to go home.

"The brother looked back and seen that dog coming and they tell me he took out a-running and run from there clear on home! That was scary. Most anybody would run from that."

I guess it probably really happened. Granddad would tell that. It wasn't really a ghost. This one Bewley boy had played a prank on his brother.

16. "Granddaddy and the Dog"

In Granddad's words:

"I was about ten or eleven years old, I guess, big enough to ride a horse and take it to pasture. What started it all off, Poppa got up there one morning about three o'clock before daylight. Moon was shining a little bit. We'd done eat breakfast. I was setting there behind the stove about half asleep. Directly, I heard that old dog roaring out there, you know. Sounded like a mill a-roaring.

"Like to of scared Poppa. He raised up. I thought if it scared him, it must be something awful bad. I got more scared than ever then.

"So Poppa went outside, and that old dog was setting out there on the stob blocks of the house. Well, that scared me pretty bad. So when he seen him, the dog run off and left. Course, he wasn't going to kill him no way.

"Well, the next day or two after that, he sent me out to take the horses to pasture. So I got ahold of one of them and I led the other one, you know, and went up there pert near a quarter of a mile. Had to come right through the woods. I never did think anything about the dog until I pulled the bridle off the horses and they took out across the field, you know. I thought, 'Well, I can't catch them no more.'

"I threwed the bridles down there by the post, you know, and started on home. And when I thought about that dog, I took off. I never run so in all my life! When I got home, I was out of breath. That was one time I run and the only time. I never did. Just the thoughts of it scared me, and the more I run, the closer I thought that dog was to me. I could just imagine he was right ready to grab me. I mean I left there!"

17. "The Ghost under the Floor"

My great-great-grandfather, Jesse Bryant, was a sort of dashing fellow in his younger days. Supposedly, he wasn't afraid of anything.

There was this certain place in Monroe County that was supposedly haunted by this weird thing. It is said that nobody would even live there on this farm where all this took place. It is said that this gentleman who came into possession of the deed to this old farm offered the farm to anybody who would spend the night in the old house.

Well, my great-great-grandfather, being the enterprising young man that he was, thought he'd take this fellow up on his offer. So he went to the house. It was quite an old log house. I don't know if it exists today or not, but probably not. The only thing that he took with him was his rifle or shotgun, whatever they used in those days.

When he got there, they bade him goodnight, so he set about to stay the night there. Well, sure enough, as he stayed there that night horrible rackets began to be heard all over the old house. The awfullest lumberments you ever did hear. The floors literally shook; the walls, too. Well, being the sensible man that they said he was, he looked around but found nothing. He looked again, but still saw nothing. So he started to get ready to go to bed. When he got into the bed, the same noises and shakings began to take place all over again. He resolved that he was going to find out whether it was a real ghost, or if it was just a prankster.

He set about to find where this noise, this horrible racket was coming from. He immediately looked around and noticed that the most noise was coming from under the floorboards of the house. Being an old house, quite old at that time even—that being nearly a century ago—he proceeded to jerk up the floorboards. There, to his surprise and to those persons who had trembled with fear for so long a time, and in fact had lost a nice farm over this, was nothing but an old hog, a sow, that was caught under the floorboards, starving to death because it could not get anything to eat.

He shot the old sow, and the next morning when they came to see if he were alive or not, there he sat on the porch with the old sow laying there at his feet. It was just a sow—no ghosts!

He nonetheless received the deed to the farm. That was quite a laugh on all those who did like to believe in ghost stories.

18. "My Cat's Ghost"

I'd had this cat named Sock for five years and a day back in July 1997. One day when I got home from summer school, I went in to do some work on my computer. All of a sudden, I heard the awfullest yelling outside that you can imagine. I went running out onto the front porch to see what that noise was all about. I looked and there lay Sock. She'd been run over by a car. She did not die immediately, but she passed away about an hour or so after we got her to the vet.

Sock was so dear to me; so very precious. In fact, she was kinda like a daughter to me. Actually, I did think of her as a daughter. Even now, some eighteen months later, when I'm walking down the hallway, I sometimes hear little footprints behind me. I believe Sock is following me. I'm very glad to know that she is still near. I miss Sock so very much.

19. "Rabbit in the Cemetery"

My grandfather said that when he'd pass this cemetery near Mud Creek while on his way home from his day's work at Boldman, just across the Pike County line, a thing that looked to him something like a rabbit would run out in front of him. And it happened over and over so many times that he finally got scared, so he started taking a pistol with him.

He shot at this thing several times, and said it looked as if the fire from the bullet would go right into the fur of this animal. It looked like a rabbit, but he couldn't be sure that it was. It followed him, even after he'd shot it several times. Never did stop following him down the road.

Even after people started to drive cars through there, they also saw something in that same graveyard. They claim that whatever it was looked as if it was a man in long underwear. He just comes out, maybe from a grave, and goes across the road in front of the cars.

As for me, I've been through there but I've never seen him.

20. "Black Dog's Ghost"

They was a Crawford fellow who killed a man. Crawford had a dog when he killed him. And, so, he couldn't step out or go to eat or nothing but what he didn't see this man's ghost. Every night when he'd step out in the yard, said this ghost would be out there with this little dog. This dog would be all around this man, Crawford. Said he killed the dog, too.

Well, he left this country and went to Missouri. Thought he would get shut of this dog's ghost, too. And said the second night after he got to Missouri, he stepped out in the yard, and the dog and this man was following him. Just worried him to death nearly. Well, he stayed around there just so long, but he couldn't rest, so he come back to this country.

He had killed this man near a pond. And I reckon he must have put him in this pond. Anyway, Crawford went and stayed all night with a man. And said they was a riding along, talking to each other.

Said this little dog come up, and they didn't know where the dog come from. And said this dog went wading out in this pond. When he come out, said he come out with a bone, with a bone in his mouth. And said he stopped in front of these two men. Crawford's friend wanted to know, "What's that dog carrying that bone around for?"

And said everywhere they would stop, said this dog would drop this bone at this man's feet. [Narrator makes a thudding noise by hitting the floor with her feet.]

And said that Crawford looked like he was just about to sink every time that dog would come around with this bone. And they didn't know where that little old dog come from—a little black dog. And said this man said to Crawford, who had killed that man, "I don't understand why that dog is a-carrying that bone around. Do you know what he's carrying it for?"

Crawford said, "No, I don't."

This other man said, "He come out of that pond with that bone. So something has been put in that pond, or somebody had killed somebody, and that's somebody's bone. That sure ain't a hog bone or nothing." Said that Old Man Crawford just sunk down.

The other fellow asked him, "Well, what's the matter with you?"

Said he couldn't talk. He just give down. Broke down over it, you know. And finally Crawford told him this man's name, and said, "I can't get shut of him. I've been plumb to Missouri, but every time I'd go anywhere, he'd be around my feet, and I can't get shut of him. Truth of the matter is that's one of that man's bones that he comes out of that pond with."

And said they went back over there and drug around; pulled all that man's bones out where they did it. And I think they give him a whole lot of time, maybe life in the pen, for killing this man and hiding him in the pond.

21. "Bullets Go through Dog Ghost"

We don't hear and see things now days like we did back yonder in olden days. There's this Kirkpatrick who killed an old scorpion or lizard, whatever it was.

They's a graveyard over yonder at Center Point in eastern Monroe County. And they said everybody that would pass that graveyard at night would see a dog—a little bitty black thing. Had a ring around its neck and feet, just a little old bitty thing. Said when you get right even with that graveyard, this little dog would come out and just run around your feet, and you couldn't kick it. Well, you could hit at it, kick at it, but your feet would just go right through it.

They had a party over there at Uncle Andy Kirk's one night. It broke up at midnight, on Saturday night. There was a passel of young girls and boys there at that party, and many of them was walking back home together. Well, just before they got to this graveyard they all begin to grab the men, you know, and hold them by their coats, just hold onto them. Afraid they would see something.

Walter Kirk said, "Now if that blasted dog comes out on me tonight, I'm killing that SOB." He had a pistol that shot six times. Said they got up about even in the graveyard when, all of a sudden, here the ghost comes right through the fence. And said it went right straight to Walter Kirk. Oh, it was just a-running around his feet. And Walter said he was just a-shooting at it, "Bang, bang, bang." And said looked like you couldn't hit it a-tall. All the women just a-screaming and hollering. It scared them to death. And said it run around his feet there, and said he emptied his pistol but never could hit it. And said all at once it just started back toward the fence.

Said it went up in the air, said it was just like a puff of wind, like a whirl-wind, "Shr-r-u-u-u-u." And said it was gone.

I don't know how many told me that they'd seen that there. My sister was in that crowd, too—sister Mary.

22. "The 'Haint' with the Hat on Its Head"

Long before I went to Muddy Gut Creek to live with my young husband, Lohren Martin, he'd told me of the "haint" with the hat. He said, "You can see the hat. Sometimes he takes it in his hand, bows and doffs the hat, as if he were meeting a lady."

While we were courting, I was told of the "haint." If you think this an unlikely subject to be talking of, walking along a lonely road at night, with siblings for chaperones, and churchgoers for censors, you've just never lived where you have to walk in moonlighted snow.

"There is a graveyard," he told me. Before I go on, let me say that later we had a child that was buried in this graveyard, and he, his parents, and all kinds of kindred would be placed here in the forthcoming years. Neither of us could foresee this, of course, or perhaps we both would have remained celibate.

"The graveyard is called Darl Jones. It is named for Darling Jones, the first person to be buried here. The graveyard overlooks our house," my husband said. "On a moonlit night when there is a snow unbroken by man or maid, the haint stands just like he's at attention, and shouldering a gun. He has on big boots, and his one arm is raised toward his hat, like he might have been saluting an officer when he was called upon to walk his sentinel turn. A Civil War veteran lies forty feet or more from the place where the haint stands. This man had his leg shot off, and his leg of wood was buck-led upon him. Some think the ghost is that of the Civil War vet, but I don't believe that. His boots show plain as his hat does, and he's only seen in the winter."

I scoffed at his story. "There ain't no such thing as 'haints' I replied. Then I told him of 'haints' supposedly seen around the graveyard on Laurel River, and how the fogs made ghosts of the vapors arising near midnight.

There was a patch of woods around the graveyard, when first I moved to Muddy Gut Creek. The woods consisted of big white oak trees, of maples, poplars, and bunches of sassafras. At the corner of the graveyard, a white oak stood. It had begun dying from the top. The white oak didn't stand out from the rest of the timber, kind of like not being able to see the forest for the trees.

A wagon road was within a few hundred yards of the graveyard and, in riding after dark, this was an eerie place, as the creek crept along here, hardly flowing enough to tell that it was moving. The creek flowed so slow that it would be iced over in harsh weather. Mr. Martin, my father-in-law, would go before daybreak in winter to break the ice with an ax, so as to let the cattle, the horses, and the mules drink. He would come back to the house and say, "I saw the haint," then he'd tell us all about it while we ate our breakfast.

Quail was not a rarity at that time. A covey of quail roosted in the corner of the rail fence just below the cemetery, at the creek's outer edge. The "haint" was the subject of conversation at group gatherings.

"They hain't no such thing as haints!" someone would declare.

Half a dozen voices would interrupt, telling of truthful incidents where the "haint" had been seen. "No doubt at all in my mind," they would say.

Myrtle Delaney would then tell some of her personal horror tales, and the hair would rise up on our necks just the same as if lightning had struck close in a thunderstorm.

We'd been married six or seven years when the ghost was spotted one night. Lohren and I were coming from his aunt's, who lived out toward the Nineveh Road. We were riding the mare double. From the time we left the rise just next to Aunt Marth's barn, we could see that ghostly man with a hat on his head!

Conditions were just right for that "haint." A seven-inch snow had fallen and Aunt Marth was ailing, so Lohren had gone to help with their chores. I'd gone, too, just to sit with Aunt Marth while the work was being "done up." Aunt Marth filled me in with the "haint's" history. "It must be thirty years or more that the haints have been close around the graveyard," she said.

"Doesn't he ever move or go sommers else?" I wanted to know. I was curious to learn if Aunt Marth and Lohren had seen the same thing when a winter snow was on the ground.

Every year, some of the birds in the covey would be left, and not shot. "Leave some for seed, Lohren," Mr. Martin would always say as Lohren left to go up the creek hunting, while the cows were driven to the barn. It just took a few minutes at that time to shoot a "mess" of quail.

We would see the "haint" with the hat, and we could see his big boots, and his huge head was kind of swaying. There was no breeze. The air was as still as a sphinx, or a rock. It was heavy. Then, all at once, I could hardly breathe. We were passing that place where the "haint" was seen dozens of times.

Just then, the hat sailed off the man's head! The mare skittered, and I landed on my bottom in the snow. I was thankful that I'd worn an old pair of overalls instead of a riding skirt.

A big owl swooped down right at the rail fence corner, where the covey of quail had roosted from time to time. After the owl left the tree, it was easy to see why everyone thought that "haint" man had on a hat and big boots. The dead limbs there looked like a man's legs, and the owl had lit on this still snowy night, when the moon was shining, to better see the quail. That owl was the "haint"!

I was trying to get up, and the snow was slick. Ice was forming on top of the snow. When the pistol shot rang out, the mare left Lohren on the ground, same as me, and the owl flopped down to the creek. Lohren was too scared to go pick up the bird, and I had no interest in seeing just where the shot had struck.

The mare ran home, then over across the creek to the log barn. Upon hearing the shot, Mr. Martin, who was just half-dressed, ran outside in the snow. As we came down the road, he hollered to see if anybody had killed one of us. He should have known better! Everyone up and down Muddy Gut Creek could hear us both, me and Lohren, blaming each other for the accident.

"I'll go unsaddle the mare, Lohren," said Mr. Martin. He was always so considerate to us all, especially his only son. It would have been harder than pulling eye teeth to have forced Lohren to go to the barn and unsaddle and unbridle the mare, just after he'd shot the "haint" with the hat on its head.

The covey of quail roosting in that fence corner never came back after that shooting, for it's sure they were scared out of their wits the same as we were!

23. "The Ghost-like Creature That Frightened Mules"

Let me tell you what me and Fred Rasner done one time. We seen this thing.

Will Jackson was making me a moonshine still. And he could make one, too, let me tell you! That was back in the late 1920s when I used to follow that kind of business. Well, me and Fred rode mules over to Will Jackson's one night, way in the night. We got over yonder by the Rich Dunham Cave. All at once, one of my mules just started snorting, and then begin to run. Let me tell you right now, something passed us, and it was just a-flying.

And here comes Fred after me. He asked, "What did you see?"

I told him, "Eh God, I don't know. I never seen nothing. Let's go back. But my mule, I can't do nothing with it."

Well, we like to have never got our mules back down there. Just as we did, there goes this ghost-like thing just kinda walking slowly across the road. And, believe it or not, that Fred Rasner got down off that mule to hunt him a rock.

He said to me, "Jim, I can't find nothing."

I said, "Get up from there; ain't no telling what that thing is."

So about that time my mule swirled again, and his'un started. So Fred jumped up on it and was riding it down the road. We went on down to Will Jackson's to get that big thirty-gallon moonshine still. I put it up in front of me there on the saddle.

When we started off down the road, the mules saw this thing again, whatever it was. Now, you never heard such a racket coming up out of that road. It scared them mules to death.

After we got home, Fred wanted to go back over there to this spot that same night. And we did see it—the only scary thing I ever saw in my life. It was black, just right down black, and it was a great big thing. That's the only ghostly thing I ever seen in my life. And whatever it was scared us and them mules to death.

24. "Midnight Scare"

Bill Sturgill of Elliott County was well known as a man that wasn't afraid of anything. In fact, people thought of him as being mean. He got drunk a lot, and when riding a horse he would nearly run it to death.

One night he was walking home after having stayed out late. About a mile from his house, an old barn stood out near the road. As he was about to go by the old barn, he noticed a calf standing out in the middle of the road. Thinking nothing about it, he started around it to pass by, but the calf walked over and got right in front of him.

He didn't think much about that either, but when he started to go around on the other side and the calf got in his way again, he began to wonder. So he took out his knife and started around on the other side. This time, when the calf got in his way he struck at it with his knife but it just went through the calf as if there was nothing there. He jumped and stabbed at the calf several times but his knife never did cut anything. And for the first time, Bill Sturgill got scared.

He started running toward home. When he came to the yard, he jumped the fence, and in getting in the house he broke the door down. When he told the story to his parents and brother, they said he was drunk but he denied it. Anyway, they went up there to the place the next morning, and sure enough, there were his tracks where he had jumped around in the road.

25. "Hollering Stopped"

Grandpa Spradlin said that his daddy had an old blacksmith shop, but he was always afraid of it because people told him that it was haunted. One night Mattie Lou's baby died and was kept there for awhile. When Grandpa Spradlin's daddy got ready to leave, he went by the shop. He heard a noise and hollered to see if it was a dog or something.

Whatever it was never did come, so he started running. Well, when he started to run, that ghostly noise started following him. He said that he went just as far as he could go, then stopped. When he stopped, this ghost-like dog went right on by him. He said that he did not know what it was at first. It like to have scared him to death, and him a grown man!

26. "Legends of Beasts at Land between the Lakes"

Land between the Lakes is a place of laughter, picnics, and history, but during the Halloween season, LBL becomes a place of mystery and legends.

Quite possibly the most notorious story to students at [Murray State] University is about the creature that roams LBL. The people who carry the most history about this legend are the ones who have lived through the decades of change in Kentucky—the ones who have lived through the history.

The old-timers are the ones to consult on the stories surrounding LBL, especially the legend of the beast within those woods.

"Shoot, people camp down there now where we didn't dare live, or even let our young'uns gather wood," said one old-timer. "We knew there was something out there," he said. "Too many of our hogs and cattle were being found torn to pieces. Wasn't no dogs or coyotes either. It left big tracks, too, like a wolf, but you could put your whole fist in it. We all went looking for it one evening. There was about twelve of us, and some of us got separated. Wasn't too much later we found something screamin' at the top of its lungs. It kept screamin' and screamin' just like a woman.

"Then it stopped as suddenly as it began. Then came the howling. I never ran so fast in all my life. Got home, bolted all the windows and doors and stayed up by the fire with my shotgun in my lap. I learned the next morning that Ben down the road hadn't made it home."

Several university students tell stories of the same nature. Some have heard the screams and others have heard the howling. LBL employees and rangers have even seen the beast . . . like a mountain lion that walks on its hind legs.

A creature of another kind has also been sighted on the grounds of LBL. Several people claim to have seen a devil-like creature near the old Tennessee House Hotel in Golden Pond. It was described as having a very large wing span, and it seemed to float as though it were flying. The last known sighting of this creature was in 1974 by a truck driver who was passing under the bridge located over the Trace, near the Golden Pond area. . . .

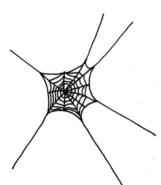

Scary Tales

Chapter 6

1. "The Old Man and the Flowers"

There was this boy scout troop in Jefferson County that always camped out in wooded places near old mansions. There was a story that claimed that an old man who lived in a certain house would always come out on the full of the moon to place flowers on the grave of his dead wife. When he would do this, she would always come up out of the grave and kiss him. This was the only thing that kept the old fellow alive.

Well, the scouts decided to explore the old house to see if this was really true. They walked over there one night when the moon was full. When they got there, they saw the old man going to a grave. There was a startling scream. Three of the scouts got scared and ran off, but one of them stayed. He watched him put the flowers on the grave. Well, he knew that the others wouldn't believe him if he didn't get something to prove what he saw, so he grabbed the flowers off the grave and ran away with them.

The old man took off after him, but couldn't catch up with him. The boy ran into his tent and quickly got into his sleeping bag.

A little later, the old man stood at the tent of the four boys with a knife in his hand. He looked at all four of the boys, but couldn't decide which one had taken the flowers. He then said, "He who shakes tonight with fear will die here."

He went down and looked at each boy, and when he came to the boy that had taken the flowers, the boy jumped up and ran toward the entrance of the tent. The old man reached out and slit the boy's back with his big, sharp knife. A little later that night, the boy died. The old man disappeared into the woods, never to be seen again.

2. "Roommate's Death on Campus"

There were these two girls who were roommates on the campus here. And one night the college here was having a campuswide dance. So the two girls decided to go to the dance, as they thought that would be a good way to meet some good looking male hunks.

So when they got to the dance they were dancing and having a good time. Then, one of the girls got sick and so she decided that she should go back to the dorm. However, to get to the dorm from where she was, she had to go through a small patch of woods. And there was a rumor out that a man had just escaped from the insane asylum located close by. Well, when she got to thinking about this, she got afraid to go through the woods all alone. She felt really bad, but she didn't want her roommate to miss out on the fun, so she told her that she was going on back to the dorm alone.

On her way through the clump of woods she heard a heavy breathing sound coming up behind her, but she didn't want to turn around and look back as she was afraid that would let them know that she had heard them, or it, whatever was back there. So she began walking a bit faster, but the heavy breathing began to get louder and louder. Well, she took off running, I mean running as hard as she could go through the woods. She got to the dorm safely, but she could still hear the heavy breathing there behind her.

She ran into the dorm and up the stairs, then down the hallway and up to her room. But she still heard the panting right behind her. She ran into her room, slammed the door behind her and locked it. Suddenly, she heard the doorknob turning. She looked at it in perfect horror, and sure enough it was turning. So she ran into the closet and closed the door behind her. She then heard the door to her room opening, but did not peep out to see who had come into the room. Well, while she was hidden there in the closet, she heard a scraping noise on the outside of her closet door, and the heavy breathing she heard was something awful to listen to.

The girl finally began to scream for help, then a dorm counselor who was on duty came running upstairs. The counselor found the girl's roommate outside the closet door with her throat slit. The dead girl had been afraid that her roommate would come in contact with the man from the insane asylum, and had followed her all the way back to the dorm. Trouble is, she is the one who was killed in the process.

3. "Old Red-Eye"

There's a tale told in these woods about a strange creature that comes out at night, scaring and killing people. That's all he lives for, according to the stories that are told. Well, "lives" isn't exactly the right word. Here's the story.

About fifteen years ago, a young man took a job with a chemical company, transporting and dumping chemical wastes at a dump site not far from here. He carried out all sorts of things to this place—broken test tubes, colored lights, and other lab garbage, including all sorts of dangerous experimental chemicals.

He'd been at this job about a year or so, and was pretty good at it. Actually, he almost liked it, and he made a good steady wage, although it wasn't very much. One day, he was showing a new guy that they'd hired, a friend of a friend of my uncle, how to dump the chemicals without getting any of them on himself. While he was doing this, he slipped and fell into a pool of chemical wastes.

Well, my uncle's friend's friend was a pretty level-headed guy, but he didn't know what to do. The chemicals started bubbling and boiling, and the guy was screaming, and little pieces of glass and metal and red lights were all swirling around in that pit. So something terrible happened. All the glop in that hole came together in a lump-like dough and started shaping itself around the guy who fell in. Pretty soon, this stuff had two arms and two legs, and a head and a body, but it was about ten-feet tall. It had sharp steel claws, and started climbing out of the pit with its claws, coming after the fellow who was there in the pit.

It looked up at him, and then this fellow really got scared. This thing had a huge mouth full of glass and metal teeth, and one huge red eye where all the red lights had come together and were magnified by a curved piece of glass into a beacon which pointed at the new worker.

He jumped into the truck and took off, with much chemical gunk falling out behind him. He looked back and saw Old Red-Eye eating the chemicals by sort of absorbing them and getting bigger. The fellow took off and didn't look back again until he was back at the chemical company.

There was a big cover-up, as lots of people since then have mysteriously disappeared in these very woods, and some of them tell of seeing a red light glowing out of the woods as they drive by. I've seen the light myself, but hope I never ever see it again.

4. "My Haunted Apartment"

All of my roommates and I believe that we live in a haunted apartment here in Bowling Green. A day doesn't go by without some strange happening. This all started off when Nickie and I were coming back to our apartment from doing laundry up the road. Our two roommates were at work and they were not expected back for quite some time.

As we drove down the road to our apartment, we noticed that the second floor bathroom light was on, yet it never was on, and the door to it was always shut. So we thought that one of our roommates was home. We were wrong; no one was home but us. When we walked into the kitchen to turn off the bathroom light, the light was already off. We found this odd. Later on that night when our two other roommates came home, we noticed that a throw blanket that was always kept on a chair in the living room was gone. JoAnna, my other roommate, specifically remembered folding the blanket and putting it on the chair that very morning. We looked all over the house but could not find it. We then started to think that someone had come into the apartment while we were gone. Later that night when everyone was getting ready for bed, we found the blanket. It was upstairs on a bed, neatly folded as if it were placed there. But just a few hours before, it was not there.

Other things that have happened include strange noises, sensing someone following one of us, and the door locking on its own. It is almost as if they do these things to show us that they are there.

Well, a few days ago, I decided to find out who these ghosts are. I played the Ouija board, and I found out that there are four spirits in our apartment and one of them is a four-year-old little boy who is there because he likes JoAnna. He likes her because she is going to be a teacher.

That is my haunted apartment. It isn't much, but for a small-town girl like me, it is a lot.

5. "Gotcha!"

One day this little boy's mother sent him to the store to get some liver for dinner. His name was Billy. She gave him $5.00 and he went to the store, but instead of getting the liver she had sent him for, he saw a roll of penny candy that he wanted. So he spent the money on candy. Well, he knew that he had to have some liver, so he went by the graveyard on the way back and dug up his aunt's body and cut her liver off and took it home with him.

His mother cooked the liver, and said to him, "My, this is very good liver. I'll have to send you to the store again sometime." So a couple of days later, she sent him back, and he again wanted the candy that he had bought when he was here last. He got the candy, then headed for the graveyard again. This time, he got his uncle's liver. He took it on home with him.

His mother said, "Son, this is absolutely delicious. I am really proud of you." Well, a few days later, she sent him to the store again to get some more liver, and again he spent the money on candy. This time, when he got to the graveyard, he dug up his grandfather and took his liver.

A few nights later it was about midnight. He was in bed asleep. All of a sudden, he heard this voice, "Billy, I'm on the first step. I'm on the second step. I'm on the third step. I'm climbing up towards you. I'm on the fourth, the fifth, the sixth step. I'm coming to you, Billy. I'm coming to get you. Now I'm on the ninth step; I'm on the top step. I'm right beside your door. Now, Billy, I'm standing right by your bed."

Well, this ghost-like creature slowly raised its hands, with fingers spread out, pointing toward Billy. With big, bloody eyes staring at Billy, the creature leaped toward him and yelled out, "Now, I gotcha! I gotcha! I gotcha!"

6. "Molly's Gonna Grab Ya!"

This ghost story was told to me by my grandma. It all started when a little girl named Molly went up to the attic one day to play. She was a brown-haired girl, with mysterious, dark-brown eyes. She was very hip and was a mischievous person also.

Over in the wall there in the attic, there was a window-like opening with a curtain that hangs over it. This opening led to an isolated room there in this old house. One day, Molly decided to go see what was beyond the curtain that hung over the window. Once she was in this old dark room, she began to look around. Suddenly she heard the window closing and locking all by itself.

Molly became terrified, because secretly she had claustrophobia. She couldn't stand to be closed up in a room with no light, no air, no life. She began beating and kicking the walls, trying to get someone to hear her and come get her out, but no one ever came.

She stayed days and nights in this old room, with nothing to eat or drink. One day she saw a roach crawling across the floor. She was desperate, so she scurried over, grabbed the roach and quickly ate it. However, the roach wasn't enough food to keep her alive. In the window, you could hear the wind blow across the porch roof, and it would drift into the attic causing the chill of death to be felt. Molly died a few days later.

Now, many years after Molly's death, people say that if you walk by the window, Molly's ghost will reach out and grab you in search for help to get out of that hole, or just to get some food. When her hands reach out, so slowly, oh, so very slowly, she'll yell out at the top of her lungs, "Gotcha! I gotcha!"

You talk about a paralyzing chill of death! When Molly's ghost does that, you just want to die and have it over with.

7. "The Bouncing Head"

One time this boy and girl that lived in the Bluegrass area of Kentucky were on a date. They were just driving around and ran out of gas near this apple orchard. The fellow decided to go for help, and the girl was supposed to stay in the car and wait for him. Well, he left, and she locked all the doors and was just sitting there scared to death, for she was hearing these thumping noises. She didn't think too much about the noises, for she thought they were just apples falling on top of the car.

After awhile the girl got really worried because her date didn't come back. Finally, a car came by and stopped. It was a police officer. He told her that she had better come along with him. When she explained what had happened, the officer told her that her boyfriend had called for help from a farmhouse about two miles away. However, the reason he had not made it back to the car was because this escaped convict had been hiding in the apple orchard and killed the boy by cutting off his head.

The noises she had been hearing was the criminal bouncing her boyfriend's head on the top of the car.

8. "The Golden Arm"

There was this elderly couple who lived in the mountains, and they hadn't gotten along very well across the years. They were poor people and getting worse off every day. The woman was always nagging at her husband, and every day he would think how rich he could be if he'd just kill his wife and have it over with. You see, she had a golden arm, and her arm was worth a lot of money. So one day he decided to do her in, and he buried her under a cliff overhang there in the mountains. That night he went to bed thinking how rich he was and all the things he could have when he bought them the next morning. He went to sleep and dreamed about these great things.

About midnight, he heard a voice, "Give me back my arm; give me back my golden arm."

The voice got louder, and he wasn't able to sleep after that. This went on for a week or more. He couldn't go into town to sell the arm; he was too tired to go. Well, one night when the voice called out, he responded that he would take the arm out there and give it back, for he was tired and scared for fear that something would grab him and do him in, just like he had done his wife.

So the voice gave him instructions to take the golden arm to where the grave of his wife was and to throw it down into the ground and cover it up. He decided that he would do just that. It was very cold that night, so he wore his long coat. He went out, and with a torch in his hand, he spotted the grave. He knelt down to bury the arm. All of a sudden his light went out, and he tried to get up as quick as he could. He was going to run away from there, but something reached up out of the ground, took hold of his coat down at his knees. The old fellow couldn't move; he was so scared that he just dropped to the ground.

Since no one had seen him or his wife for a while, some people went out looking for them. They found him lying on the ground dead, with a frightened look on his face. His coat was caught on his shoe buckle. That was the ghost that had scared him to death!

They never found his wife.

9. "The Hook"

One night, a couple of summers ago, Jeff went out with his girl friend, Denise. They went to the movies, then to the Pizza Hut; then they went to a party.

After the party was over, about three or four in the morning, Jeff and Denise left the place and drove way back into the woods in his convertible to a place where Jeff liked to take his dates. It was really secluded, way back on an old dirt road. At four in the morning, these woods are kinda creepy. The moon was about half full. When they got to the spot that Jeff had picked out, Jeff cut the car engine off and turned on the radio to D98, and the two of them began kissing and squeezing each other. While they were doing this, the radio on the car blared out that a deranged mass murderer had just escaped from the transport that was hauling a load of prisoners to the state pen. He was believed to be somewhere near Bardstown, unarmed but very dangerous. The escapee was described as being about five feet, ten inches, 165 pounds, wearing blue work pants, a blue jacket, and work boots. He was unshaven, but his most distinguishing feature was the hook on his arm where his left hand was once located.

Hearing all this scared the dickens out of Denise. After all, the two of them were parked way back in the woods—and where would be a better place for a deranged murderer to hide from the cops? Jeff tried and tried to calm Denise down, but try as he might, there was nothing that he could do to calm her down. So he told her that they were going home.

When he started to pull away, he turned on the headlights. There in front of them stood a beast-like man. He disappeared into the woods almost immediately after the lights came on. Jeff didn't get a good look at him, but it looked as if the figure had something like a knife in its hand. Jeff gunned the engine and took off down the road, but he heard a loud "thump," and the cloth top of the car had a big sagging in it as a result. Then he heard something that sounded like "rip, rip." He looked up and saw something like a knife with a curved blade ripping through the top of his car. He swerved suddenly and the man fell off the top of the car. There was a "slam" on his door, and he looked out the window and saw the face of something that looked half animal. No sooner had he seen it until it was gone. Disappeared! Then he heard a loud scream, but didn't look back. Instead, he sped into town to Denise's house. Whew, were they ever glad to be safe at her house!

Jeff got out of the car and walked Denise to the door without looking back at his car. When he went back to the vehicle, what did he find stuck in his door? A hook!! It had been ripped off the convict's arm.

Incidentally, the escaped criminal—the Hook—was never found. However, on certain nights he can still be heard screaming at the top of his lungs there in the woods.

10. "The Hook"

One time there was this guy and this really neat girl, who were really in love with each other. One Saturday night when they were out on a date together, they decided that they wanted to be alone in the woods somewhere. So they went driving down this long, lonely country road, on out into the dark woods. I mean the night, coupled with the woods and the fact that there were no stars in the sky, made it a very dark spot where they went to park.

About the time that the boy was getting ready to kiss the girl, all of a sudden they heard this "sktch," sktch," "sktch," a scratching-like noise on their car. Well, both of them just about jumped out of their seats, but they decided to ignore it because they didn't want to find out what it was, nor to get out of the car.

All of a sudden, they heard this "sktch," sktch," "sktch," again. The guy felt that perhaps he should get out of the car and check to see what it was that was making the weird sound, and that it was not something that was going to bother them. So he told the girl, "Now look, when I get out of the car, you lock all of the doors and don't open them for anybody but me, and don't you get out for anything. Just stay right where you are. I don't want anything to happen to you, and I'll be back as soon as I can."

Well, he got out of the car, and she locked all the doors. After he was gone for a little while, she began to get worried about him and also about her own safety. So she decided to just close her eyes and think about good things so that she wouldn't get scared. Well, he was gone, and he was gone, and he was gone.

After a while, she began hearing the "sktch," "sktch," "sktch," "sktch" again. She tried not to think about the noise. She managed to stay awake for a good while, but being so sleepy and tired by now, she finally fell asleep, just worn out waiting for her boyfriend.

Well, the next thing she knew, it was daylight and she was awake. She decided that it was okay to unlock the car doors and get out of the car. So she got out to look for her boyfriend or, if necessary, to go get help or something because she was really worried about him. Just as soon as she was out of the car, she looked up over the car and there, hanging from a tree branch, was her boyfriend. His feet were hitting the top of the car, going "sktch," "sktch," "sktch."

She never knew who it was that did that to him, or why they did it. Immediately after he was buried, she vowed to never again go into a patch of woods like they did the night he died.

11. "I Want My Big Toe"

Once upon a time there was this man and his wife and their two children. This was a very poor family. One day, they were out in the garden digging taters, and the man dug up this big toe. He said to his wife, "Let's have this big toe for supper. Just cook it in the pot with the beans."

His wife said, "All right."

That night they had the big toe for supper. After they had eaten, everyone went on and got in bed, because they were tired from digging taters all day.

Late that night when everyone was asleep, the old man woke up to what he thought was a strange noise. He told his little boy to go to the henhouse to see what it was. The little fellow went out to the henhouse, but he didn't hear anything, so he went back to the house. Told his daddy, said, "I didn't hear anything."

The father said, "All right, just go back to bed."

The father went to sleep, but he again heard something. This time he sent his little girl out to the woodpile. Maybe it was something out there. She went out to the woodpile, but came back to say that she hadn't seen or heard anything.

The daddy said, "Well, I heard something, but just forget it and go on back to bed."

So she did, and the father laid down again and went off to sleep. A few minutes later, he thought he heard it again, so he woke up his wife and told her to go around the house to see if she could find anything.

So, she got up and went around the house, but soon came back to say that she had not seen nor heard anything. She said to her husband, "You must be crazy, so stop imagining these things."

He responded, "Okay, just get back in bed."

So they both got back in bed and went to sleep. In a few minutes, he was awakened again by some noises. He decided that this time, he'd go out there himself to see what it was. So he got up and went around the house, but he didn't see anything. He then went to the woodpile and the henhouse, but didn't see a thing or hear any strange voices. So he went back into the house. There in the front room, right there in the fireplace, he heard it, and it was saying, "I want my big toe. I want my big toe."

The man looked up the fireplace chimney and there was this big black thing saying, "I want my big toe."

The man said to the black-like creature, "You can't have it. I've done eat it up."

Well, the creature said, "I'm going to come down this chimney and get my big toe."

The man responded, "No, don't do that. Wait a minute."

While the thing was climbing down the chimney, the man grabbed a kerosene lamp and threw it onto the firewood that was ready to be ignited the next morning. When he did this, he lit a match and threw it onto the kerosene-soaked wood. The fireplace interior was suddenly ignited with the fire.

Well, whatever the thing was, it fell right down into that fire and was burned up. They never saw or heard it again after that.

12. "Wha-wha-wher-e-r-e's My Gold?"

This old woman died that had a lot of gold. This other woman often dressed like her and would pretend that she was coming back from the grave as this old woman's ghost. She'd ask people where her gold was. She'd come up to these young people and ask them, in a scary, quivery voice, "Wha-wha-wher-e-r-e is my gold? Wha-wha-wher-e-r-e is my gold?"

Then she'd yell real loud, "W-H-E-R-E-'S M-Y G-O-L-D?" and then leap out at them with them bad looking eyes.

That would scare these young people to death. They would end up in a daze.

I used to tell that to the kids I taught at school, to see them jump. They always liked stories. Children just love stories like that.

13. "Dividing Up the Walnuts"

There was an old schoolhouse here in Greensburg that stood close to the Greensburg Cemetery. And right by the old school building was a large walnut tree. There was a fence around the cemetery. A fellow by the name of Tressinrider lived just over the hill from the cemetery. He liked to get walnuts from the big tree there.

Well, the kids there at school also liked to get some of the walnuts each year, so this fellow thought up a plan to scare the boys and girls away. One Saturday afternoon, there were these two little black boys gathering the walnuts. It just so happened that the other school kids had a big stack of them over by the schoolhouse. There were some of the walnuts on the other side of the tree, too, so the two boys decided to sit down and divide these up.

One little boy would say, "You take this one; I'll take that one. You take this one; I'll take that one."

When they got through dividing this stack of walnuts up, one of them said, "I'll get over on the other side of the fence there and get some of them."

As he stood there close to a gravestone, he began to count them out, "You take this one, and I'll take that one. You take this one, and I'll take that one."

About that time, Mr. Tressinrider, who had a sheet on him so that he could scare the two little fellows, raised up from behind a gravestone and said, "I'll take T-H-I-S O-N-E," as he reached out pretending to grab the little fellow.

The boy climbed back over the fence, then both of them took off running down the street. They never again tried to take any of those walnuts.

14. "Dividing Up the Dead"

Not far from here, right here in Clinton County, there was a little grave house in this old cemetery. The little building was located right beside the fence. Well, this Arshman [Irishman] was going down the road, and there was these two other Arshmen down at this graveyard picking up walnuts. They'd picked up a lot of walnuts and put them in this little grave house to keep them dry.

So these two Arshmen was in this graveyard, by this little grave house, counting and dividing up the walnuts.

One of them said, "You take this one, and I'll take that one."

Then the other feller said, "You take this'un, and I'll take that'un."

Well, this Arshman that was passing by heard them, and he stood there a while beside the gate to listen to them dividing up. He thought they was dividing up the dead.

They kept saying, "You take this'un and I'll take that'un."

Finally, one of them said, "There's another one on the outside of the fence, and you can have it."

Well, this Arshman got skeered and took off down the road a-running jist as hard as he could go. He kept running until he got to a neighbor's house. Shaking all over, he says to the neighbor, "God and the Devil are up here at the graveyard, and they're dividin' up the dead. When I heerd one of them say, 'There's another one outside the fence that you can have,' I took off a-runnin,' 'cause I knowed I was the only one standin' there. And it was the Devil that'uz after me. Boy, did I ever run!"

15. "I'll Take This One; You'll Take That One"

One time these two young boys went out possum hunting, and they started to pass by this graveyard where there were trees in it. It was dark, and shadows were to be seen every which way they looked.

Unknown to these two boys, there were two men that had been out gathering up walnuts. They had a falling out over the divide. One of them said, "Well, let's just go over in the graveyard and divide these up so that nobody is cheated.

As they went into the cemetery, they laid a walnut on each gate post. So they went on in and they began to divide up the walnuts. One of them was saying, "I'll take this one; you'll take that one. I'll take this one; you'll take that one."

While they were counting out the walnuts, these two young boys leaned up against the gateposts. One of the men said, "I'll take this one on this gatepost, and you take the one on that other gatepost."

Well, when the boys heard that, they took off and left there. They had the idea that it was the Good Lord and the devil counting up the souls and bodies in the graveyard. They would divide up the dead people. The boys thought that they just might reach out and grab them, too, maybe even stick them down in a hole there in the ground. Whew, did they ever run from the Lord and the devil!

16. "The Lord and the Devil in the Cemetery"

Two boys here in southern Barren County went hickory nut hunting. They filled their paper sacks full of hickory nuts as they walked down this old road. Then they came upon this old cemetery where no one had been buried for years and years. One of the boys said to the other, "This would be a good place to divide up the nuts that we've picked up along the way. After all, we need to have an equal number of the nuts. What's good for the goose is good for the gander."

So they crossed over this old fence surrounding the cemetery, but two of the hickory nuts dropped out of one of the bags as they crossed over the fence. As they divided the other nuts, they'd say, "This one's for you, and this one's for me. This one's for you, and this one's for me."

While they were dividing up the nuts, a man walked down the road past the graveyard, but he was so scared that he began walking at a much faster pace. On down the road a few yards, he met this other fellow. Told this fellow that the Lord and the devil were down there at the graveyard dividing up the dead. Said, "They're saying, 'You take this one; I'll take that one.'"

The other fellow said to him, "Now come on; you know they're not dividing up the dead on this old road."

The first fellow said, "Yes, they are. Follow me, and listen when we get there."

In the meantime, the two boys were just finishing dividing up the nuts. When they finally got through, one of them happened to think of the two that they had dropped as they crossed the fence. He said to the other boy, "Now, let's go on the other side of the fence and get the two that are over there."

Well, these two men were scared to death that the devil might get one of them, so they took off running in the other direction. And the last I heard, they were still running.

17. "Is He Lean, or Is He Fat?"

Near a lonely graveyard in the backcountry section of Breckenridge County was this little country store where farmers would gather at and tell ghost stories relevant to the old graveyard. These farmers would gather in around an old pot-bellied stove, tell tales, whittle on benches with their Barlow knives, spit on the stove and even on the floor to the disgust of the woman folk. They would tell tales that would make young people's hair stand on end.

When it came time to go home, and the merchant had closed the doors, most of these loafers were afraid to pass the lonely graveyard on the way home. A tale was often told by loafers who had reputations for telling the truth that several of them had seen objects moving about in the graveyard. They swore that this was true. One night, two particularly sensible citizens decided to test this tale out so that they, too, could see the ghosts. One of the two was a crippled young boy who volunteered to go, provided a strong man would go along to help him walk. This is a true story.

Against the advice of the others, late in the night they proceeded cautiously and quietly as they slipped up beside the graveyard fence to watch for a ghost at the precise time they had always been told that the ghost appeared. Crouching together behind some bushes by the fence, they looked, and sure enough, in the dim light objects could be seen also crouching on the ground in the midst of the old white and gray headstones at the graves.

The boy and the man grew more and more frozen with fright. The man began attempting to lift the crippled boy in his arms to run with him when, all of a sudden, they heard a ghost yell out, "Is he lean, or is he fat?"

The man dropped the crippled youngster and started running away from the graveyard. He was scared to death of having an encounter with a ghost. And, would you believe it, the crippled boy jumped up and ran for the first time ever in his life, back to the store nearby.

Naturally, the braver, older fellows there at the store immediately went to the graveyard to see what it was all about. And to their amazement, there were two men skinning sheep close to the cemetery. The truth was, one of the sheep skinners confessed, they had been stealing sheep and taking them to the graveyard to skin them in this ark of safety.

The sheep-skinning man who had seen the fellow lifting the crippled boy earlier and had asked, "Is he fat or lean?" thought that the crippled boy was another lamb or sheep that was being cautiously carried to them by another sheep thief.

Like a lot of other things, a ghost has its values, even if imagined, for the "ghost" in this story caused a cripple boy to walk. And he has been walking ever since that happened.

18. "Headless Lady of Iroquois Park"

About a year ago, one night at one o'clock, I was walking down this dark road near Iroquois Park. I was in a cemetery, so that is what makes this somewhat of a scary story.

As I walked along, I could hear somebody else walking. I was on the asphalt road, but the other steps sounded as if they were in leaves. I kept looking around and I kept hearing these other footsteps. They were in the leaves and were getting faster and faster, keeping up with me. So when I started trotting, it also started trotting to keep up with me. I ran a little bit harder, and it also ran harder. So I said to myself, "I'm going to figure out one way or another if it's just me that I hear."

So I ran as fast as I could, then came to a complete stop. But whatever it was didn't stop right then. It ran on a few feet farther.

Well, there I was in the middle of the dark road, all alone but not really. So being kind of foolish, I went over to the woods to investigate. At first, I didn't hear anything, but then I heard footsteps again. The steps got closer and closer, but still I didn't see anything. But then I felt some cold chills going down my backbone. I turned around to look, and there stood the famous headless lady of Iroquois Park.

I didn't know what to do at first, because all I could see was a woman holding her head with blood dripping out of it. Believe you me, I ran like a madman until I finally got away from there. I wouldn't advise anybody to ever go there alone. No telling what might happen if that headless lady reached out toward you and yelled out, "I gotcha!"

19. "Ghostly Gun Appears in Photograph"

My mother was going to school when she was about twenty years old. She and a couple of other females that she went to college with decided to investigate this old house that everyone claimed to be haunted. It was way out in the country, and there were signs that read, "Keep Out."

The three of them went in the old house, and it was just totally covered with dust and cobwebs. No one had lived there in a really long time.

They walked around through the house, taking pictures of each other. And after exploring the downstairs, one girl got the creeps and she went on out to the car. But Mom and the other girl were determined to look upstairs in the old house. As they walked up the steps, one of the steps cracked under their feet. They went on up and looked all around, but never found anything in any of the rooms.

One of the doors would not open, however. They shook and shook, and tugged and pulled on it, but they just couldn't get it to open. The other girl took a picture of my mom in front of that door, then they left.

A week or so later, the other girl came running up to my mom, yelling, "Look at this!"

In that photograph, the door that they couldn't open was cracked and there was a gun pointed at Mom's head. The girl swears that the door was not open when she took the picture.

20. "Screams of a Murdered Girl"

One night after the burial of one of the murdered jailers in LaGrange, we were sitting around in a car talking about the escapees from the state prison who had murdered the jailers. We were less than two miles from the prison.

One of my friends heard someone knocking on the back window. The first thing everybody thought of was the murderers. The reaction of my friend was to start the engine and get out of there. He turned the ignition key but nothing happened. We were scared. All we could think of was the murderers. Then we heard a shriek or a scream, but we didn't know what to do. We decided to lay on the floor and stay as still as possible.

We stayed there for two hours without moving. After two hours, we decided that whoever it was out there was gone, so we all jumped out to see what had happened. We found a girl who went to high school with us stabbed to death. And there was blood all over my friend's car. The only thing that we could figure out was that the murderer was still around. At that notion, we decided to run to the nearest gas station.

When we got there, the only objective seemed to be to call the prison and tell the officials of the incident and that we had heard the girl scream when she was murdered. The prison officials told us that the prison escapees had been caught that afternoon.

The murderer of the girl was never caught. The only thing that comes to my mind when I pass that place now is the scream that we heard that awful night. Other people now say that each year from the day of her death, there are weird happenings at this same spot.

Ghost stories, especially those with a "gotcha!" ending, were favorite forms of entertainment for children, especially youngsters who grew up in storytelling families and communities. (Photograph by Michael L. Morse, 1974)

21. "Three Young Girls and the Boogeyman"

When I was a child about eight years old, we lived in Ashland. The neighborhood I lived in was very small, and had only about three children my age. That being the case, I played with many older kids, twelve, thirteen, fourteen years old. Close to our house was a creek with large trees lining its banks. It seemed to be sort of a secluded place. At that time, I was always scared about going around the creek to play. See, those older kids told me time and time again that the boogeyman was going to get me. They seemed to take pleasure in trying to scare us young kids. None of us young kids would ever dare go down to the creek at night.

After this boogeyman stuff had gone on for years, it came to be what people sat around campfires and told to scare others there. Well, one time there were these three girls, Beth, Julie, and Kate, who went down to the creek one night. They were playing in the water, and seemed to have lost track of time. It was about 10:30, and the moon was full. And there was a light fog floating low in the air. The three were talking, when all of a sudden they saw this ghostly form in the fog. The creature had a white face and was wearing old, blue walking clothes. The three girls were so frightened that they thought they could not move. But, believe you me, when this thing started running after them, they ran and ran until they became lost. They were so scared by then that they started crying. It was then that the boogeyman extended its long, boney fingers toward the girls and shrieked, "I gotcha! I gotcha!"

They told me later that they were so scared that they all wet in their pants.

22. "Rawhead and Bloody Bones"

The conventional way of telling ghost stories is around a campfire or in a dark environment. Yet, there are some ghost stories that are told in broad daylight.

My mom was told by her grandfather about Rawhead and Bloody Bones when she was a little girl. Rawhead and Bloody Bones are two men that used to live in a one-room barn house before my grandparents lived there. Legend has it that these two men were brutally murdered by another man who discovered that they had a secret fortune. One of the men was found later with no skin on his head, hence the name Rawhead. The only clue that another man had been living in the house was a skeleton that lay on the floor of the barn house. It came to be that these two murdered men later haunted the old structure. My great-grandfather would tell my mom and all her cousins that if they did not behave, Rawhead and Bloody Bones would come to get them.

Mom and all her cousins spent the night there one night after he had told them all of this. Mom said that she woke up because she heard footsteps. She raised up in bed but saw no one there, so she laid back down.

Once again, she heard footsteps, only this time they sounded as if they were right by her head. She did not want to move, but she just had to see who was there. So she looked up and saw this figure of a skeleton dripping with blood. She started screaming real loud and woke everyone up. My great-grandfather ran in there and turned on the lights. When he did this, there was a drop of blood right next to where my mom had been lying.

My great-grandfather thought that it was just a coincidence, because a raccoon had scratched up the hunting dogs earlier that same day. But the truth of the matter is, the dogs had not been in the house all day.

23. "Two Little Crying Girls"

Sometimes ghost stories are fabricated, but seem to be so true that one cannot forget the events that are told as part of the story. I personally had an incident like that.

I was at my friend Amy's slumber party back in October. We were in the basement, which was her rec room, when her parents came down and said that they needed to tell us something.

The first thing that they told us was that we should not get scared at the little girls that are in the garage that was sealed from the outside. They said that they probably would not hurt us if we were nice to them. Amy's parents then proceeded to tell us that an insane couple once lived in the house. They had two daughters, Milly and Molly.

One day these little girls did not behave like they were told to, so their mom put them in the sealed-in garage. Well, the girls just screamed and screamed to be let out of the garage. They pounded on the door leading into the rec room. Their mom got tired of listening to them scream at the top of their voices and pound on the door, so she went down and tied them to a post in the middle of the garage. This did not keep the girls from screaming though.

The father came in from his daily excursions. He heard the girls screaming, and it just about drove him crazy. So he went down there to gag them so they could not scream. But before he did this to them, the little girls asked him if they could have some bread and water. He brought this to them, gagged them, then went back upstairs.

The little girls remained there for two weeks before their bodies started to weaken. Six days later, they died. It was two months before someone discovered their bodies. This was a real estate agent who came by to look at the house because it had been abandoned.

Amy's parents told us that if we heard clanking and maybe some screams, that we'd better get some bread and water for the girls. They then left us there all alone. At first, none of us thought it was true. But after we went to sleep, we changed our minds in a hurry. We were awakened by a loud clanking noise in the sealed-off garage. We all started screaming, and I began to cry. I ran up the steps and screamed for Amy's mom. Her dad and mom both came running down. That immediately canceled my thoughts that it was one of them making the noise just to scare us. The really bad thing is that the clanking noise continued to be heard. Amy's dad ran upstairs and got some bread and water, then came running back downstairs. He said that one of us had to take the bread and water to the little girls. My other friend, Sebrina, opened the door and sat the food in the garage and took off running. She was too afraid to stay close to the door. Right after that, Amy's brother came running out of the garage screaming and laughing at us. They had that all rigged up to scare us, and, wow, did they ever do a good job!

24. "Boyfriend's Fingernails Heard Scratching the Top of the Car"

In Sleepy Hollow in Louisville, and this is true, it's very dark. There's no light anywhere. And this couple was parked down there in the hollow. They were both very Puritanistic, except they were at Sleepy Hollow, drinking quite a bit. It was getting late, so they got ready to leave but their car wouldn't start. So the fellow didn't know what to do. He told the girl to stay in the car and to keep the doors locked.

So this guy goes on and leaves the car, and his date was sitting there in the car with all the doors locked. It was pitch dark. The guy is gone to get some gas. She waits and waits for him, but he doesn't show up. She doesn't know what to think. Then she hears this scratching on top of the car and thinks that it must be a tree limb on top of the car. She waits and waits and nothing happens. Finally, she falls asleep.

In the morning she wakes up when a policeman begins pecking on the window of the car. She opens the door and the policeman says to her, "We're going to have to get you out of here."

So she starts walking away, and the policeman says, "Please don't look back at the car."

She couldn't resist looking, so she looked back at the car, and there's her date hanging there by his heels, with his fingernails scratching the top of the car.

25. "The Grandparents' Haunted House"

Amanda and Sami were on their way to visit their Grandma Kay and Grandpa Matt. Their grandparents' house was quite a drive from where Amanda and Sami lived. After a long trip, Sami looked at her older sister and asked, "Are we almost there?"

"Yes," said Amanda, as they pulled up into the driveway. Both of them glanced up at their grandparents' two-story house that they had moved into about two years ago.

"So this is the place, huh?" Sami asked.

"Yep, it sure is," Amanda responded, as they proceeded to walk up to the door.

After greeting each other and talking a little while, the grandparents began to tell the girls some very strange things that had been happening in the house. The grandparents had felt no reason to move out of the house, as they had not felt threatened by any supernatural presence. Yet they knew that the place was haunted. Grandpa Matthew said to them, "There is a main ghost that we see around here more often than the others. It's a ghost of a little boy."

All the two girls could do was to look at each other, strangely. Yet they were not convinced that some of the things that their grandparents had told them were really true. The girls thought that maybe the grandparents were just trying to scare them in a joking manner, maybe to startle them.

Before Amanda and Sami started up the stairs for bed, they said goodnight to their grandparents. Then Grandma Kay spoke up and said, "If you get scared, come down and get us. It's no problem."

The girls chuckled and went on upstairs. Their bedroom had a hallway leading to it. Across from the doorway was the bed. Thus, anyone who slept there could see out the door right into the long, dark hallway.

Both girls crawled into bed, but decided to stay awake and talk for awhile. Suddenly, Amanda asked, "Did you open the door, Sami?"

"No, why?"

"Well," Amanda said, "I shut it just a minute ago, and now it's open. It's probably an old door."

Sami then asked Amanda, "Do you really believe Grandma Kay and Grandpa Matthew are telling us the truth?"

"I don't know," Amanda responded. "I think they may be losing their minds. It happens with old age."

While the girls were talking, Sami saw a glowing in the corner of her eyes. She looked in the direction where it came from, which was on the other side of the hallway. Being too scared to speak, Sami grabbed hold of Amanda's arm.

Amanda by then had her eyes fixed on what appeared to be the image of a little boy's ghost. "Oh, my gosh!" she said.

Both girls watched the misty figure as it came closer and closer to their room. Both of them became very silent for a moment. Then, an over-whelming fear of the little boy came over Amanda. She sat straight up in bed, intending to plead to the little boy not to come any closer to them. However, only the word "Stop" came out of her mouth. As soon as she had said it, out of the hallway wall came a remarkable large hand, or what could have been a huge claw of some sort, and it snatched up the little boy ghost and pulled him back inside the wall.

The girls sat and watched with disbelief what was taking place. They waited a few minutes to see what else was going to happen, but nothing did. Needless to say, the girls told their grandparents that the next time they came to visit them, they intended to stay in a hotel or motel.

I guess by then they believed in what their grandparents told them about the ghostly things in that house.

26. "Knife in the Skirt"

There was just a bunch a-having a party at a girl's home one night. They were just making a bet, you know, what each one would be afraid to do. There was a graveyard right close by this girl's home and some of the other girls and boys told her that they'd bet she wouldn't go to that graveyard. And she said she would go, that she wasn't afraid. So, one of them told her, says "Well, you take this butcher knife," says, "You stick it in a certain grave over there so we'll know then that you've been there."

This girl, she took the butcher knife and when she knelt down to stick it in that grave, she unknowingly stuck it through her skirt, and when she started to raise up, naturally that butcher knife held her skirt down. That scared her so bad, why, she died. So that's where they found her, there by that grave.

27. "Revenue Man with Ghostly Hands"

My grandparents lived in the big brick house there in Tompkinsville at Fourth and Main Street. That's where my daddy grew up. They'd always sit there at night with the lights off. My granddaddy was Dr. Billy Richardson, and he'd sit there and tell a lot of the old stories, or they'd talk about the stories that he'd already told.

Grandfather lived at Judio in a big white house at the foot of the hill below Coe Ridge, the black community back then. Grandfather raised his family there. That house looks ghosty, just to look at it.

The black people up there on Coe Ridge would call "Dr. Billy" to come up there on Coe Ridge to doctor them. The path that he had to travel over was steep and went right up the side of that mountain. He'd ride his big brown horse up that mountain to go up there where those black people were, no matter what was wrong with them. But no matter how sick they were, he would not go into their house to doctor them. That had something to do with ghosts, but they would never tell me what they were talking about.

Anyway, they'd bring the sick ones out in the yard. Two or three people there in the family would carry them out and sit them either on a stump or on a big log. And Grandfather would doctor them like that. Then, they'd carry them back in the house.

Well, one day, these blacks were down making whiskey at their moonshine stills. Said they had a run nearly ready to ship off. And they were talking about how much money they'd make by selling it, what they'd do with it, and which way they were going.

One of the blacks said, "Now, wouldn't Old Man Huddleston, the revenue agent, like to know this."

Said Huddleston had been lying there under a pile of leaves, hidden from them. Well, he just reached out and grabbed one of them black moonshiners by the leg, and pulled him down. Granddaddy said that Huddleston caught everyone of them that way. They all thought that it was a ghost that got them!

The idea behind all this was that it was thought that all the houses there in Zeketown (another name for the Coe Ridge colony) had ghosts in them.

Chapter 7

Hanged or Murdered Persons' Ghosts

1. "The Woman in a Pink Nightgown"

After we moved out of the gray house in Brandenburg, we moved into another house owned by the same woman. It was a white house. Had no upstairs. It was also in Brandenburg, and still is.

When you walked into the front door of that house, you went into the living room. Off the living room was a kitchen, and the kitchen had a back door leading out onto a carport. Mom and Dad's room was off the hallway on the left; the second room on the right was the bathroom. But before you got to the bathroom, there was another room on the left. It was my room but I didn't use it. At the end of the hallway was Granddad's room.

I slept on the couch in the living room. That's where the TV and all was. Had an electric lamp on a table behind me, and my dog Krypto was still with me. One night I was laying there on the couch close to midnight, reading a book. I happened to look up over the book and standing at the corner of the living room wall and the hallway was a woman looking at me. She was wearing a pink nightgown and she had pink hair curlers in her hair. She never said a word. I thought it was my mom, who was there to see what time I was going to bed.

So I just said, "I'm going to bed now." And I just reached behind me and turned the light out. Didn't think a thing about it. Went to sleep. Well, I did notice that the dog was acting kinda peculiar. His hair was standing up on the nape of his neck, and he was trembling and doing a combination of a whine and a growl. I couldn't figure out why he was acting that way, knowing Mom was standing there.

So the next morning, I got up and got ready for school. While I was eating breakfast, I asked Mom what she wanted the night before.

She said, "What do you mean?"

I said, "What did you want last night?"

She said, "I don't know what you mean."

I said, "Well, you was standing there looking at me reading my book, but you didn't say anything."

She said, "I didn't get up last night."

I said, "Yes, you did. You was standing there looking at me. You had on a pink nightgown, and you had pink hair curlers in your hair."

She said, "Well, first of all, I don't have a pink nightgown, and another thing, I don't have any pink hair curlers. You can go in there and look."

So I did. I went into the bathroom and looked. She had hair curlers, but they were yellow and green. No pink hair curlers at all. I couldn't figure it all out. Well, we had a next door neighbor that lived there in front of us at the time. Her name was Thelma Miller. She has since died, but was alive at the time.

Well, I went over there and talked with Mrs. Miller about what I had seen that night.

She said, "Well, I wasn't going to say anything, but now that you've told me on your own, I'll tell you probably what that was." She went on to say, "At one time, a few years ago, there was a young couple lived in that house—a young girl and her soldier husband. I knew he was a soldier because he had on a uniform."

She said that he was stationed in Ft. Knox. I guess that he apparently just married this girl but didn't know anything about her family. I guess they eloped. So he went back to Ft. Knox, where he was stationed. Of course, that girl was there. Mrs. Miller said that this girl got sick and was in bed. The girl's brother came to see her and visited with her for a while. Well, on the day that the brother came to see her, this girl's husband got out on a surprise furlough. He was going to come home and surprise his wife with a visit. Didn't call to tell her that he was coming in or anything.

Well, when he walked in the front door, this girl's brother was getting ready to leave. When he came through the front door, he opened the bedroom door to surprise his wife. When he opened the door, he saw this man bend over his wife and kiss her. Well, that was just her brother kissing his sister goodbye, but the man didn't know that the man who was kissing his wife was her brother. What he saw was a man that he didn't know kissing his wife, and his wife was in bed in a nightgown and all. So her husband thought the worst. Well, he run this guy off, then ran back in the house and beat his young wife up. Didn't even give her a chance to get up out of bed. He just beat the stuffings out of her. Then he went out on the carport and got a can of gasoline and took it back in the house and completely drenched his wife from head to toe. Then he set the whole thing on fire.

He didn't kill his wife when he beat her up, but he did knock her out. But when he set her on fire, that killed her. When he saw that she was burning, he ran out of the house yelling things like, "She will never cheat on me again," and things like that.

Well, Mrs. Miller saw what was going on, so she called the police, then called the fire department because she saw smoke coming out of the windows. Well, the police got there and caught the soldier and put him in custody. But by the time the fire department got there, it was too late to save this girl. She was dead.

Mrs. Miller said that when they carried the girl out on a stretcher, she was dressed in a pink nightgown, or what was left of it, and it looked as if she had pink hair curlers in her hair.

She said that every time that somebody new moves into the house, this girl will come back to see who it is and to see if it's her husband. I guess that she's wanting to get revenge on her husband.

I don't know what ever happened to him. I don't know if he's still in prison, or if he died, or what. I don't even know who he was. I never found out what this girl's name was or what this guy's name was.

But the way that Mrs. Miller described the girl that got murdered, she looked exactly like this woman that appeared to me that night. That house is still standing there in Brandenburg.

2. "The Ghostly Sounds of a Teenage Boy"

One night, there was a birthday party being thrown for Chris. He and Sam were the best of friends. Sam couldn't be late, as it was Chris's sixteenth birthday. He was three days older than Sam. Sam was in such a hurry that he ran off without picking up Chris's birthday present. When Sam got to the party, he explained what happened and told Chris that he'd bring it to him at school tomorrow.

As soon as Sam got home that night, he went straight to bed. The next morning he got up and got dressed for school, then took off. Well, Chris wasn't there when he got there, so he knew that Chris had to be pooped or maybe sick. So Sam thought that he would drop it off at Chris's home that afternoon after school. When the bell rang to dismiss school that afternoon, Sam ran out the door, got on his bike, and rode over to Chris's house.

He knocked on the door, and Chris's mother came to the door. Sam asked her if Chris were there. The mother burst into tears. Sam asked her, "What did I say wrong?"

She stopped crying and asked him to come in. She told him, said, "I've got some bad news. Chris fell out of his bedroom window last night. Killed him. We don't know how it happened. When we woke up this morning, I went up to get him up to get ready for school. He wasn't in his bed. I looked over toward the window and the glass was shattered all over the floor. I peered down at the ground and there he lay."

Sam was devastated. He left and went home and went straight up to his room. His mother came and asked him what was wrong. He said, "Mom, Chris is dead."

"Dear God, what happened?" his Mom asked.

Sam explained to her what happened.

The next day they had the funeral and buried Chris. His Mom says that when it rains or storms, she hears glass shatter and a piercing scream. She says that one night she ran upstairs and saw Chris being pushed out the window. She said that she ran over to grab him, but her hand went through him and he fell to the ground.

But it looked like he was being pushed. To this day, no one knows what really happened.

3. "Peripheral Vision Detects Ghosts"

I worked for a pharmacist in Caneyville, and he is still there. But he did move his family to Leitchfield where they bought a home. I guess it had been twenty years or so before they moved there that this woman was murdered in the house that they bought. This is a fact; a woman was murdered there.

This pharmacist had heard numerous reports that this house was haunted, but he refused to believe in anything like that. But he did say that after they had been there for a while, strange things began to happen. They heard noises, but not just noises like you can hear in an old house, such as the creaking and all that takes place in old houses. The noise was like thumps, loud thumps and a bang on the wall, or something like that, something out of the ordinary. He does not believe in anything like that really, so it is chilling to hear him tell it.

So after they had been there for a while, they had begun seeing these apparition-like things or just glimpses out of the corner of their eyes. And the whole family from time to time reported seeing these things.

Their children were kind of small, so it could have been that they picked up on their parents' ideas, but I don't know. He said that one night he was going up to bed, climbing the steps, when all of a sudden out of the corner of his eye he saw this thing go around the corner there in the hallway. It happened twice after that, and once he saw the whole figure of a woman. But he said that they all just sort of learned to live with it and accept it for what it was—a ghost.

4. "Ghost of the Old Iron Bridge"

Just south of Leitchfield, Kentucky, there is a supposedly haunted bridge where local teenagers and, for that matter, older people go to try to give each other a good scare. This bridge is locally known as the "Old Iron Bridge." It is located about four miles from highway 259–South on Bloomington Road.

Legends claim that, years ago, a young mother took her baby down to the creek that flows underneath the bridge and drowned it. The reason for this grizzly murder is to this day unknown.

As to why it is that people go there to the bridge, they say that at midnight, strange things begin to happen. It seems that every person who comes back from the bridge has a slightly different version as to what takes place while they are there. The original story claims that one, and sometimes two, things happen while a person is at the bridge.

The first of these two things is by far the most disturbing. It is said that, at midnight, the water that flows under the bridge turns either reddish or bluish in color. While the water is of a different color, it is said that you are supposed to be able to hear the baby crying.

The second of the two things that happens is that people sometimes see the ghost of the baby's mother wandering around in the woods looking for her child. Stories are still being told that if one wanders in and around the woods surrounding the bridge, they just may encounter the mother of the child. I was once told a story by an older fellow that was quite unnerving. He told me of a night when he was a teenager that he and some of his buddies were down in the woods around the bridge, just goofing off and trying to raise any kind of trouble that they could. As he continued with his story, this fellow, a Mr. Davis, had to get up and start moving around. I believe that he was beginning to scare himself badly just by retelling the story.

He continued by stating that about midnight certain things began to happen that were just unexplainable. First, he said that he and his friends faintly heard what they thought was a baby crying. They then hurried back through the woods in the direction from which they heard this crying. As they got back to the bridge, they noticed that the water had turned into a bluish color. It was then that they really started to become scared. They realized that it was here that the cries of the baby are supposed to be heard. With this in mind, they very quickly decided that it was time for them to get away from there. They retraced their steps back to the woods where they had parked their car.

While walking back through the woods, Davis felt a peck on his shoulder. Reluctantly he turned, and guess what he said he saw? He said that he saw a very white and almost translucent outline of a female. Needless to say, he and his friends froze in their tracks. He said that the ghostly woman then asked the question, "Have you seen my baby?"

Davis calmly replied, "No, I haven't. Sorry."

The apparition then turned and slowly walked away. Then, after it was about twenty yards down the road, it slowly disappeared.

I can't say whether I really believe this or not, but here's what actually happened to me when I went there. It started off as just a regular summer week night during my high school years. Three of my friends and I were sitting around one night just talking about ghosts and hauntings about which we had heard. After an hour or so and many stories later, the subject of the Old Iron Bridge came up. So, after some contemplation, we decided to head over to the bridge just before midnight.

The drive out to the bridge was normal, if you could consider doing anything like this normal. Anyway, the drive out was accomplished without any mishaps, but these things were to happen later. We got there just before midnight, but left the car running just in case we needed to get away from there in a hurry. In the minutes that passed, we remained silent, except listening to the radio turned down low, which we kept on to help pass the time until midnight.

At 11:59 we all began to get a little fidgety. As we watched the clock, there was total silence except for the hum of the motor and the playing of the radio turned down low. When the clock finally read 12:00 midnight, the water did not turn red or blue, the baby didn't cry out, and we didn't see a ghost. Actually, we didn't stay around long enough to see. When the clock switched to midnight, one unnerving thing did happen. The radio that had been playing all of a sudden just cut off. Nobody had turned it off, and no one had touched the volume control. The radio just simply cut off.

As soon as it cut off, we hightailed it straight out of there and headed back to town. Oddly enough, the radio came back on just the second that we entered the Leitchfield city limits.

I'm not saying that I believe everything that I have heard before about the Old Iron Bridge, but I do believe what happened while I was out there. I guess that all it takes is one trip out to the old bridge to make believers out of us.

5. "The Ghost of a Man Who Was Stabbed to Death"

This happened in Franklin. One night I was coming home after seeing a girl that I was dating. She lived across town from me. I was young, so I walked over to see her. I stayed with her for quite a while, then had to walk back home. By the time I got home, it was 1:30 to 2:00 a.m.

There used to be an old junkyard on the left side of the street close to where I lived. Now, it is just an open lot. When I got to the junkyard that night, I saw a man walk out of the entrance to the junkyard, wander over to the main street, and then wander into the yard next to the junkyard. He walked maybe ten yards into that front yard, then disappeared.

It shook me up pretty bad. I went on down the street to our house, and went on inside. The next morning I told my mother what I had seen. It wasn't very strange to her. She said that she, too, had seen him, and that she knew a little bit about him.

It seems that this man got into a fight at the junkyard and was stabbed and cut up pretty badly with the knife. He had stumbled out of the junkyard trying to get some help, but died in the process. She said that the man had died in the same yard in which I saw him disappear the night before.

6. "Indian Joe's Ghost"

One night me and my best friend Vada were out cruising in the county, just something to do after the drive-in movie was over. We decided to take the long way home from Morganfield to Sturgis, by way of Boxville. The night was really nice. The sky was as clear as a bell, and the moon was so bright that it was almost like daytime. We were cruising along without a worry on our minds with the windows rolled down and the tape player blaring out Hank Williams Jr., when all of a sudden we heard a noise outside the car. We didn't know what the noise was, so we cut off the tape to see if something was going wrong with the old car I was driving.

The sounds weren't coming from the car, and all around us we could hear horses running, the sounds of whips cracking, and chains rattling like they were being dragged on the pavement. We looked all the way around us but we couldn't see a thing. The sounds got louder and louder until we couldn't hear ourselves talk or even think. Needless to say, we weren't sticking around to investigate any further, and thanks to my old 1976 Mercury Comet and my heavy tennis shoes it didn't take but about two minutes flat to finish out the fast journey home.

The next morning when we got to school, we found out about the Indian Joe story, a story that apparently everyone else at school at heard about, but we hadn't. Indian Joe was accused of stealing horses in Union County in the late 1800s and then hanged by local men in the area where it took place. Whether or not Indian Joe actually stole horses is still an unsettled argument with the area locals. Guilty or not, he was hanged for the crime, and ever since he was hanged people have been too scared to travel that road much at night because of the unexplainable noises they often hear. It is also said that at night on the far side of Daisy Mae Lake, sometimes you can actually see his body hanging from the tree from which they hanged him almost a century ago.

7. "Baby, Baby, Cry for Me"

When I was growing up in Uniontown, located in Union County along the Ohio River, one of my favorite scare-you-to-death booger stories that us kids would tell in order to scare each other until we didn't have a lick of common sense left was the story about a man named Moses Staton [pseudonym]. He was an old fellow who lived down in a river bottom.

According to the story, Staton and his wife had a farm in the river bottoms. One day when he was out in the field working, a storm quickly blew in. Moses was running from the middle of the field toward the house when lightning struck a tree in front of him, sending a large limb right down on top of his head. He was knocked unconscious and was never the same man again. Legend has it that after the accident, he totally went crazy. He locked his wife up in the attic of the house, and every time she had a baby, he would bash it against a tree, then feed it to the hogs. The townspeople went and gathered him up one afternoon, and he was hanged in Morganfield in front of nearly everybody from the entire county.

When we all started getting up in our later teen years, we decided to be brave and go to the house and scream, "Baby, baby, cry for me," to see if we could get the babies to cry like we had heard others say that they got the babies to cry.

We drove out one night, and about four of the six of us got out of the car. We were pretty scared but said the words anyway. No sooner had we said, "Cry for me," until sprays of tiny river rocks came pounding down upon our heads. We got into the car and drove so fast that I thought the engine would blow any second.

We never knew where the rocks came from. At first, we thought that a group of our rowdy friends had followed us out there, but we soon found out for sure that they hadn't. And after all that happened, none of us were brave enough to take a second trip to that old home place where the babies reputedly died.

8. "The Ghost That Carries Its Head in Harry Webb Hollow"

There was a black man named Harry Webb who was killed in a crap game there in Harry Webb Hollow. He was probably a slave that belonged to William Caldwell. And this might have happened while he was still a slave. Anyway, our folks would tell us children that on a rainy night Harry Webb's ghost would walk down through the hollow by the spring carrying his head. And it truly was a dark place when you walked down Greensburg Street by that stream of water. When you did that, you were sure to think about the story and be inclined to believe it, even if it weren't a rainy night. I don't know how much our people talked about that in order to keep us kids from going to town, but I'll tell you right now, it was a tale told to *all* children in this section of Columbia. And it was told for many, many years. I know that. I remember my father telling that when he was a boy he heard it, and what he did so as not to see the ghost.

From all indications, it was already a legend by 1885. I don't know when it happened, but it was being told then about this man who was killed up there in that hollow, and his ghost was seen at nights.

I remember coming home from town one night with Lucille Patterson. We weren't too old, yet we couldn't have been very young or we wouldn't have been out by ourselves after dark. Anyway, we'd passed Grandpa's house, and between his house and this spring branch was an empty lot. There was a fence and a dirt bank down by the sidewalk. We were starting to walk down the hill when something rose up out of this bank. We screamed and shouted and grabbed each other. But guess who it was? It was Todd Jeffries, the boy that lived next door to us. He wouldn't admit it, but he was too scared to go through the hollow by himself. He had heard us coming, so he waited for us, then decided that he would scare us as we walked by. He leaped out at us, waving his arms and yelling, "Boo! Boo! Boo!"

And, believe you me, he scared the heck out of both of us.

9. "Lewis Bedford's Ghost"

The Ross family moved into an old house in Mortonsville, which is a small community near Versailles, in 1978. At that time they began remodeling the old house that was approximately 200 years old. And although there were widespread rumors that the old house was haunted, members of the Ross family weren't worried. However, the construction crew began to hear footsteps on the stairway. It seemed as if they were disturbing something or someone. So the Ross family investigated and began finding some very interesting things, ghostly even.

Lewis Bedford had built or at least had lived in the house. However, he met an early death. His early death was never researched, but it is thought that it was his third wife who murdered him. This is what people felt, because she was to receive his fortune, and she remarried after only a few days following his death. When my mother and I were reading Lewis's will recently, we heard doors latching of their own accord, and the lights went out. Also when my brother Laith saw a book fall from a shelf, he laughingly commented, "Oh, Lewis, stop that!" Then, many more books fell off the shelf.

Another interesting point is that our family dog will not walk past the stairs, as footsteps are frequently heard going up and down the steps.

Lewis' ghost also opens doors and rattles pans there in the house. My mother tried to drive the ghost away by saying, "Anything that will not bow down to the name of Jesus Christ must leave this house."

Lewis' ghost did not leave, but it has proven to be non-malevolent. But believe you me, that ghost is truly mischievous.

The last time that Lewis' ghost was active was during minor remodeling of the house in 1988. Since that time, his ghost has not been seen or heard.

10. "The Mandy Tree"

Mandy Holloman, who has been dead for many years, still keeps silent watch over the countryside she loved so well, barely outside the western city limits of Madisonville. At least this is what everyone says.

Mandy led an average life, and officially filling a suicide's grave, Mandy has come within recent years to be a legend. Near the spot where she was found twenty-eight years ago, dead either from her own hands or by a bullet from a murderer's gun, stands now a white oak tree, the branches and leaves of which have formed themselves into a perfect image of Mandy.

The case was entered into the records as self-murder, but there are several people who believe without a doubt that she was murdered and that Mandy's spirit has come back into the tree to stand there watching for whoever caused her death.

As for me, the nearest thing to truth, I think, is the story told by Albert Taylor, her brother, who lives just outside Madisonville. Albert has been a coal miner for fifty years, and his story may not hold much water. Anyway, he told that one morning his brother-in-law Ed Holloman ate a hearty breakfast which Mandy had prepared. Then he took his dinner pail and went off to work in the coal mine. A few minutes later, Ed's son, or Mandy's stepson, who also worked in the mine, was seen leaving the house in a run. He reported to the mine, which was Bell and Zoller. But before he left home that morning, the other children had been sent to the spring to get some water.

The stepson was probably the last person to see Mandy alive, for when the children returned they found Mandy lying on the floor wrapped in a quilt. Two feet away was a pool of blood, but there was no blood on the quilt, nor was there a bullet hole through it. The bullet had entered her right side near the armpit.

Neighbors around the Holloman house heard no commotion that morning, nor could they give any reason for suicide. To add more mystery to the affair, the stepson was only a short time later killed in a mine at Clay, Kentucky.

Mandy was well liked and well respected by other black people of the community. They say that she was forever working in the garden, or planting shrubs. They also say that she had planted a tree in her back yard, a white oak sapling, which she cared for. It is this tree which, today, bears her resemblance.

There are two reasons for this resemblance of Mandy in the tree, so they say. "Mandy's blood was spilled under this very tree" is one. The other is that "Mandy's clothing, worn on the morning of her death, was buried on the very spot occupied by the tree."

The tree is on a place owned by V.H. Taylor, and is just a short distance from an old Negro college [Atkinson College], founded in 1892 by John B. Atkinson [who was President of St. Bernard Mining Company, located in Earlington]. The school was closed in 1930, and Taylor was its last president.

Since the Mandy tree has come into view, Taylor has made a tidy sum of money selling pictures of the curiosity. For ten cents, one could get a printed picture with a few words telling about the tree. But of all the excitement that has surrounded the spot, nothing has been like the excitement raised when students park under the tree and the moon is just right to cast a silhouette of Mandy's monument. Her chin is up, and she is looking silently across the countryside.

11. "Nun's Ghost at Bethel Academy"

There is an old building seven miles outside Elizabethtown that used to be an all-girls' school, taught by nuns. The name of the school was Bethel Academy. It has been abandoned for fifty to sixty years.

This academy was a good distance from any houses or barns. So during the first days of school, the girls had to live there through the school period. When the school was finally closed down and abandoned for good, three nuns stayed there in their quarters until they could be transferred to someplace else. Well, winter came on, but back at that time of the century there was not a whole lot to do at night. Therefore, every night one of the nuns would go to the assembly room on the third floor to play the organ for practice and entertainment.

One night while one of them was playing the organ, the other two nuns heard a scream from the third floor. It was a blood curdling scream, and it terrified the other two nuns so badly that they would not go to the assembly room. They told themselves that it would not be wise to go up there, as there had been talk of a mad man on the loose.

The next day, the two nuns got some neighbors to come over and check the upstairs. When they reached the room, there lay the third nun over the organ without her head. It had been cut off and was laying there on the floor in a big pool of blood.

Now the old academy building is considered to be haunted by the nun who was murdered. One thing that is truly eerie is that the trees in front of the academy have never had leaves on them since the nun was killed. Also, on a really windy, cloudy night, her ghost is said to be seen and still heard playing the organ.

12. "Spirit Returns to Reenact Death"

These two friends of mine from Louisville got married and moved to Lexington. They bought an old house there and proceeded to renovate the old structure. When they got the house finished, they called to ask me if I would like to come to Lexington and be their first overnight guest in their newly renovated house.

I was truly thrilled, so I told them that I would come. The very next Saturday night, I drove to Lexington to be with my friends. We had dinner, then sat there just talking away until around 11:00 p.m. It was then that the fellow said, "Well, I can see that we're all getting tired. Let's go to bed." He then said to me, "We sleep downstairs, but your room will be the first room to the left at the top of the upstairs steps."

Well, I went on up to my room, and since there was no one else up there but me, I did not close the door when I walked into my room. I flipped on the light switch, then went over and put my night clothes on, turned back the covers on the bed, then walked back over and turned the lights out. I hopped into bed.

Just as soon as I was lying down in the bed I heard this noise out in the hallway, "Squeak, squeak, rock, rock."

I raised up in bed, looked out into the hallway and, would you believe it, that rocking chair was rocking of its own accord. It was moving back, then forward, back, then forward. I could see it moving, because the light from the street was shining through the window. But no one was in the chair! And there was no wind coming in from the outside, for the doors and windows were all closed.

Then, the rocking stopped and I heard footsteps coming into my room. And you've never heard such loud, painful breathing in all your life. Then, whatever it was put its hands on the mattress there at the foot of my bed and mashed down. I could feel the pressure there on the mattress. And that breathing, you've never heard anything like it! I was scared to death.

Then, whatever it was walked on around and stood at the side of my bed. Then it bent over the bed, still breathing that awful breathing sound. Then it put its hands on the mattress there at the side of the bed. And, would you believe, my body rolled over into the cavity created there in the mattress. My first thought was to get up out of that hole and get over on the other side of the bed. So I crawled out of the hole and got over on the other side of the bed.

Then, it walked on around and stood between the wall and the head of my bed. When I heard it breathing as it bent down over the bed, I chickened out, I turned over on my stomach, pulled a pillow over my head, then pulled all the bedcovers over my whole body. Just as I did this, I felt a very painful stab right between my shoulder blades, just like a very sharp knife had stabbed me. I was scared to death, and said to myself, "My God, It's going to kill me right here." Then I felt two more stabs right between the shoulder blades.

I just knew it was going to kill me, but suddenly I heard footsteps leaving the room, and the breathing was much less pronounced. It wasn't long until I heard the rocking chair once again rocking out there in the hallway. I was so relieved that I was still alive that I did not call out to my friends downstairs.

The next morning when I went downstairs, I said to my friends, "I want to know what in the world it was that I experienced last night? Who was it that tried to kill me? What was that thing?"

The fellow responded, "What in the world are you talking about? We don't know. You're the first overnight guest that we've had in this house."

I told them what I had experienced up there in that room. Well, that morning my friend went down to whatever office you go to to find out about a possible homicide in this old house. He came back two hours later and said to me, "Guess what? Fifty years ago, a man's body was found in the closet under the stairway leading upstairs. And guess how he died? He was stabbed three times between the shoulder blades."

Well, I must have experienced how that man was killed, and felt the pain that I guess he felt as he was being stabbed to death. This is not a made-up story. It is very real. I felt that pain.

13. "Ghosts of Crying Babies That Were Murdered"

I heard these babies crying. Everyone in this country around here in this part of Wayne County has heard them crying. My brother Clarence who is a gospel singer and preacher, went up on the mountain over here across from the house with his wagon to get a load of wood. But he got scared up there on the mountain and left without getting the wood.

There were these two babies killed up there. Well, one day, I came into the front room here in my house because I kept hearing a baby crying. I got up and looked out the window.

At that same time, there was an old man, Paul Hancock, who lived over there in our house, coming down the road. I saw him stop to listen to the same crying that I was hearing. I went out in the yard and asked him if he had heard something crying.

He said, "Yes, sounds like babies somewhere." Said, "Sounded like the babies come right down the mountain."

He went on down the road to get his grandson, Paul, to go with him across the footlog that crosses the creek right over here. Well, whenever Paul Hancock stepped onto the footlog over here, the crying hushed up all at once. There wasn't another sound when he stepped onto that footlog to go across the creek to look for those babies. That was the last of the noise.

There were two babies killed up there on the mountain about sixty, seventy years ago. One was killed with a stick of wood and then was hid under the house. Well, a local doctor went up there and made them bring the baby out. I guess he had heard what had happened. He got these six local men to hold an inquest that night. So the doctor cut the baby's lungs out and floated them in a bucket of water to show them that the baby was not born dead; it had lived after it was born. Some people claimed that the doctor's son was the baby's illegitimate father.

The next baby that was killed up there on the mountain was killed by its mother while it was being born. That was a different woman, two different families entirely.

They got an indictment against the mother of the first baby I told about, and she went away never to return home again. Nothing was done to her and nothing has been said about her, because her people still live here.

Something I have studied about a lot is why these two babies that were not kin to each other were always heard crying together. Both babies were killed in the same house, though, and both are buried in the back yard, not in a regular cemetery. And their ghosts are always together; always crying out in agony.

I never heard them crying except that one time. These noises were still heard in the 1940s and '50s. Many people claimed that they heard them back then. Robert and Opal Hancock, who live right up here above us, have heard the crying many times since then.

The chimney of the old house is still standing, but the house itself has fallen down. We used to go up there on a tractor all the time. But I always had a weird feeling when I'd look at the spot where these two little babies are buried. I guess I'd cry, too, if somebody had killed me.

14. "Ghost of Little Girl Dressed in White"

When my Aunt Malie was a little girl here in the mountains of eastern Kentucky, my Grandma saw a little girl dressed in white. Grandma hollered at the little girl because she thought the little girl was my Aunt Malie. But when Grandma hollered out, the little girl just disappeared. A week after that happened, it was in the newspaper that a little girl had been kidnapped and killed. I guess Grandma saw the little girl's ghost.

Last year, I was playing in the mountains and I found a piece of white cloth. I showed it to Grandma, and she said it looked like material from the dress the little girl was wearing many years ago when she was killed.

Since that time, people around here have told about seeing the little girl's ghost just floating along the roadways, or up at the foot of the mountains. I don't know who she was, but I guess some people do.

15. "Bloody Handprints of Murdered Man"

Up Terry's Fork here in Harlan County, there's an old house where a man was murdered several years ago. I don't know just when. He had been shot, and he was trying to get inside this house. He got as far as the front porch, but didn't make it any farther. People say that there was a splotch of blood left there on the porch, along with a bloody handprint on the steps leading up to the porch. Whew, that would scare me to death if I saw that.

Of course, they say that they took the body away and cleaned up everything, but the place on the porch that had the pool of blood on it, and the bloody handprint on the steps, keeps coming back. When it rains, the blood stains show up again. They have scrubbed these spots, but they keep coming back. They have also painted over these stained spots, but the blood oozes right through the paint. They have tried putting new planks on the porch, but the blood continues to appear.

I've never seen any of this for myself, but I have seen the old house where it happened. People swear that it's true: that you can see the bloody spots on the porch.

16. "The Revenge of a Girl's Ghost against Her Killer"

It is claimed that in the early 1900s there was a large house on Center Street here in Henderson that was occupied by a mother, a father, a daughter, and a maid. The father and the maid were having an affair. The daughter found out about their affair, and she told her father that if it happened again, she and her mother would leave forever.

The father loved his wife and daughter very much, so the affair ceased. When he stopped seeing the maid, the maid became angry, even furious, and plotted to kill his daughter.

Christmas time was approaching. One day as a beautiful parade was coming down the street, the daughter leaned over the balcony to watch as the parade passed by. Upon seeing the girl leaning over the balcony, the maid sneaked up and seized the opportunity to push the little girl over the balcony and into the yard below. She hit the ground with a deafening thud.

At that very moment, her face's image appeared on the house at three different locations, one each on the sides of the balcony from which she fell. Her parents tried to remove the images but they were unable to do so, as the images kept reappearing.

Ten years later, as the maid was leaning across the edge of the balcony, two arms reached up, grabbed her, and threw her off. She died immediately when she hit the concrete sidewalk below. The images of the girl's face who was killed when the maid had pushed her off the balcony disappeared from the walls of the house and have never been seen there since that time.

17. "Whose Ghost Sits at the Organ?"

The October wind blew the lacy white curtains at the window of the room that my grandmother called the music parlor. My great aunt often played the organ in that room in the early afternoon. The times that she chose to play sometimes seemed strange. Later, we learned that there was a message in her music and her timing.

This great aunt was not liked very well by neighborhood ladies in Clinton County. One of the many reasons was the way that she wore makeup and the dresses she ordered from a mail order catalog. The dresses that she wore usually had bright colors in them and were cut to show her pretty, petite figure. Her long black hair curled softly about her pretty face and down her back. Although she was petite, the way that she held her head and with the brisk way she walked, she seemed taller and even more striking.

On this particularly warm October afternoon, my great aunt Amelia had all the windows open. She could see the Cumberland River and its rolling waters from her window as she played one of her favorite love songs.

Three-fourths of a mile down river, a man was waiting and listening for the familiar sound of Aunt Amelia's playing. This was her signal to him that her husband, Bill, was away on one of his many business trips as a salesman.

By twilight, Amelia saw the three familiar flashes of a lantern from the woods south of the house. She played one more chorus of the familiar song, then hurriedly took her shawl and left by the back door to meet her lover, who was waiting in the grove of pine trees behind the barn.

This was not the first time they had been together. They walked quietly back to the big white house on the hill overlooking the Cumberland River. They discussed the love they had for each other, but Aunt Amelia was afraid to leave Bill. She was afraid that he would kill her. Just before midnight, Aunt Amelia's lover got on his horse and rode away, never to see her again.

Bill was not supposed to return for three more days, but as Amelia was getting ready for bed, Bill appeared in the bedroom doorway. Three days passed; no one saw Amelia. Bill went about catching up on his farm work. Neighbors asked about her, but he replied that she had gone north to Cincinnati to visit relatives there.

On the third day of her disappearance, a neighbor man became very curious about some fresh dirt behind the barn. After going to get the sheriff, a doctor, and two other men, he began digging. There in a shallow grave lay Aunt Amelia, her skull smashed, according to the doctor, by an object resembling a shovel.

One of the two other men asked Bill, "Who would have done this, since you weren't home?"

Bill dropped his head, stating, "I don't know."

After a quick funeral the next day, Bill went straight from the graveyard to the barn, shot and killed himself.

Bright white lights have been seen around and by the window where the big organ sits. No one has been able to live in this old house very long since then. The property is still in my family. Most all the furniture is gone except the organ. Many people have wanted to buy the organ with its red velvet seat. But each time it is approached, a strange bright light appears around the organ, and a red light can be seen there on the organ.

18. "Ghosts Plot Revenge"

There was this man and woman who had just gotten married. They moved into this house that had an 80–foot-deep water well in the back yard.

I don't know why, but this man soon killed his wife and threw her in the well, then went to town to establish an alibi. The court decided that it was suicide on her part, thus let the man go free.

Later that night after he got home, he heard howls and screaming from out in the yard. He went out to see what was going on. It was then that he saw the figure of a young woman jump into the well. He saw it several times after that.

Later that year, he remarried. One night, his new wife heard the same screams and groans that he had been hearing. When she went out there to see what in the world those noises were all about, the ghost of the man's first wife grabbed her rival and threw her into the well. Now, almost every night, you can see the ghosts of both women sitting there on the well-top together.

Maybe, just maybe, they're plotting to kill that rascal husband.

19. "Ghost Haunts Death Site"

There is a ghost story about a man who appeared along the stage coach road that ran between Hopkinsville and Columbus, located just a few miles west of Mayfield. Where this took place was in what is known as the old Wright's Chapel neighborhood.

It is the tradition that someone had been slain near the old road and that sometimes, while driving through that section, a man is reported to have been seen coming out of the woods and heading off in the direction of where he was slain. He then disappears.

As far as is known, there was never any explanation of this matter. Superstitious people believed that the ghost of the slain man was simply wandering around in an effort to perhaps frighten the people responsible for his death, or to warn others that the soul of the slain man would haunt them as they ventured near the point of the killing.

This report comes from some older people who had heard of the so-called apparition, but never heard how or why it ceased to be seen.

20. "A Killing"

This happened when I was a very young girl. But it seems as if it only happened yesterday because it is so vivid in my mind. This one brother that lived near the Laurel River killed his brother. I had never seen either one but I sure heard a lot about them.

We had two farm houses, and mother was always sending me up to the one on the hill to stay alone. My stepfather was afraid that someone would come and steal the farm tools if someone didn't stay up there. In this very house was where one of the brothers had killed the other. He was killed in a downstairs room near the front porch. He had bled a lot, and the blood had really stained the floor. My mother told me to clean up the blood as well as I could.

The more I scrubbed, the redder the blood got until the blood was a very bright red. So mother decided that the only thing we could do was to spread what we called a sand rug over the spot. In those days people who were poor would spread sand real thick on the floor and this would be used for a rug.

My mother was scared to stay up there after the murder, so she made me stay by myself. I was about nine years old then and, you know, just too little to stay alone. I did have my dog with me, though, name of Traitor, but I couldn't pronounce that, so I called him Taylor. I spent a lot of my time in the barn with my dog.

There were panthers in the hills and I had been taught just what they sounded like so I could recognize one when it was near. I was sitting in the barn when I heard something go like this, "Ki-t-t-t-y-y," and I ran with my dog real fast to the house. I didn't see anything so I decided it was only a bird. I went to bed that night as soon as the sun went down.

Sometimes mother would come up to see about me, but she would never stay very late. She always said that she would never let the sun catch her there while it was going down.

That night, I heard a noise. There were some holes between the logs near the floor of the porch. My stepfather had put some board over the holes, about four by six. On one side of the porch was one board torn loose. The bed I slept in was in the rear just next to the porch. This hole wasn't very far from my bed. After I heard that noise, I jumped up and I saw this man's head sticking through the hole in the wall. He was looking straight at me. He had big blue eyes, a red moustache which was clipped near the lips, and a red complexion.

I jumped up and ran out on the porch to see for sure. I first thought that some of the neighborhood boys were trying to scare me (they were always playing tricks on me), for they knew I was scared. When I got out on the porch I didn't see a thing. I ran around the house a few times but still didn't see anything. I then went back to bed and waited for morning.

My mother came up that morning with a neighbor, and I told them what I saw. Mrs. Hood, the neighbor, said, "Oh, my God, that was the boy that was murdered."

He had come back to haunt the house.

21. "The Ghost of Town Branch"

Long years ago when I was just a little bit of a girl, and the town wasn't nothing but a village, there was a drummer come to town and went to drinking and gambling with some of the men. Well, sir, along toward dark, when he was plumb drunk, one of the men took that drummer up to the head of the holler, right here on Town Branch and knocked him in the head and took his money.

The drummer commenced trying to get up, and this fellow that took his money cut his head clean off with a big old knife he had. After he had set there for a while he buried the body and throwed the head down in an old well, leastways that's what everybody figgered when they found that drummer's body with no head on it. . . .

In the summer along toward dark there was this round ball of fire that come up out of that old well and went to traipsin' all over the holler like it was looking for something.

For years some of the boys from town would get to feeling brave every now and then, then have to go see what that thing was. Well, sir, they may have felt brave as they went up the holler, but I'll tell you right now, there wasn't a one of them that would stop running long enough to speak as they passed our house. There wasn't none of them that would ever tell what they had seen either.

One summer my Uncle Rufe came to stay with us and he allowed that he was going to find out what that thing was. Now Uncle Rufe had been in the War with Gen'ral Morgan and he wasn't going to have it said that no little ball of fire was going to scare one of Morgan's men. So this one evening Uncle Rufe went up the holler to wait for that thing to show itself. It wasn't a half hour after dark when Uncle Rufe came back, and I'll tell you he was as white as a sheet and every hair on his head was standing on end and he couldn't hardly talk. All he could say is, "The devil hisself is up there."

The next day when he had calmed down a bit, Rufe told us what he had seen up there. He said that that ball of fire was that dead drummer's head looking for its body. Now Rufe had known that drummer before, and he said he would have knowed that face anywhere. And, do you know, inside of a month Uncle Rufe's hair had turned as white as snow.

It wasn't long after that that Uncle Rufe and Pappy went up there in the daylight and filled that water well up so that that head wouldn't have no place to stay. But it didn't do no good, 'cause to this day, in the summer along toward dark you can still see that drummer's head trapsin' around in the hills and hollers looking for its body.

22. "The Ghost of Moberly's Drain"

Near where I live in Clay County is a stream that flows down into the South Fork of the Kentucky River, known as Moberly's Drain. It was near this small stream where a runaway slave was supposed to have killed himself to avoid capture and return to slavery. The road where it passes over the stream is hanted, and if you pass there alone riding a horse at night, just as you pass the drain, the old slave's ghost will jump up behind you and ride a short distance with you. Horses know of this hanted place, too, and when they come to it they will begin to act funny and will run away if you are not very careful and hold on just as tight as you can.

A few years ago, a neighbor boy by the name of Wilson Rodgers passed this spot frequently late at night on his way home after spending the early hours of the night at the home of his future father-in-law in the company of his sweetheart. But the last time he passed, just as he approached the drain and began to take a firm hold on the reins, the old slave's ghost jumped up behind him. Wilson, being scared speechless, never made so much as one effort to control the frightened horse that set out for home at a dead run. When the horse reached home, Wilson was still aboard, but he fell off senseless in the yard, while the frightened animal continued on to the barn without slackening its pace.

Wilson's father, being awakened by the noise, came out to see what the matter was. After he had taken Wilson into the house and revived him by throwing cold water on him, he got the story of what had happened by piecing together the fragments of sentences the boy was able to say. The father had to go to the barn and unsaddle the horse, which he said was still scared half crazy.

Even though Wilson is now an old man, he still maintains that the ghost of Moberly's Drain rode home with him one night.

23. "Billy Damorn's Ghost"

One of the times when I was the worst-ever scared was when my grandpa told me about the ghost of Billy Damorn, who was killed several years before I was born. Grandpa said, "When you bring a horse across that one water hole across the creek down there, that horse would just about bow down when it got in that water." He said that there was a ghost of somebody who would get on that horse and ride it.

Well, I always thought that that was a story that somebody had told. So me and some boys got up there one night on our ponies. We were riding the ponies through that hole of water. That was about eleven or twelve o'clock that night. Well, those ponies would get spooked at that hole of water. We never could get our ponies to go through that hole of water. To get home, we had to go back up this hill and get on another road.

Since those ponies would not go through that hole of water, I always believed what Grandpa said about that hole of water was the truth. He said that at one time a lady came down through there, and said she heard something groaning around this hole of water. This woman said that one time they was coming through there, and they saw a man there at the edge of the creek, then he just disappeared. Several other people said that they seen that ghost, or whatever it was, travel up through there.

Well, sure enough, at that time there was someone killed there. Somebody shot him off his horse in that hole of water.

Well, a horse is one of the most easily spooked things you can get on. I do know that those ponies we had there cut up the awfullest you ever seen. They started squealing, looking right down just like they was looking at something, maybe a ghost.

Grandpa has told me that he and Billy Damorn was very, very close. Grandpa lived to be 105 years old. I kept him and took care of him until he passed away. By the way, he told me one time that he went to Pikeville, the county seat town, only twice in his life. He was a mountain man who just loved to work on the farm. He never held a public job in his life.

Back to the story, many times I heard him say that he'd go out of a morning to feed his cattle before he went to the field to work. And he said he could hear a man up in the barn loft a-praying, and he always said it was Billy Damorn up there in that barn loft a-praying and begging people not to kill him. Said this voice would say, "Lord, let me go home and see my kids. Let me go home and see my wife."

Grandpa said it was the most honorable prayers that he ever heard anyone pray, begging them not to kill him. He said that Billy's prayer was the beautifullest prayer he ever heard.

What happened was, they shot him off his horse, and he fell off his horse and rolled to the edge of the creek. Grandpa said that was where Billy had begged them not to kill him. That's why that hole of water is spooky now.

The reason they killed him according to Grandpa, was that this other party was making moonshine whiskey at a moonshine still in the foothills of the Cumberland Mountains on Elkhorn Creek, located about eight, ten miles down below Shelby Gap. And somebody always said that Billy Damorn give their still away, and that the officers, or marshals, caught the moonshiners. Then, later on these whiskey makers laid there waiting for Billy at that hole of water and shot him off his horse.

I never knowed of my grandfather telling something that was not true.

24. "The Weird Noises of Ben Caudill's Ghost"

My granny used to tell ghost stories many, many times. One that she told was about Ben Caudill, who was shot and killed at Big Branch, Kentucky, here in Pike County. She said that she went to stay all night that night with her brother. She said that her brother was supposedly the one who did the killing, or at least was in on it. She said that her and Grandpa was laying there in the bed, and she heard this lumberment that fell down out of the loft. That's what woke her up. Then she heard the pots and pans rattling in the kitchen just like somebody was washing dishes. It was about four o'clock in the morning.

She said that nobody was up. Not a thing was moving in the house until she heard that lumberment. But all at once, after she heard that big noise she could see something that looked just like a hog in front of the fireplace. She said that about a quarter 'til five, right on the fireplace hearth she could see this thing that looked just like a hog laying there struggling, trying to get its breath.

She said to Grandpa, "Did you hear that noise?"

He said to her, "That's Ben Caudill in there getting your breakfast ready for you."

Well, they had just shot and killed Ben Caudill a little ways above the house, there in the creek branch. Her brother was in on it, and also these two other fellows were, too.

Her brother told her that Ben Caudill had laid out there in the branch and begged them to give him a drink of water, but they wouldn't give him any water.

Granny said that you could be in her brother's house of a night, and said, "I don't care what we would put against that door, that door would open." She said, "I don't care what we would put against that door, that door would push itself open. And when we'd lock that door, we'd hear knocks on that door." She said, "Those was the scardest times that ever was."

She told that many, many times. She swore it was true, and I've never known her not to tell the truth.

Now back to that hog-like thing that she saw in front of the fireplace: she said that was the way that Caudill laid and struggled in the water when he was dying. He was strangling and struggling just like a hog will do when it's dying.

25. "Ghost at Zion Brick Church"

I was seeing this fellow from Slaughters, and we were out riding around one night. He had had two or three beers to drink. Well, out in Webster County in the Slaughters area, there are a lot of backcountry roads. After we had driven around for a while, he had to stop and relieve himself. We were near Zion Brick Church, so he pulled in the lot and drove around the back of the church and stopped the car there on the other side of the church. He was going to get out and do his business.

He leaned over to kiss me before he got out of the car. Well, the car started shaking violently. It was just really violent. I said to him, "Stop shaking the car."

He said, "I'm not shaking it."

It shook for about a minute, then it stopped. I got this cold feeling on the inside of me. He said, "I'll bet it's some of those old boys around here hiding, and they shook the car."

See, Zion Brick was still a hangout for teenagers. They'd go out there and drink and smoke their pot. We figured that some of the guys were hanging around, had seen us pull in, and decided to come over and scare us.

This fellow I was with got out to look around, and of course there was nobody there. He went ahead and did his business, then got back in the car. He was going to sit there and talk for a moment, but I was feeling more and more uncomfortable by that time. So I told him, "Let's leave here."

Well, we left there right then, and I will not go back out there. I'm scared of that place.

I was working in the restaurant in Slaughters at the time. One of the girls I worked with was a teenager, and she hung out there a lot. She said that a lot of times when they were out there partying, they could hear organ music coming from the church, or a light would come on in the church. She said that a lot of times when they were sitting out there, they were just waiting for something strange to happen. And it always did.

26. "The Ghost of a Man Murdered in the Kitchen"

Once we moved into a house in Keene. That evening the moon was very bright and my husband was outside. Suddenly, he came running in with his eyes as big as saucers. He told me that he had cast two shadows and that something was mighty wrong around here. I went out with him to see, and when I was there he cast only one shadow.

Well, I went back inside and began to scrub up the blood in the kitchen. Before we had moved in, someone had been murdered in the kitchen. The blood had run across the kitchen floor and had stained it. I scrubbed and scrubbed, but the more I scrubbed the redder the blood got. I used lye on it and everything else, but it just wouldn't come up. So I gave up.

We went to bed that night, and all of a sudden the whole house began to vibrate. It sounded like all the dishes, pots, and tableware and the whole cabinet fell over on the floor. I thought that one of them Keenes had got into the house. We got up and lit the lamp and began to search the house, and lo and behold, everything was in its place, and there was nobody in the house. We went back to bed and tried to get some sleep. The next day we moved out of there.

27. "Airdrie Ghost Searches for Her Head"

On a hillside near the banks of the Green River about a mile west of what once was the town of Paradise, in Muhlenberg County, lie the crumbling remains of an iron foundry built in 1855.

Named "Airdrie" by its founder Robert Sproul Crawford Aitcheson Alexander, the iron smelting operations were abandoned after only three runs, never to be reopened.

The hand-hewn stone buildings and fortification-like walls resemble a deteriorating medieval castle and have been the inspiration from which have arisen many stories and superstitions.

Tortures of convicts working the coal and iron mines near the foundry, murders and the sightings of ghosts are a few of the more colorful tales about Airdrie. Some historians claim the stories are not true. Others, claiming firsthand knowledge, just as adamantly claim they are true.

Possibly none of the tales recounted of happenings in Airdrie in the days of its prosperity is more thrilling or more gruesome than the story of a young woman said to have been murdered in the old hotel there.

A journalist who in 1922 visited the now nonexistent hotel, gave this account of the event:

"The hotel is a rambling old structure, neglected and falling into ruins. Leading to the second floor is a rickety old stairway and the visitor with temerity to risk his neck may ascend to the second floor and see the room where the murder took place.

"It is a bare and musty place and an indefinable air of mystery seems to linger in the dimly lighted interior. It was here that a young woman, traveling unescorted through stress of circumstances stopped for the night. It was bitter cold and a roaring fire burned in the big fireplace. The weary traveler had slept only a few hours when two robbers entered the room. The girl was given no chance to make an outcry, being throttled by the larger of the men while she slept.

"Not content with killing their victim, the murderers cut off her head and threw it into the fire, where it was partly consumed before the burned-down embers sunk down into ashes and caused her head to roll out on the floor. A hole in the flooring, the edges charred and black, still remains to show where the head rested after rolling out of the flames."

It is reported that people who pass through the Airdrie area between sundown and dark, can see a woman in an evening gown, with a shawl over her arm, walking through the canyon without her head.

Another tale about Airdrie relates that, on certain nights, one can hear the sounds of iron chains being dragged over the stone steps as the ghosts of convicts who slaved in the mines relive their unfulfilled past.

Still other residents of the area insist that prisoners were held there during the Civil War. The prisoners were said to be an unruly lot, and legend has it that a prisoner was thrown into the furnace as an example to the others.

Some present residents claim that at various times, screams from the dead man can still be heard.

28. "The Traveling Salesman"

Once upon a time there was a traveling salesman, who traveled through the country. He came to this farmhouse and decided to spend the night. As he walked up to the house, he smelled food cooking and saw a fire in the fireplace. He went up and knocked on the door. There was no answer, but he decided to go on in and wait for the folks to come home.

He sat down by the fireplace and took his boots off to warm his feet. He was enjoying the comfort of the fire when all at once he heard a terrible racket. He looked behind him and what he saw was unbelievable. He saw a white woman with a butcher knife in her hand striking a black woman. He watched for a while, not knowing what to do. Then, all of a sudden the black woman fell to the floor. She was dead, of course, cut to pieces with the knife. The white woman picked the black woman up and carried her body outside, then she put her in a big open well by the side of the house.

The traveling salesman watched, then all at once he got up and ran away to the next farmhouse as fast as he could. In his haste to get away, he forgot his boots.

When he finally got to the next farmhouse, he told the farmer what he had seen. The farmer told him that that couldn't be true because there was no farmhouse within fifteen miles of there. The farmer told the salesman that there was once a farmhouse not far down the road, but that it had burned many years ago. The salesman told the farmer to come with him and he'd prove to him there was a farmhouse not far down the road.

So the farmer went with the salesman to see the farmhouse that he knew wasn't there. On the way down the road, the farmer told him about the house burning down and about the people who lived in the house.

He said there was a white woman who had lived there with her black maid. The farmer said the white woman had disappeared, and so had the maid. He said the house had burned down later on, and that the people living in that section of the county had often wondered what happened to the two women.

The farmer and salesman were approaching the place where the farmhouse was supposed to be, when, all at once the salesman said, "It's gone."

But, believe it or not, the chimney was still there, and on the hearth set the salesman's boots that he had left just a short while ago.

The next morning, the salesman and the farmer dragged the well, and what do you think they found? They found the black woman's bones!

29. "The Unwilling House"

Once upon a time a man and his wife moved into this old house. They had fixed everything up and had settled down when the sound of moving furniture could be heard. The two of them got up to see, and sure enough the furniture was all rearranged. His wife was awfully scared and wanted to leave, but he wouldn't.

They went back to bed. They had just gotten settled in bed when they got disturbed again by the sound of something dripping on their bed. They jumped up and turned up the lamp, and the light reflected on a large, dark stain on the bed. His wife was so scared that she ran out of the house and left her husband there.

She ran all the way to a distant neighbor's house and told them what had happened. They told her that the house was haunted and that the people that had previously owned this house were killed and put up in the loft. And no one can live in that house because of the ghosts of the murdered people.

30. "Local Character Ghost"

Before his death, this Courtney fellow never allowed fishing in the large pond there in front of his house in Christian County. The favorite fishing spot was a fence running out to the middle of the pond. Whenever Mr. Courtney caught anyone fishing, he would wade out into the pond and try to knock the fishermen off the fence with a stick.

After his death, one of the hired men went catfishing one night. While he was fishing, the water began to move as if someone was wading in it, then something pushed the man into the water. Everyone claimed that Mr. Courtney pushed him into the water. After that, no one around there would go near the pond after dark.

Just before his death, Mr. Courtney told his wife not to bring her people into his house to live after he was dead. A short time after his death, Mrs. Courtney's brother's house burned, so he moved into Mr. Courtney's house. One night not long after that, Mrs. Courtney heard three knocks under her window. She called her brother, but he said it was only the dog that was sleeping under the house.

A few minutes later, Mrs. Courtney claimed that a cold hand slapped her on the cheek. This unnerved them so that they called Mr. Cayce to bring a lantern to search the house. The next day, Mr. Courtney's brother began plans to rebuild his house and refused to stay another night in his sister's house. . . .

After Mr. Courtney's widow moved, Mr. Cayce took full possession of the farm. He had sold a cow to a nearby farmer and was expecting the farmer to drop by and pay him. Late one afternoon, while he was in the barn feeding the cows, Mr. Cayce heard someone open the door and walk in. He thought it was the farmer bringing the money for the cow.

When he started down from the loft, he saw a ghostly figure that looked like Mr. Courtney going out the back door of the barn and then past the barn window. He rushed outside but couldn't find anyone. When he got back to the house, he asked if anyone had been to the barn. Everyone said "no."

From that day forward, Mr. Cayce believed that he saw Mr. Courtney's ghost that late afternoon.

31. "Wailing Sounds of Wife and Daughter"

On Livingston Creek in Lyon County there once stood a gristmill, its exact whereabouts is not known. A miller once inhabited it, along with his very attractive wife and daughter.

He found out that both of them were being unfaithful. He took them both out to the mill and bound them, then raised his millstones and ground them both to death.

Today, if people can find the spot where the mill once stood, they can hear the weeping and wailing of the wife and daughter.

32. "The Murdered Girls"

Once upon a time there was a woodsman who had four daughters. Each day, this man went far into the forest to cut wood, and his eldest daughter took him his noon meal. One day she prepared lunch for her father and started on the long journey into the woods. As evening turned to night, the father came home very angry because no one had brought his lunch to him. His other daughters told him that their older sister went off into the woods with his lunch early that morning and had not returned.

The next day, the next oldest daughter went into the forest to take her father's lunch to him. That evening, the father came home and wanted to know what had happened to his lunch. They told him that it was sent to him by his next eldest daughter.

The same thing happened the next day to the third daughter. That way, the man had only one daughter left and he didn't want her to go into the forest. He went back to work and left his daughter to tend the house.

The daughter became lonely there by herself, so she decided to take her father's lunch to him even though he had told her not to go into the forest. She set out through the woods to find her father, and as she walked she didn't notice how thick and dark the forest had become. When she did, she had lost her way and it was getting late.

She had traveled some distance when she saw a blue light shining through the forest. When she had gotten to the source of the light, she saw a small cabin in a clearing. She knocked on the door and a huge man opened the door and let her in. She told him that she was lost and could not find her way home.

He told her that she was not to look into any of the locked rooms or outside buildings. She agreed, and the next morning she decided to clean the house while the man worked in the forest. She had cleaned most of the house when she spied a set of keys on a chain hanging on the wall of the cabin. She remembered what the man had said about not looking into the locked rooms, but her curiosity got the best of her, so she took the keys from the wall.

She tried all the doors but the keys wouldn't fit, so she went outside and tried the buildings there. When she came to the last one, she tried the keys and the lock snapped open and the girl screamed, for there was three headless girls.

She stepped inside and saw the rings on the fingers of the dead girls, and she knew that they were her sisters. As she turned around, she dropped the keys in the blood there on the floor. She picked them up and wiped them hastily.

When the man returned, he noticed the keys were missing, and he told her that she had disobeyed him and for that reason she had to die, too. He started toward her with a long sharp knife, and as he came closer she ran out the door and down through the woods. As she ran blindly, she tripped and fell. Before she could get up, the man had found her. He dragged the screaming, crying girl back to the cabin where she received the same fate as her three sisters.

When he had cleaned up the blood and locked the door of the outside building, he heard a knock at the door. It was a girl who had lost her way and was attracted by the blue light. I guess we can imagine what happened to her.

33. "Bloody Dishes"

My great aunt lived in a very old house. One day one of her sisters came to see her and they were talking. They had a snack, and then the sister was going to do the dishes, but my great aunt told her, "Don't do the dishes now, because when you get up in the morning we will just have to do them over."

So they let the dishes go, and went to the garden to get some potatoes for breakfast the next morning. They brought the potatoes in and peeled them.

By now it was ten o'clock, so they went to bed. In the middle of the night the two women woke up and began to talk, when all of a sudden they heard sounds like dishes falling and potatoes rolling around. My great aunt was used to this, but the sister said, "I'll bet we will have dishes to wash and potatoes to pick up in the morning."

My great aunt said to her, "No, they will all be just where they were before we went to bed."

When they got up the next morning, everything was in its place but the dishes were all to be washed and the top had to be taken off the milk and butter. The reason for this was because they were all covered with blood.

The mystery of it all was that a Negro boy had been killed in this house, and the prints of his face and hands were still on the wall, and they had placed the dish cabinet over the boy's bloody handprints. That was the cause of all that commotion.

34. "Hell's Half Acre"

There's an area of pine and cedar that is thickly grown together and hanging over a country dirt road ... about twenty miles southwest of Madisonville, and twenty miles south of Providence. . . .

This old narrow road goes around a graveyard, which is about 100 yards from the only building within three miles—a log dwelling house and pack-peddler hotel. I've heard my uncle and neighbors tell tales about this old place from ghostly graveyard stories to murder tales. It was a common thing back in the 1890s for people to ride through this area and hear a horse following them, then to look around and see the horse carrying a man without a head. Back then [just after the Civil War] two men were hanged near this old graveyard. For several years it was told that you could hear these two men screaming when you passed there late at night.

The best story I remember was about the traveler. He had stopped at a hotel about half way between Providence and Dawson Springs. This old hotel was a place of lodging for peddlers of all kind, and they were plentiful in Hopkins County around 1875–1900. It seemed that this particular peddler had a large sum of money in his suitcase when he stopped at this house for a night's lodging. Some of the neighbors were in to chat, drink, and tell tales until bedtime. After this, the peddler was never seen. No one thought much about it for several months, and the caretaker of the lodging house moved away. The neighbors began to notice that he had quite a lot of spending money.

The next people who moved into this house heard screams and saw peculiar things at night, such as lights and fire rolling across the road. They moved out soon. For a long time, no one would live there very long, and finally the structure was torn down.

Blood was found under the floor, and tales of all kinds were told. One was that the peddler had been killed and buried under the house.

I never saw the old house, although I have been around the graveyard and along the road that went past the old house place, but I didn't hear any screams or see any ghosts. If you were to go through this place on a horse in daylight, you would expect all of these graves to open up and the spirits to come out and trail you. As you pass by the old house, the pines and cedars overlapping the road would make you wonder if the peddler were going to stop you just around the next curve.

35. "John Neville's Ghost"

One of the most diabolical murders ever committed in Metcalfe County occurred near the Barren County line, August 25, 1871. The victim, Mrs. Lucy Perkins, had left home with a small sum of money to make some purchases at Turner's store, a couple of miles distant.

The family at home, becoming alarmed at her prolonged absence, went to see what could be the cause of her prolonged detention. Between her home and the store, her lifeless body was found. The head was almost severed from the body, but a small ligament still connecting it, and the body itself ripped open down to the navel.

Who could have been so vile as to perpetrate this awful deed, and what could have been the motive, are questions agitating the minds of those living in the vicinity of the murder, they yet having no positive evidence as to who was the murderer. Should anyone be arrested, on the slightest evidence, the people will take the law, it is feared, into their own hands and visit summary punishment on the villain.

John Neville was charged with the murder of his mother-in-law, Lucy Perkins, who was a Franklin. Neville was taken from the Metcalfe County jail, August 28, 1871, by a community mob about four o'clock in the afternoon and carried to the place where Lucy's body was found. He was lynched at the same spot where she died. John Neville went with Lucy some before she got married. He wanted her to marry him, but she wouldn't have him. So he married Bill Perkins's daughter, whose mother died. A few years later Bill Perkins married Lucy Franklin. This made her Neville's mother-in-law, and he always said he'd begrudge Bill Perkins's happiness with Lucy.

At the time of her death, the 'sociation [Baptist Association] was a-going on at Dripping Springs, and Lucy was making a new dress to wear to the 'sociation. And she was going to this store in Randolph to get some thread to finish up her dress. He [Neville] met her over here and killed her, and then he was mobbed. They took him from the jail in Edmonton and brought him back and hung him at the same spot where he killed the woman; stood him up on a big mule, then hung him on this dogwood tree. The tree has been gone now for about thirty years.

It has been said that the Dalton Brothers of the Jesse James mob said that if they could get to him before the mob did, they would take him and never let him be hung. Said they would carry him with them.

This community mob had Neville standing on a mule almost ready to make a full confession. Then they heard a gun fire, and when they heard

Trees such as this large oak are often described in ghost stories, especially if a gruesome lynching took place here and the spirit of the hanged person returns to commemorate the death process. (Photograph by the author)

this, that scared them. They thought it was the Dalton Brothers coming to take him away from them, so somebody hit the mule and the mule jumped out from under him, hung him.

Over here in the second field from right here is where John Neville was hung. I've always heard it said that when people would go down this road that went through the woods there, when they got close to where he was hung, a big ball of fire would rise up out of the ground. They'd just ride on by until they got past the dogwood tree where he was hung, then the ball of fire would disappear.

36. "Ghost of Small Baby"

There's a farm on Highway 90, that old crooked road that runs across northern McCreary County. On that farm is where a girl killed her little baby. It is said that she took the infant outside behind their house and throwed it over the cliff.

On stormy nights, these people who live there now can hear a baby crying out there behind their house.

37. "Ghostly Spot at Matthews Fork"

There's a "hainted" place out here on the ridge; it's called Matthews Fork. There's a man got murdered there, and a long time after he got killed, there were things heard out there.

There's an old mill out there on the ridge. And when people went to this mill, they had to pass that place where he was killed. But, boy, when they passed by there, this man's "haint" with no head would get up on their horse behind them and ride a long ways with them down this ridge.

Once, there was this fellow who was excited so bad when this ghost got up behind him he lost his turn of corn meal. He had to go back by there the next morning to get his turn of meal.

One time later, me and this other woman was walking down this ridge, and we heard something following us, making lots of noise in them leaves on the ground alongside the road. We kept walking, but we thought we'd slip over to see what it was. We expected to see a dog, or a squirrel, or something like that. When we looked, we couldn't see nary a thing.

When we'd stop, it'd stop. Then, when we'd go on, it'd go on with us. Finally, it got just up real close to us. Well, we just stopped, and in a few minutes it just left all at once.

Ever since that man was killed there, there's been things like that that was felt or heard when the people passed by.

Now, that's the truth.

38. "Dying Shriek of a Woman Killed by a Stage Coach Driver"

An old stage coach driver in the early forties was John E. Winters who drove the stage from Louisville to Nashville. Reaching Bardstown a change of horses was made and dinner partaken of. On one of his trips, while stopping at what is now the Bardstown Hotel, the passengers told the following experience which occurred while on the road a few miles out of Bardstown with Winters as driver.

The stage had been delayed, and it was some hours after nightfall that it passed a lonely spot, shaded by trees which grew on both sides of the road. All the passengers in the coach were men. As the stage entered the dense shade, suddenly a loud, piercing, thrilling scream of a woman sounded through the car. For a moment pandemonium reigned. When the coach got out into the moonlight all the passengers were groping about inside with open eyes and blanched lips. All could have sworn that the woman was not four feet away, and each felt as if they could have leaned forward and touched her. In the direction where the voice had sounded, the seat was empty and the astounded looks bent upon those seats showed that every occupant of the coach had heard the same sound and from the same direction. Suddenly one of the passengers told the driver to stop the stage, as a woman had been run over back there in the shade. They all got out and taking a lantern went back to the spot and examined the ground closely but saw no sign of any crushed and mangled body nor any signs that anyone had been injured. The passengers were a puzzled set and went back to the stage and resumed their journey. One of the passengers named Williams, more curious than the rest, decided to stop off at Bardstown and go back at his leisure and investigate. The next day he walked out to the spot but could see nothing. He remained in the vicinity of the place until nightfall to make another effort by moonlight. He went through the shaded spot singing and shouting to find if there was not some peculiarity in the way the sound was caused which might produce the effect the passengers had heard. The next day he spent a number of dollars in getting a farmer to pass the spot and sing while he stood still and listened, but as yet he had not discovered the cause of the blood curdling shrieks heard in the stage. Still not satisfied, Williams returned to the spot the following evening and while walking about staring at the trees he heard the rumbling of the stage a few hundred yards away. Standing well within the shadows of the trees, he waited for the coach to pass. Just as the stage was opposite him, suddenly out of the roar and din came a woman's shriek almost like a knife plunged into his ears. And it came from the coach: the same piercing, agonizing scream he had heard a few nights before. Williams left the spot and returned to town as quickly as he could. He packed up his things and acted as if he was crazy. The next afternoon he boarded the stage for Louisville and soon discovered that he was in the same coach and the same driver that he had come out with a few evenings before. He saw that the driver avoided him, and he determined to have it out with him. Seating himself by the driver's side Williams asked, "What is the matter with that spot?" The driver began to tremble and could scarcely answer. "Did you hear it again?" he said hoarsely. "I don't know anything about it, and you better not say too much. We can scarcely keep any drivers on this line as is. Every one of them has been changed in the past year, and I am the only one to stay."

Williams was quick to jump at conclusions and said: "So the trouble is with this coach that she was probably killed in that shaded spot." The driver winced as if someone had struck him a heavy blow. Then Williams continued: "What a terrible thing it must be for the murderer to pass that spot week after week and hear that dreadful shriek. I should think he would go forward." The driver gave a great gasp and got down from his seat saying he was sick. Another driver was found to take his place and that was the last ever seen of Winters on that line. A few years later he died at Nashville and confessed to murdering and robbing a lone woman passenger on the road from Louisville and packing her body in her trunk until Nashville was reached where he interred the remains of the victim. Where the woman came from was never ascertained, and the dreadful shrieks were never heard again after Winters left the road.

Chapter 8

Ghosts of Persons Killed Accidentally

1. "Penny's Spirit Seen at High School"

It all started one dark evening. The janitor at this high school, located here in central Kentucky, was sweeping the dirty floors. All the people had been out of the building for hours, and no one was in sight except Carl, who was the janitor, and his "friend." As Carl turned to go toward the back of the room that he was cleaning, he saw a girl sitting there. He asked her what she was doing there and told her that she should go home. The girl never said a word to him, yet she sat there. When Carl started on toward the back of the room, the girl slowly disappeared.

The next day, Carl told of his adventure the previous night. He was asked to pick out the girl in the yearbook. He carefully searched for her, and after finally locating her picture, he and the others realized that she had been killed in a car accident a few weeks back. What happened was that she and her best friend had skipped school to go see their boyfriends several miles away. On the way there, the driver lost control of the car and ran off the road. She wasn't killed in the wreck, but the other girl who now haunts the high school died there on the road.

The death of the girl, whom I'll call Penny, greatly upset the one who was driving. The next day after Penny had come back, the word "Alive" was found written on the blackboard in the schoolroom where Penny's spirit had been seen. The unusual thing about the word was that it was written backwards on the board, just as if someone had written it from the other side. The school had been locked all night and no one knows how anybody could have gotten in to write that on the blackboard.

In the next few weeks, people were aroused by all the strange happenings that were going on there at the school. During this time, another occurrence happened. The yearbook staff had a deadline to meet but they weren't quite finished at that point in time. They had all gotten together in an English room to try and finish their scheduled work. It was late, and the school and office doors had been locked for some time. All of a sudden the intercom came on, and someone's voice called Penny to the office. The office, of course, was locked and nobody around had the key.

Little things happened off and on. Teachers would get to school in the mornings, and their classrooms would be rearranged. Things also started to disappear. A couple of other people also claimed to have seen Penny, which they should never have done. About a month after Carl had seen Penny, he was killed in a car wreck on the same road where Penny had been killed.

This high school has not been the same since. During ball games, certain doors will be locked so that people won't venture down the long, dark hallways. If for some reason someone needs to go down a dark spot at the school, that person is cautioned not to go alone.

Not only the unfortunate ones who have seen Penny have died; others have, too. Since Penny's death, there have been at least two persons in every class who have been killed in a car accident. I for one have never seen Penny's spirit, and I sure don't want to.

If you, the reader, ever happen to be at this high school, be on the lookout for Penny. She may try to scare you, but just try to not let her get to you. If you do, you could be the next in line.

2. "Ghosts of Both Husband and Wife"

I had a friend who claimed that when she was eight years old, her parents bought an old house that was pretty well run down and in need of repair. She said that she hated the house because sometimes during the night she would be awakened by something, and at the foot of her bed would be an old woman standing there. My friend would lie there until she finally had enough wind to scream out for her parents. Every time they switched on the lights, the old woman disappeared before the parents saw her.

At first, the parents didn't think too much about it because a lot of times girls that age like to tell a lot of ghost stories that are made up. Thus, the parents thought that their daughter and her friends were just getting a little carried away with such things.

This went on for some time, until the baby that was only three years old started saying that a man walked around in his room with tools in his hand.

One day while the mother was hanging out laundry, a lady neighbor came over to say hello to her. They stood around and chatted about different things for a few minutes. Then the mother asked the neighbor about the previous residents of their house. The neighbor responded that they were real fine people, but they had died in freak accidents just a day apart from each other. The man was remodeling the house when he fell from the ladder and broke his neck. The very next day, his wife, who was on her way downstairs to go sit with her dead husband's body, missed a step on the stairway and fell to her death.

My friend, who had seen the old woman standing at the foot of her bed, and her parents moved out of this house shortly afterwards. They didn't want to stay there any longer.

3. "The Ghost of a Man Who Died a Painful Death"

Back in the 1800s there was this black fellow who lived in a humble little cabin here in Meade County with his wife and two children. The story claims that he went hunting on one cold winter day while his wife and kids stayed home. She was cooking supper. While the man was gone, his wife lost control of the wood-burning oven and it exploded and set the cabin on fire. She and the kids were trapped inside the cabin. While there in the woods, the husband saw the black smoke coming out of the cabin, so he raced back to save his family.

When he got there, most of the cabin had already burned to the ground. He tried in every way to save his family and finally leaped in as a last effort, only to be penned in behind a large wooden beam. All four of them perished in the flames. Neighbors came in to investigate the situation. They found the bodies and ashes of the man's wife and children, but they could never locate his.

The family of this friend of mine built a house on the spot where this black family's cabin once stood. When they moved in, weird things started happening. Electrical switches would turn off and on for no reason. One night, J——, who is this friend of mine, along with her sister, A——, went to bed only to be awakened by a whistle from the corner of the room.

When they looked over in the corner, they saw this black man looking back at them. They screamed out in terror, yelling, "Mother, Mother, where are you? Come here, Mama. We need you!"

Come to find out, their mother had seen the man's ghost but had not told her two daughters, so as to keep them from being scared and worried. Sometimes, the mother would purposely leave the stove oven on and the ghost would turn it off. Finally, they couldn't stand the thought of being in the house with a ghost, so they moved away to a different community. Eventually, they moved back to their original house, but the ghost was gone.

The youngest of these two sisters had a baby born out of wedlock when she was sixteen. The ghost of the black fellow then came back and moved the baby around through the house, trying to take care of it.

This is a friendly ghost. I feel that he is still there because he is roaming around after such a painful death. They had the house blessed recently, but the ghost has not left. It is still there much of the time.

4. "The Ghost of a Woman and Her Dog"

On June 15th of every year between 11:00 p.m. and midnight, if you sit at the four-way stop in Sturgis, you will see a sight that will absolutely raise the hairs on the back of your neck.

My grandfather, G.W. Holt, was ninety years old when he died. I'm twenty-nine years old, and all the years I knew him, he never told a lie. And he told me about this.

Back when he was a little boy, there was this woman there in Sturgis who walked her dog every night about 11:00 p.m. There in the middle of town there's a four-way stop now, but it used to be a stop light and a through street. On one corner there's the Presbyterian Church; on the other corner was a service station.

This woman walked her dog, a big white German Shepherd, from this Presbyterian Church across the street and on down to her house. She'd walk up and then walk back home to give her dog exercise before she went to bed. Well, one night, on June 15th a long time ago, as she was walking across the street, a man ran a red light. He hit her and her dog, and the woman died. The man didn't stop, didn't even slow down.

Every night since that took place, if you go down there and sit on the opposite corner, you can hear the woman walking across the street from the Presbyterian Church to the gas station. By the time she gets from one corner to the other, you can see her and the dog. Then she disappears.

5. "The Ghost of a Baby That Died in a House Fire"

The Holt Mansion is in a place called Holt's Bottom, which is real close to Stephensport, Kentucky, between Addison and Cloverport. The mansion belonged to Joseph Holt. He was the one that had it built.

There were two mansions there, but the first one burned down. Then they rebuilt the one that's standing there now. Nobody lives in it, and nobody has lived in it for years and years. But when we lived there in a little white house that sets there between the mansion and the Holt family cemetery, my job was to mow the yards.

I would mow the yard around the house that we lived in and then mow the yard around the old Holt mansion. I could mow in back of the mansion without any problem. According to legend, Joseph Holt Sr. died when he fell down the back steps of the mansion and broke his neck.

I could mow in back and on both sides of the mansion without any problem, and I could mow most of the front yard without any problem. But there was one spot there in front of that mansion that I couldn't mow with the riding lawn mower. When I'd get to this one spot, the mower would just quit running and wouldn't start back up.

When I got to this spot in the yard of this Holt Mansion, I would set there and cry just like a whipped kid. I couldn't keep from crying. The tears would just flow. It was such a feeling of sadness that you just couldn't hardly stand it. It would last for quite a while. The only way that I could get the mower to going again was to get off of it and push it away from this spot. Then it would start like a brand new mower, and I could finish mowing.

The explanation for the sad spot is that a one-month-old baby, Joseph Holt II, perished when the first mansion burned down. He was in the nursery on the second floor and couldn't be saved.

6. "The Ghost of a Man Who Loved His Farm Animals"

My grandmother told me that her father, when he was young, worked for a man named Will Wright. Mr. Wright owned a large farm in Boyle County. On the farm, he had three sawmills and plenty of animals. He loved all of his animals, and had plenty of different kinds of them. He just had these animals around because he loved them so much. However, he made most of his money through the three sawmills.

The Holt Mansion in Holt's Bottom, Kentucky. (Photograph provided by Elbert Cundiff)

All the animals, including sheep, ducks, cows, horses, chickens, cats, and dogs, were all housed in one big barn. Every day he would go to the barn at five o'clock, taking my grandfather with him, and talk to the animals as he fed them. Each time he entered the barn, the animals would make sounds to let him know that they liked his being there. He would feed and pet all the animals, always telling grandfather that if you become friends with the animals, they will always do as you wish, and how important it was to be near them. Grandfather kept this in mind.

One day as grandfather was making the rounds to the sawmills with

Mr. Wright, an accident occurred. Mr. Wright's coattail got caught in the grinder and pulled him into the blades. He died on the spot.

After the funeral, Mrs. Wright asked grandfather to stay on with her and help with the farm. Realizing how much Mr. Wright loved his animals, grandfather decided that he would feed them at five o'clock, just like Mr. Wright did.

Not long afterwards, he went into the barn and started to feed the animals when he heard an eerie, even scary, strange noise. The noise started out softly then grew into a regular human-like pitch. He said the noise was something like, "Pu-u, m-o-o-o, pu-u-u-u-u, m-o-o-o-o." All at once the animals started walking and making a lot of noise in their stalls. It was animal noises, but sounded ghost-like. At first, grandfather said that he was scared, then he realized that it must be Mr. Wright in there with the animals. His ghost had come back to talk to them.

Every day at five o'clock, as long as my grandfather worked there, he always heard the same noises. He never saw Mr. Wright's ghost, but he was sure that it was there in the midst of the animals. They sure loved him.

7. "Shadows beside the River"

This is the story about Irvan Bunch and his love for his two dogs. It tells of their times spent together and of the mysterious and tragic end of the old man and the only family that he ever had, his two dogs, Jud and Jake.

Ruth Williams, a farm owner in Hart County, told that Irvan moved onto their farm in the early 1950s. He lived in a small four-room shack that was just about ready to fall down. All he had in his living room were two small chairs next to the fireplace. In his bedroom was a put-together cot with a chest beside it that contained what few clothes Irvan had. The shack, which overlooked the Green River, had no electricity or plumbing. He had to cook over the fire in the fireplace.

Irvan was a tall, skinny man whose only clothes were overalls, a ragged shirt, and a long blue-jean coat that he wore during the cold months. He was a loner and had very few friends, if any.

The only real friend that Irvan had was the Green River. Irvan was a river rat. About all that he ever did was go fishing. Every morning he would go down to the river and get into his green, man-made, wooden boat. He had to bail water out of the boat each morning and then get in it to go out and set his fishing lines. Irvan also trapped animals in order to make extra money needed to buy his liquor. He was a heavy drinker and spent most of his money on whiskey.

John Wilson told me that he could remember as a kid seeing Irvan walking across the fields twice a week to the bridge that crosses Green River into Munfordville. He would walk into town to get his groceries and liquor. Wilson said that Irvan was a very quiet person, didn't like to talk much. Wilson also said that kids used to laugh at Irvan and make fun of him all the time, but for some reason it never bothered him. He never expressed anger or even unhappiness when they did this.

Mrs. Williams recalled the one day when Irvan seemed happy. As he was walking back from town, he approached her with a box in his hands. She could hear sounds coming from inside the box. He opened the top of the box and on the inside were two puppies that someone had given to him while he was in town. Both pups were brown with white spots and of no certain breed. They were just plain old mutts. Irvan named these two dogs Jud and Jake.

John Wilson told me that he recalls Irvan and Jud and Jake walking across the fields together for three or four years. The dogs especially liked to go fishing with Irvan in his boat.

In or around November 1963, Irvan approached Mrs. Williams and asked if she had seen Jud and Jake recently. He told her that they had been gone since last night.

She told him that she hadn't seen them, but that she would keep an eye out for them.

Irvan seemed to be really nervous and scared. Mrs. Williams said that she had never seen him so upset. She remembers clearly what he said as he left. He said, "If anyone has taken or hurt Jud and Jake, I will kill them. They are all I have."

The rest of the story is, for the most part, what is believed to have happened.

Irvan went out across the fields and down the river banks in search of Jud and Jake. After hours of searching, he finally found them dead. Supposedly, they were shot and killed by some teenagers who were out hunting. Irvan carried the two dogs back to his small shack, then evidently went crazy because of their death. It would have been like losing a child for someone else. He took a knife and cut both of the dogs' bellies open and collected their blood and used it to paint a cross over the door leading into the cabin, and over the doors leading into each room. The design was strange, they said, as he painted crosses and a half moon over each of the crosses. Once he finished all this, he began swearing, cursing, breaking bottles, and tearing the cabin apart.

Later, he took the bodies of the two dogs down to the river and put them in his boat. Then he climbed into the boat and went down the river crying and swearing revenge. He started drinking and continued to drink for a long while. The story goes that his boat flipped over, and being too drunk to swim, he drowned.

It is said that, now, if you go back to his cabin or down to the river's edge, you'll be able to hear two dogs barking, Jud and Jake.

"Fish" Butler, another river rat, claims that late one evening when he was coming home from fishing, he noticed three forms on the river bank. He said that it was very dark. He yelled, "Hello," to the figures but got no answer. The figures were those of two dogs and a tall skinny man. Legend has it that Irvan, Jud, and Jake walk together along the banks of the river, and if someone goes down there about dark, he'll be able to see them.

If you ever visit Hart County and decide to go down to the river where Irvan died, listen very carefully and look around. If you see the shadows of two dogs and a tall skinny man or hear the dogs barking in the distance, you can be sure that it is Irvan and his two beloved dogs, Jud and Jake.

8. "Girl's Ghost at Top of Steps"

The haunted house that I'll be describing is the one that I live in. It is located in Ohio County, and is about 112 years old. Many of the rooms were added on in no apparent pattern. The house has both an upstairs and a basement. My sister and I shared one of the upstairs bedrooms, and our brother had the other one.

When the ghostly things that I'm talking about happened, I was about fourteen years old. At that time, the stairwell of the house ran from the living room straight up into the bedroom that my sister and I shared. One night when my aunt was staying with us, I woke up in the middle of the night and looked over at the top of the stairs. When I looked, I very clearly saw a tall, blonde-haired girl in a white-flowing dress standing at the top of the steps. I could see her very well because we had left the light on at the bottom of the stairs for my aunt.

I shook my head and closed my eyes, then reopened them to see if this ghost-like girl was still there, and she was. I thought to myself, "I'm not scared, so I must be dreaming." Then I turned over and went back to sleep.

The next day I didn't think anything about it until my sister asked me if I had seen anything odd the night before. I had not mentioned seeing what I saw to anyone, so I asked her what she meant. She described the same thing that I had seen exactly, except that I had seen this figure in a white dress, with high-top black and white tennis shoes on. People may laugh, but that is what I saw.

My sister did not have as good of a view of the face as I did, so when I described the girl, she told me that I had just described one of her best friends, Nancy. Then it hit me that the figure was Nancy. The dress was more out of place than the shoes, because she never wore fancy dresses, but always did wear those shoes.

What happened is, Nancy had accidentally shot and killed herself four and one-half years earlier.

We never again saw anything like this. At the time we saw this, neither my sister or I had been ill or experienced an emotional crisis.

9. "The Dwale Hill Ghost"

There's this guy who took his date to the top of Dwale Hill, located just above Allen, and parked his car. He told his date that he had to go relieve himself but that he would be right back. He locked his car with the girl in it, took the keys with him and walked down the hill.

In a few minutes the girl hears someone trying to jiggle open the door to the driver's seat. She knew that it wasn't her boyfriend because she could still see him at a distance walking back up the road. She saw this ghost and began screaming.

Before I go any farther, let me say that this story is still told by many people in the Dwale Hill community. But generally it's the girl who parks her car and goes off to relieve herself. On her way out, she loses her footing and falls down the face of the hill onto the railroad tracks just as a freight train is coming around the bend. The engineer doesn't see her in time to stop the engine. The train hits her broadside and cuts off her head.

Now, the story gets interesting. In one version, the girl is parked by the side of the road with her boyfriend. It's midnight, and they've been there for some time before she feels the need to get out and go relieve herself. Well, the train does hit her, and she dies there on the spot.

Every year on the anniversary of her death, her ghost is seen on the road there on top of Dwale Hill, trying to find her boyfriend's car. She thinks that any car parked on top of the hill is his and will try to open the door to get in.

Truth of the matter, the anniversary of her death is whatever date Prestonsburg Community College students feel like making it. That way, some college students, myself included, will park our cars on the hill and wait for the lady to appear. So far, she hasn't shown up.

10. "The Railroad Flagman's Death"

There's a tale about a flagman on a railroad, who was to retire after his last trip home. He was going home, riding this caboose. What his job was, he was to ride on the caboose, and every time that the train was to start or stop he was supposed to lean out and wave his lantern. Every time they went by a road or some big byway, after the train was clear, he was to wave the lantern out of the caboose, so that the engineer would know that the train was past.

Well, they were going past this road, and they had just got past when he leaned out to wave his lantern. But they were going around a slight curve, and he had to lean farther out than usual so that the engineer would know that they were past.

All the engineer said that he saw was just the lantern flying out through the air. He went back later and found the flagman with his head decapitated, where he had fallen. Leaning out, the flagman had lost his grip and fell underneath the caboose and had his head cut off.

They say that still to this day you can see the lantern swinging back and forth as he was swinging it down the railroad track, and finally it flies out into the underbrush and is never seen again that night. And every night of this same week, this same occurrence happens.

This has been validated by many people: all the folks of this town and the country around here, and even by a person known as the Ghost Hunter, who makes his living verifying or denying these things.

11. "Boy Ghosts"

When you go through the Hicks Road stretch, where a Perry boy got killed in the summer of 1966, you can sometimes see a ghost or two. It's truly a weird thing to encounter. What happened goes like this. About thirty years ago, there were these two boys, a Davis and a Taylor, who were out there riding around on their motorcycles and had a wreck.

It is claimed that a speeding car came zooming down through that hill-country road, on the wrong side of the road, or in the middle of it, and ran into the boys there in the woods. They were both killed on the spot.

During the summer on a rainy night or a night clouded with fog, you can see these boys' ghosts.

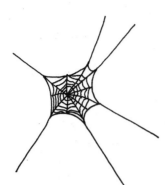

Chapter 9

Ghosts of Suicide Victims

1. "The Ghost of a Teenage Girl"

There is an old story that goes around 'til this day about the old fire tower that was located not far off Highway 56, going out of Morganfield. The tower was on one of the old abandoned gravel roads that used to run along through there.

It is said that years ago a young teenage girl climbed to the top of the tower for reasons unknown to anyone, even her own family, and jumped to her death. That was a long time ago, so the story goes, but on occasion her ghost is still spotted by local teenagers who go out to cruise and hang out in that part of the county. The ones who claim that they see the ghost of the girl will insist that periodically around midnight on certain nights of the year, the dead girl repeats her act of suicide all over again. They swear that you can hear her blood-curdling screams as she falls. Sometimes, even, you can see her falling to her death from the tower. But she always disappears just before her body hits the ground. They swear that's a true happening.

2. "Ghost of College Student"

My cousin, who lived in Madisonville at one time, told me this story. It seems that there was a young man who went to college at Lindsey-Wilson College in Columbia. People said that he was a little strange. He never hung out with anyone, nor did he go to parties and things. No one ever saw him except when he was in class. Even when they did see him, they said he never did speak a word to anybody.

One weekend, when everyone had gone home, this fellow stayed there on campus. About midnight that first night that everyone was gone, some people who lived close to the campus reported that they heard screaming and piercing cries in the darkness. When they went to check out what was happening, they found that this strange young man had committed suicide by jumping off his dorm roof.

Since no one knew his name, nor his family, or where he was from, they tried to look these things up. And, would you believe it, there was no record of him at all.

Every year since then, there have been strange sightings of a man's ghost walking around the campus, but it never bothers or hurts anyone. Never bothers a soul. What a sad fellow he must have been.

3. "The Gravestone That Refuses to Stand Erect"

Some of us were out messing around in old graveyards one day. We'd heard of this gravestone that would not stand up, even after it had been braced. We asked a grave digger about this odd gravestone, and why he would never fix it so that it would stay up.

He said that they had tried for the longest time, using all kinds of methods. However, it always fell down after only a few days of standing erect. Once he told his wife about it, and she told him that in Scotland, where her ancestors were from, that the grave marker of a person who had committed suicide could never be made to stand up of its own accord.

I mean, man, we found that to be truly interesting!

4. "Teenagers' Ghosts"

On December 3, 1979, two Jeffersontown High School seniors, Tommy and Terri [pseudonyms], committed suicide together. They were members of the Drama Society and devoted many hours working as both cast and crew for the drama club. During their three and one-half years of high school, Tommy and Terri carried leading roles in many of the plays and sang in several of the musicals.

Despite their devotion and experience, Tommy and Terri were both denied leading roles in the final play of the year, their senior play. This came as a great disappointment to them, and in the final analysis, they decided to take their own lives out of revenge for not getting the parts they wanted. So later that night, they drove out to a desolate field, parked the car, and slowly died of carbon monoxide poisoning. Since that night, the spirits of Tommy and Terri have haunted the other students involved in plays at J-town.

Several incidents involving their ghosts have occurred. Many times each year, students have seen a faint, shadowy trace of a girl and a guy standing in the chorus room. These ghost-like figures have also been seen in the dressing rooms and on the catwalks above the stage.

Six years later, in 1985, the crew put together some scenery for a play, using backdrops and props that were made in 1978. One of the 1985 crew members was touching up the paint on a backdrop when he discovered Terri's signature. Being totally ignorant of her story and suicide, he painted over her name. A friend watched over his shoulder and commented, "You shouldn't have done that."

The painter thought nothing about what had been said until later that evening. Once he had finished securing the light fixtures, and was moving the ladder, the ladder collapsed and barely missed his head as it fell. He then realized that he had ticked the dead girl off. And believe it or not, three hours later he tripped over a loose wire, fell off the stage, and broke his arm. He later dropped out of the drama club.

The most recent incident happened after school one day last year. A young girl, Jenny [pseudonym], was sitting alone in the chorus room doing her homework, when she was approached by a girl described to be about eighteen years of age. The girl introduced herself by her real name and said that she was a senior at J-town. Jenny told her that she was studying for a test, but did ask the one who had just come in if she would like to sit with her.

They talked for only a few minutes, then Jenny said that she needed to go catch her bus. As Jenny attempted to exit the room, the door slammed in front of her. And a yearbook that Terri had been carrying flew from her hands and headed toward Jenny. After a few minutes of screaming for help, Jenny was let out of the room by a student who had heard the screams. The spirit of Terri was still with her.

Other students came by to question Terri, or her spirit. After a few minutes of conversation, they soon realized that Terri must be the one who committed suicide back in 1979. One of the students then picked up the yearbook that Terri had thrown at Jenny. Looking through it, they soon recognized her as the one who had indeed killed herself back in 1979. And believe it or not, Terri's name was inscribed in the yearbook.

Many people believe that as long as there is a drama club at J-town, Tommy and Terri will continue to haunt the school's dramatists.

5. "Apparition of Former Newsman"

This happened at the *Henderson Gleaner* newspaper office about 1991. A new employee was working in a rear dark room in the news office. He was scanning a photo at a light table, and all the lights were off. Suddenly, he felt a presence at his left elbow. When he looked up, he saw the apparition of a man in a work uniform. The apparition moved behind him to the other side, and continued to look over his shoulder. Eventually, the spirit faded away.

The employee was scared, but he wasn't in a panic. Gathering his wits, he went out into the light and told his foreman what he had seen. The foreman took him to a printed poster of employee photos from a few years back. The man who had just seen the apparition immediately pointed to the photograph of the man whose apparition he had seen. The foreman then said that the man in the photo, who had been a longtime employee at the news office, had committed suicide only a few months ago.

6. "Greta's Ghost"

The house in which I live in Anchorage is a nineteenth-century Victorian house. And, it's the truth, the house is haunted by the spirit of the widow of Benjamin Harris, a Civil War colonel.

Colonel Harris's wife, Greta, died in the room that I use as my bedroom. She died as the result of a self-inflicted gunshot wound. And she comes back quite often to move things around in the house. Things are continually being moved, or they simply disappear.

One time I woke up in the middle of the night and saw Greta standing beside my bed, looking at me. Suddenly, her hand reached out toward me as if she wanted something. Then, all of a sudden, Greta screamed and then disappeared. I don't know what that was all about, what she wanted from me.

7. "The Misty Creature"

The first experience that I ever had with a ghost was the night that I was spending the night with my Aunt Joyce in Russellville. My aunt had invited my family over to her house one evening to visit. We got there during late afternoon, back in the summer of 1982. I was thirteen years old at the time.

That night we ate supper, then sat around and talked for quite a long time. It was late before we finished talking that night. When we all decided to go to bed, we were told that everyone would be sleeping on the first floor of the house, except my sister and me. Our bedrooms were upstairs.

As everyone went to their own sleeping rooms, my sister and I walked up the steps together to our bedrooms. The door to my second floor bedroom was an overhead door that a person had to push open. As I opened the door, I looked into the room and saw something very bizarre. I saw what appeared to be a mass of glowing mist.

As soon as I saw this, I pushed my sister back. She couldn't see it. I knew that if she had, she would be scared to death. I told her to stay outside of the room as I went in.

The misty creature was hovering directly over the bed, and the light switch was exactly on the other side of this ghost-like creature. I didn't know what I was going to do, but I knew that I had to do something before my sister saw it. So I decided to try to turn on the light. As I approached the bed, the mist stayed nonmoving over the bed. I collected my courage and proceeded through the creature. Boy, did I ever feel funny and strange. Scared, you know. I had a feeling somewhere between being cold or being electrocuted. I can't explain just how I felt. Anyway, when the light came on, the apparition disappeared. I decided to wait until the next morning to tell other members of my family about it.

When I told what happened the next morning, my mother said that her brother had killed himself in this house. I knew that Aunt Joyce had had a husband, but I thought that he had died of a natural cause. When I heard that my uncle had committed suicide in this house, the word "ghost" immediately formed in my mind.

My mother and I thought it would be best not to tell anyone else about it, especially my Aunt Joyce, because it would likely upset other family members.

My mother also told me that someone else committed suicide in this house before my uncle did. She didn't know his name, but she knew that he had owned the house before my uncle and aunt had purchased it.

I asked her how the other man had killed himself. She told me that he had run out into the front yard and shot himself with a shotgun. It was then that she told me that my uncle had killed himself with the same weapon that the previous suicide victim had used, a shotgun.

8. "Bloodstains on the Wall"

When my mother was young, she was told about an old man who lived across town from her, lived in a house that sat on a high hill. Said it was hard to get up to his house in the wintertime when snow and ice were on the ground. Winter or summer, the old fellow would come out of his house about one time each week, but when he did he only stayed on the outside for just a few minutes.

One night, when Mom was a young girl, a little neighbor boy said that he heard a gunshot at the old man's house. Everyone said that it was thunder, but the young boy said it was not thunder.

Finally, the boy and some of his friends went up to the old man's house. When they walked in, they saw the old fellow sitting in a chair, dead. He had shot himself to death. The bullet hit him in the head. Well, they said that blood was on the walls everywhere.

The kids ran home and told their parents about what had happened. The people that lived close by took care of cleaning up his body and burying it, then cleaned up the house. They got the house all ready to sell. New people bought it and soon moved in. Then, on a stormy night, all the old man's blood appeared on the walls and on the chair in which he was sitting when he killed himself. Ever since that first time, the blood still appears on the walls on stormy nights.

9. "Ineradicable Bloodstain of Suicidal Victim"

Granddad said that these people lived in this old two-story house close to Bewleyville. Uncle Harold and Cindrella Albright Cundiff, my Granddad's mother, lived there a long, long time. Mama knowed the man that lived there. He was Roy Paine. His parents lived there with him. He had money. Mama said that he lived there—owned the farm. He decided to sell the farm. So he sold it, and the fellow paid him for it. After he sold it he decided that he wanted it back.

Well, that fellow wouldn't let him have it back. So he got worried and bothered about selling his farm and not being able to get it back. So he killed himself. He was upstairs, as I've always heard it, in one room upstairs. He took a razor and cut his throat. But when Mom and my brother Harold lived there, they said you could hear scuffling upstairs there every once in a while. Said you could go up there and look on the floor and there was blood on the floor. Said you could go up there and look for yourself. It was suicide blood. They could never wash it up. That's what I've always heard. Of course, I never did go look. But that's what they said when they was living there. Mama knowed the man when he was living. Of course, that's been a long time ago. That was back when my mama was a young woman.

Mama, nor Harold, nor Poppa, none of them were ever afraid of ghosts anymore. They just didn't believe in them. They'd hear ghosts tales and all like that, and live in a house that was "hainted," and all, but they didn't pay any attention to it.

10. "The Woman Who Went Insane"

There's an old, old house on Casey Road here in Logan County. The old house is right on top of a hill, and there is a brook behind the house. The yard around the house is middle sized and in it is located a small building.

There were seven people living in this one-story house. This included a woman, her parents, and her children. The woman's husband fell ill and died, and it was then that she moved in with her parents.

It is said that she slowly lost her mind, and one night as she was cooking supper she slipped match heads into the food. She did this in order to put everyone to sleep so that none of them would wake up or hear anything happening.

After everyone was asleep, this woman went into the kitchen and got a butcher knife and then slipped into her and her kids' bedroom. One by one, she slit her own children's throats. After she made sure they were dead, she went out back to the brook where they got their drinking water, and there she slit her wrists and died.

Forever after that happened, a bloodstain was on the floor. They painted it but it kept showing up, so they tore up the floor and turned it upside down so they wouldn't see it. But even to this day, that bloodstain is still on the bottom side of the floor in that house. People still say that after 11:00 p.m. if you go up there and listen very closely you can hear the screams of the dead children.

We live down the road from this old house, and, boy, is it ever scary looking.

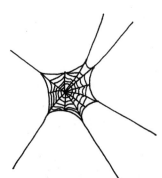

Chapter 10

Weird, Eerie, Ghostly Lights

1. "Ghostly Lights in Sloans Valley Railroad Tunnel"

Sometimes there are certain happenings that make you wonder about the possibility of ghosts. I've been down in a cave in Sloans Valley, a cave that they once called the Old Moonshiners Cave. It was located just at the north end of the Sloans Valley bridge.

I'd stayed a little longer in the cave than I had intended, and when I came out it was beginning to get dark. It looked like it might rain, so I started down the railroad track towards the Sloans Valley tunnel.

Everett Hilton was night watchman at the tunnel. And Everett and I always passed the time of day talking to each other. When I came up to the south end of the tunnel, Everett was sitting just outside his little shanty there. When I started to pass on by, he yelled out, "Hey, where are you going?"

I answered, "I'm going to Burnside. Are there any trains due to come by soon?"

He told me that there was none any closer than at Somerset and Alpine. I then asked him if he had ever heard of the immigrant train wreck in the Sloans Valley tunnel.

He said, "Yes, many a time. What do you know about it?"

I told him that at that time my grandfather owned a restaurant just above the railroad tracks there in Burnside. My grandfather told me later that on a particular day, the immigrant train stopped, and some people got off the train and went in to get them some food to eat. When they got finished they went back to the train. All the people on the train got off, all except the immigrants that were on it. I guess they didn't have enough money to spend at a restaurant.

My grandfather said that when the train pulled out, a strange, strange feeling came over him. He just looked at those immigrant people and he had a feeling of dread. The train pulled out, went on up the grade, then vanished. Now, this is what happened.

At that time, Alpine was called Summit. That was the place where the fast trains passed each other. On this particular day, there was a north-bound passenger train that pulled into Summit. The train crew got off and went to the telegraph office for orders. The operator already had their orders written out. He handed them to the conductor. The conductor glanced at them and handed them up to the engineer with the remark, "Well, we go to Somerset for Number One."

So the engineer started the train and they went off down through Sloans Valley.

In the meantime, the immigrant train climbed the hill, and had just passed Rodamore Cut, and was making up time on the downgrade toward the Sloans Valley tunnel. The two trains met with a terrific crash right in the middle of the tunnel, and the wooden cars immediately caught fire.

Because there were so many people in the immigrant cars whose names were not known, the number of people killed in the wreck was never known. Over the years, the section hands and other railroad employees began to notice something peculiar about the tunnel in Sloans Valley.

I might mention that that tunnel was 1,000 feet long, and it was as straight as a rifle barrel. However, at each end there was a curve. Because of the curve, you couldn't see very well beyond the tunnel, going either north or south.

Well, back to me and Everett. On this particular night we sat there and discussed that train wreck for quite a while. Finally, he said, "Well, you better be careful going through the tunnel. The rock is still falling where that wreck happened fifty years or more ago.

So I finally took off. I didn't have anything with me but the flashlight and a few candles I had used down in the cave. I started through the tunnel, thinking about all the people who had been killed in the wreck.

Just as I started, Everett called out to me, and I went back to see what he wanted. He asked, "Do you see something there in the tunnel?"

I told him that I didn't see a thing.

He said, "Looked to me like a man walking."

I turned on my flashlight and started walking again towards the tunnel. When I got to the tunnel and got a little ways into it, it seemed as if I heard someone calling. I yelled back, "Everett, did you holler at me?"

He says, "No, but you'd better hurry. That train that was in Somerset when we started talking is coming through Burnside right now."

I responded, "Yes, I had better hurry." So I started out walking pretty fast. About two-thirds of the way through the tunnel I could feel a cold breeze on the back of my neck, just as though a train were entering the tunnel. I turned around and looked, but there was nothing in sight. I hurried along. Then, all of a sudden it sounded as if I could hear wheels clicking on the rail joints. Then it started getting closer and closer. All of a sudden, I heard what sounded like a low mournful whistle, way off in the distance. So I imagined that I was hearing the train coming down Rodamore Cut. I began to hurry up again. I decided to look around behind me. When I did, I saw what looked like a reflection of a headlight in the south end of the tunnel. I thought to myself, half scared, here I am in this tunnel and there's two trains coming, one northbound and one southbound.

Well, I started trotting, but the more I trotted, the longer that tunnel got. Suddenly, I could see train lights coming through the north end of the tunnel, and I could feel a hot breath of air or something. It couldn't have been a natural breeze. Then something rushed by me and the rails were clicking. Suddenly, I heard a loud, devastating, explosion-like noise back in the tunnel. But when I looked around, the tunnel was completely clear. The lights were gone, and I stepped out into the cool, fresh, night air at the north end of the tunnel.

From that point in time, I have always believed that I saw ghost-train lights, and heard the sounds of the ghosts of the people who died in that awful train wreck.

2. "Indian Graveyard Lights"

The house over here on the state line where my grandmother and two uncles used to live has always had the name of being spooky. No one ever knew what these ghostly lights and things were all about, until one day when my grandfather plowed up some Indian bowls and cups. And believe it or not, he also plowed up some bones. He didn't know that a graveyard was at that spot on the ground. There must have been Indians buried there, and I guess these were Indian bones that he plowed up.

One night as my uncle was coming home from Celina, Tennessee, he saw a light going around that old house where he lived. Scared, he went running into the house and told my grandmother and my uncle what he had seen. They didn't know what to think or do. The next day they told a neighbor lady about the weird light, and she told them that this was not the first time that someone had seen strange lights around the house. This lady went on to say that on some nights you can stand on the front porch of the house and see a ghost-like light over on the hill. I was in the house the night my uncle saw this light. I'm glad that I didn't know this then, because I would have freaked out.

Do you suppose that this old house they lived in was built over some Indian graves? People say that if you build over a grave, that person's spirit will come back to haunt you.

3. "The Mysterious Light"

I've seen something that I don't understand, and maybe I'm not supposed to understand. I was not ill at the time, nor was I imagining it.

It was a warm July night when I was about nineteen. At that time, about 1:00 a.m., I had just pulled my car up into my driveway. My dog was lying there on the steps as I walked into the house.

Everyone was asleep, but Mom had left the air conditioner on to cool the house. All the lights in the house were turned off. I went into my room to change clothes, then went back into the den and fell asleep on the couch. I woke up about an hour or so later, feeling strange, as if there were something else there in the room with me, watching me. I started to get up and turn the light on just as the dog started barking. Then, in the upper corner of the ceiling, a small light appeared. I stared at it in amazement, as it was getting brighter. It was like a star shining in the sky.

I looked around the room to see if the light was coming from outside, but the window curtains were all closed. I stared at the light trying to figure out what it was and why it was there. I was not afraid. Suddenly, the light started fading away and soon it had disappeared from sight.

A strange thing happened after the light was gone. The dog stopped barking, as if someone had left the dog's presence. I haven't seen the light since, but I will always remember the night that it came.

4. "Strange Lights and Noises"

On several occasions, this older man has said that there was a little rise of the ground just out front of this little old house they lived in when he was a boy there in Clinton County along the state line. On top of this rise was an oak tree and a very old graveyard. He said that they would sit on the front porch at night, and several times they'd see a light rise up out of that graveyard and go up into the tree. It would set there for a while, and then ease its way down the hill and come to their house. It would pass right by them as they sat there on the porch and go right through the front door.

That light would go through all the bedrooms, work its way all through the house as if it were checking things out. Then it would come back outside, work its way back up the hill, sit up there on that big old oak tree for a few minutes, then it'd ease its way back down and disappear into the ground, right into that graveyard.

He said that on other occasions, that they would be sitting there on the porch, when all of a sudden dishes would come crashing out of the kitchen and land there on the porch. Said it sounded as if they were breaking into a million pieces. They'd get up and run into the kitchen, but all the dishes would be in place, nothing disturbed. Couldn't find anything wrong.

5. "Ghostly Light Streaks into the Sky"

This story is about my grandmother when she was traveling from Cumberland County to Barren County. Back in her day and time, they didn't have any cars and trucks and buses, or anything like that. They either walked, rode horses, or rode in wagons.

Because she had been walking all day on her way to Glasgow, she became very tired and sleepy. She passed this old house on the side of the road, where weeds and everything had all grown up there in the front yard. She thought this would be as good a place as any in which to spend the night, so she stopped and went up on the porch. There was nobody around anywhere. It was a totally empty old house that was about ready to fall down.

She had a few clothes with her, and she made herself a pillow out of a blanket that she had. Well, she laid down and went to sleep. Late in the night, she woke up and looked out and saw this great big, really bright light that was rising out of the ground and going up into the sky. It did this several times.

She was scared, but she stayed on there in that old house that night. She didn't see anybody around, and she could never explain what that ghost-like light was all about. But she was insistent that she did see it, that she was not dreaming.

6. "Ghostly Light Enters House"

My grandmother's name was Belle Brizendine. When she was a child, they lived in an old house built in 1867 in Muhlenberg County, not far from Greenville. I remember her telling about the Union soldiers that were in the neighborhood when she was eight or nine years old. And she used to tell me a ghost story about that old house.

She said that when she was a little girl, they used to sit on the front porch in the evening. There was a dirt road that passed in front of their old house, and there was a cemetery just a short distance down the road from the house.

Grandmother said that one night when she was out on the porch, she saw a very large ball of light rise slowly from the cemetery and come very slowly down the road in the direction of the house. She always told how scared she got when it got closer and closer.

One time, when this light got directly in front of their house, the front gate opened and the ball of fire passed through the gate and came up the sidewalk directly toward my grandmother. She said that she was simply paralyzed as she watched it. As it passed by her, the front door of the house opened and the big ball of fire went into the house. It then proceeded to go up the long flight of steps to the upstairs area, then it disappeared.

7. "Mom Sees a Light"

My mom told me a story of a true experience that happened at the Tommy Triplett red-brick siding house near Bewleyville. Her name was Virginia Ann Cundiff; she was born in a little bitty community called Mystic, Kentucky, August 17, 1937. She died April 12, 1988.

This happened to her upstairs in the Triplett house. Mom and Dad got along fairly well, as married couples go. But, as married couples tend to do, they did have their arguments and fights and all. When this experience happened, Mom and Dad had had a rather rambunctious argument. And when they would have an argument, she wouldn't sleep with him at night, but she would find other sleeping places.

On this particular night, she decided that she was going to sleep upstairs. She went up there and took me with her. She put what's called a pallet down on the floor; had pillows and covers, but there wasn't a bed, just a pallet on the floor. She was going to sleep upstairs with me that night. I was real little at the time.

The way the house was designed, there were two windows in front of the house upstairs facing out toward the gravel road, which was quite a distance from the house. There was another window at the end of the house facing an old tree that was out there in the yard. There were no windows on the back part of the house.

Mom was laying there in bed, thinking about the argument and all. Said it was dark upstairs. I was asleep, so I don't know anything about it. Mom said that she saw a light about the size of a basketball. It was outside the window toward the tree. Well, the light came into the room through the window, floated over the bed, and went out one of the two windows facing the road. It circled the house and came back in this window facing the tree. Well, when it came back in the window that time, it was above the mattress where she and I were laying. She said that the light started to grow, getting bigger and bigger and bigger. Said the bigger it got, the brighter it got. Said she knew it wasn't a car light, because a car light wouldn't act that way, and besides there wouldn't be one car a day go down that road toward Rosetta.

The bigger the light got and the brighter it got, it scared her. So she got me and went downstairs and got in bed with Dad. She never did figure out what that light was. But we did hear that at one time a doctor lived there in that house. For some strange reason that no one understands why, he took a rope, tied it around one of the rafters and jumped down this stairwell and hung himself and died. We don't know who he was or why he done that, but there was part of a rope that was still tied across one of those beams upstairs when we were there. We don't know if he was the one who was haunting that house or not. We never could find out.

8. "It Wasn't the House Afire"

When I was about five years old, my daddy and mother and two or three of us kids had gone to church. That was back in the days when we did not have electricity; just used coal oil lamps for light. Anyway, this was in the summertime and it was dark on our way home from church in this old road wagon.

When we came within sight of our house, lights were shining out the windows just as bright as could be. And my dad thought the house was on fire, so he spurred up the team of mules. When we got to the front gate, daddy jumped out of the wagon and ran into the house. But it was just as dark as midnight in there, no lights at all. And there wasn't no one else around, because it was out in the country and the rest of the family was not at home. If anyone had been there, we could have seen them as they ran out of the house. There wasn't anything that could have caused this light.

Now, that's a "haint" story from back in the old days, and it really happened.

9. "The Ghostly Green Light"

One time this girl went to camp for her first time, and she was real lonesome because she'd never been away from home before and she was missing her parents something awful. She was always sorta quiet and shy and she didn't make friends very easily, so at camp she stayed by herself most of the time.

One night, all the other girls were sitting around the campfire singing, and she got homesick and decided to take a walk. She walked by the cabins they were staying in, and she thought she saw a light under one of them. She crawled under the cabin to see what was making the light, and she got stuck.

For a while, nobody missed her. In a few days, her parents came to get her to take her home. And everybody got really upset when they learned that the girl was missing, so they looked all over the woods for her but could never find her. All of a sudden, her father heard this noise under a cabin and went to investigate.

So, finally, they found her under the cabin, and she was still alive. She was not dead yet, but she had eaten the green moss under there so long that she had turned green, and her fingernails had grown real long. The poor girl had gone crazy, so when they got her out from under the cabin, she ran off into the woods and they never could find her.

They claim that you can still see her at night in the woods in the form of a green light moving all over the place but disappearing when anybody gets very close to this green light.

10. "Off and On Lights and Television"

About thirty miles from Sturgis, there's a little town of Marion. On the main drag at Marion is a big, beautiful white house with a screened-in front porch. It's really a good-looking house in real good shape. But no one will live in it more than two or three days. I've talked with one person who lived in it for one day, then moved out the very next day. She couldn't take it. I personally have gone over there and sat in front of the house at night to watch what went on.

It appears that the spirit of a man who lived there is still there. The night that a bunch of us girls went over, we told our moms that we were going to stay all night at each other's houses. We ended up at Marion across the street from this old house. And the weirdest thing happened.

There's no lights or water in that old house. They're never turned on unless someone lives in it. The house was totally empty, and we were sitting there. All of a sudden, the lights came on upstairs and down. The water sprinkler came on out in the yard, and we saw shadows moving in front of the windows in the house.

I talked with one of the women who had lived there, and she told me about the time when she was sitting in front of her television set. They'd just moved in, and she was taking a break, drinking a cup of coffee. She had a coffee table in front of the couch and an end table at each end of the couch. And she had, of course, little knick-knacks sitting around.

Well, she was sitting there watching TV, when all of a sudden this little candleholder on her right side there on the end table just picked up, floated over, and then set down on the coffee table in front of her. She thought that maybe she had been working too hard and was seeing things. So she picked the candleholder up and put it back on the end table, but then the same thing happened again. She called her husband in there, then put it back over on the end table. Believe it or not, the same thing happened again.

He said to his wife, "Well, we're tired. We've worked too hard, moved in in one day, and we're still working. Let's go to bed."

They got ready for bed and went to turn off the TV, but the TV went off of its own accord. He walked over and checked the plug. It was all right. So he turned the TV on again and was standing there looking at it; then all of a sudden it turned back off.

So whatever it is that is in that house turned the TV off. I guess the spirit of the old man who once lived there heard them say that it was time to go to bed, so he was just trying to help them out.

11. "Ghostly Lights"

I might tell you a little experience that happened to me once. This happened several years ago on election night. And, of course, people usually drank a little back then on that special day each year. I hardly ever drank, but I drank a little that night. And I wasn't very easy to scare. I drove back out to Mt. Gilead with Norman Miller. And there was a path—it was in the fall of the year, November election—and muddy. There was a path that cut through—it was a narrow cut-through by the back of the church house—and you could keep out of the road.

So it led up pretty close to this church house. And I saw a light in the

Eerie sounds, ghostly lights, and headless beings were often heard or seen by persons walking along country back roads and trails. (Photograph by David Sutherland, 1972)

church house door in the back. And seemed like while I was a-walking I could hear somebody talking. But I'd stop and look at it, couldn't hear a sound. And it didn't throw out any rays like a lamp or a flashlight or anything like that. It looked more like a ball of fire. I'd walk a piece, and my nerves were sort of built up, so I wasn't a bit afraid.

Naturally, I didn't go up to it, but I went pretty close by where it was at. And I'd walk a piece there and hear something a-talking, seemed like. And I'd stop; you couldn't hear a sound. It still stayed there, that light did. And I never did know what that was, but it didn't scare me a bit in the world. I just went on up, had to cut right across the corner of the graveyard there. By the way, that graveyard didn't scare me much, because I was used to it. I went to school there. And many a night I've went right through the middle of that graveyard. I'd go down there to Mt. Gilead to play pitch, rook, and the like. If it was in the wintertime, usually we'd be playing pitch or rook. And I'd go up through that graveyard and it didn't scare me one bit, and it didn't scare me that night, but I never did know what it was, don't 'til this day.

12. "Ghostly Light in Graveyard"

I can tell you a real funny story about my good friend Buford Page. Dr. George Bushong had just built them ponds up in that holler there behind his house in Mt. Gilead. The ponds had fish in them, but the Bushongs didn't want nobody fishing in them.

Buford and his wife, Clarice, come over to our house one night. Well, me and him slipped over there to fish in Dr. Bushong's ponds. And there is this little graveyard with two or three graves in it right at the back of the big pond. I used to walk along there from Mt. Gilead, and I've seen jack-o-mo-lanterns I don't know at the times they would dance up out of that little graveyard there.

The two of us got down there to the lake that night with our backs to that little graveyard. We was just fishing away. Well, directly it got so light you could have picked up a pin there from off the ground. Now, I'll tell you, when we left to go down there to the lake, it was as dark as all get out. But it turned light, just as light as this house is in here right now.

That light scared both of us. We didn't know what to think about it. Buford, he's awful scary anyway, said, "Wh-wh-wha-t was that?"

And I said, "I don't know unless it was the light from that graveyard right there behind us."

And, man, he like to have went off into that pond, and that's all there is to it! I never did know what it was. He wanted to leave right then. He didn't know the graveyard was there until I told him.

It was a funny thing, just as clear as it could be. It got as light as this house. You could have picked up a pin. Well, he was scared to death. He's the scaredest fellow you ever seen, anyway. Scared of boogers, and him a grown man!

The last thing he said right there was, "I'm leaving here, and I'm going to stick to it, too."

13. "Unexplained Lights"

Back in the 1940s, Metcalfe County was like most rural areas of Kentucky just after the Great Depression.

Mud Slash School was located on Highway 68, also known as the Greensburg Road. It was located near Sulphur Creek, and people have talked about mysterious lights that come from the gases and vapors surrounding such creeks. The old school building no longer stands, but for many years it was occupied by the Roscoe and Amy James family. The area around the school was supposed to have a headless horseman who traveled up and down the road.

In the fall of 1941, Maxie Martin, who is the father of Greg Martin of the Kentucky Headhunters, was twenty-one. Maxie was on leave from the army, visiting his parents, Claude and Ora Martin, who lived there on the Greensburg Road.

None of the houses or country stores at that time had any electricity, and the headlights on cars weren't really bright. Maxie had been in the CCC and later joined the army. He had brought with him a friend, J.W. Boles, twenty-two, of Glasgow. The two of them were out, and around 2:00 a.m. they had a flat tire near Mud Slash School. At first, they had intended to sleep the night in the car, but they became hungry and decided to go down to Gilbert Sneed's grocery store to get something to eat. They woke Mr. Sneed up and got some food. Then they headed back to the car, where they intended to stay for the rest of the night.

What happened next is something that Maxie says to this day that he cannot find a logical explanation for what occurred. As the two approached the school, they could see bright lights coming from behind the building. Since the school wasn't wired for electricity, they assumed that there was someone behind the school causing the light to flash. The two of them walked around in behind the school, but they didn't find anyone there, nor did they hear any evidence of anyone located around the school in any direction. "I think we'd better get out of here," Maxie said to J.W.

J.W. responded, "I think so, too!"

The pair left the school, and just as soon as they could, they drove their car up the bank until they came to Gilbert Sneed's store once more. They were in such a hurry that they even tore the inner tube in one of the tires in their haste to get to the store where they would be safe. They parked the car near the store and slept outside in the car for the remainder of the night.

Maxie Martin knows with absolute certainty that no one except him and J.W. were around the school that night. They didn't hear or see any evidence of anyone else's presence, but as close as they were to the school, they certainly would have. The lights were very bright and they did not come from any car lights, the moon, or anything else that people would consider normal.

14. "The Light That Shined Where Money Was Buried"

This story took place on my father's place on the Fairview Road here in

Christian County. A woman by the name of Miss Cobb had hanged herself in the well house one night. She had taken a lantern and buried her money down in the field below the house and then hanged herself in the well house.

Every rainy night a light [from a lantern] will come out of the well house and go across the fields and down into the ground at the foot of the hill. The lantern travels just about the same way a person would carry it. The popular belief is that the light goes down just where Miss Cobb buried her money.

Several people have dug around in the daytime looking for the money. People believe that if anyone would follow the light and mark the place, they would find the money.

15. "Ghostly Light at the Old Morgn Perry Place"

I believe that what we call the Old Morgan Perry Place, which is the next house on the big hill after you pass Ron's Market, is haunted. Or, as the old folks used to say, "hainted."

No one lives there now, but every night there is a lamp which comes on in one of the rooms at the front of the house. The room is to the right of the front door. This is the only light that can be seen in the house, and it has a yellow glow to it. It comes on about 10:00 to 10:30 every night.

No one around there can explain it. They just say it's a ghost light. Sometimes it stays on all night; at other times it's gone in a few minutes.

16. "The Glowing Ball"

My mom said that one time when she stayed all night with her sister at Parker's Lake, up near Cumberland Falls, she was awakened by a noise. She looked up and saw a glowing ball just floating there in the room. She said that she laid there quietly, just scared at seeing whatever it was.

She watched it as it floated into other rooms there in the house. She declares that she was awake when this was happening. Finally, it just disappeared when it floated through a wall.

She said that it didn't seem to bother anyone who was asleep. But it sure gave her a weird feeling.

17. "Lights Seen Coming down the Mountain"

There was this elderly lady from over in Carter County. She lived out in the countryside most of her life. Back in 1977 or '78, she was my mother's roommate in the St. Claire Medical Center here in Morehead.

One day I was there visiting my mom, and her roommate was in the bathroom, Mom told me that the other lady had mentioned, in general conversation, some ghostly goings-on. When the roommate returned to her bed, I talked her into telling me what had happened.

She told me that while she and family were still country dwellers there in Carter County, all of them had seen lights coming down the mountain, and they had always disappeared at the same spot. They knew that these lights were ghostly presences, but they had no idea what they were doing on the mountain, or why they always disappeared in the same spot.

She declared that these were ghost lights, and claimed that she typically got a weird, eerie feeling ever time she saw them.

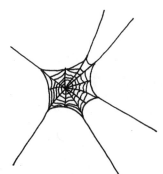

Chapter 11

Haunted Spots on the Landscape

1. "The Ghost of a Little Girl Killed in Bloody Harlan"

It was a rainy day on October 13, 1956. Back then, my grandfather, whom I shall call Cawood, drove a Greyhound bus. Early that morning, he was getting ready there in Harlan to run his route for the day. Like any other rainy day, it was just miserable and gloomy. Cawood's first bus stop was in Pine Mountain, then on to Evarts and Baxter. He picked up passengers in those places and took them back to Harlan so that they could do whatever. Cawood then went to lunch but got an unexpected telephone call from his boss telling him that he had to work a double shift, the reason being that the second shift driver had called in sick. Actually, Cawood was pleased to hear this because he had a wife and three kids, and a little extra money wouldn't hurt a thing.

It was late evening, around 10:30 p.m., when Cawood dropped off his passengers at Baxter and Evarts. He had one passenger to haul on over to Pine Mountain. The two of them started up this steep mountain slope, when suddenly the rain picked up and the fog got real bad. They were about half way up the mountain when Cawood saw a little girl about eleven or twelve years old, just soaked from the rain, and she appeared to be terribly cold.

Suddenly, the passenger began screaming at Cawood, telling him not to stop to pick her up. Cawood was terrified at the screaming, but being his

A ghostly fog hanging over the Hensley Settlement, now in Cumberland Gap National Historical Park. (Photograph by the author, 1972)

normal stubborn self, he stopped on the mountain and opened the door for the little girl. Well, he didn't see her when he stopped, so he went down the steps and started looking for her. She was nowhere to be seen. So he stepped back into the bus and sat down in the driver's seat with a look of fright and confusion on his middle-age face.

He turned around and asked the passenger what was going on. The passenger told him to get the bus moving on up the mountain, that he would tell him when he did. With the bus moving once again, the passenger told Cawood that the little girl had been killed along with other family members at the beginning of the miners' conflict called Bloody Harlan. He said, "The little girl is often seen on nights when the weather is like it is tonight."

Well, Cawood saw her that one time and he kept on looking for her as he would pass by that spot. But he never saw her again after that.

2. "Horses Spooked by the Spirit of a Vampire Woman"

A friend of mine from Edmonson County told about this vampiress that was killed on the road not far from where he lives. And supposedly she was buried close by in an old cemetery. My friend claimed that horses can sense a ghost or a vampire, so they won't go near where she was killed.

That was a while back when this woman vampire was buried. Anyway, these guys were on horseback riding down the road. All of a sudden their horses stopped and wouldn't move. The riders didn't beat the horses, but they couldn't get them to go near the spot where this vampiress was supposedly killed.

It is said that on certain nights you can see a white light right in the middle of the road, and also up there around her grave. They claim that people on other horses have ridden them up there in the woods where she's supposedly buried, and when they get there their horses will just rear up and throw their riders out of the saddle. Then, these horses will take off running in the other direction just as fast as they can.

3. "The Ghost That Rode behind a Rider on His Horse"

There is a ghost tale told by people over in the western part of McCreary County. The story claims that there was once two boys who frequently went places on horseback.

They were out together one night and got to drinking some moonshine whiskey. I guess they had too much alcohol, for on the way home these two boys got into a quarrel with each other, and one of them killed the other.

After that killing took place, the surviving boy said that every time he rode past the place where the killing had occurred, the ghost of his one-time friend would appear right there on that spot. Actually, he said that as he rode by there the fellow's ghost would walk out of the woods, hop up behind him on the horse, and ride for a while. Said these ghostly arms would be firmly wrapped around his waistline. After a few minutes on the horse, the ghost always disappeared very quietly, just as quietly as it had come to hop on the horse behind the rider in the first place.

4. "The Ghost That Wasn't"

One dark night I went for a drive to sort out some thoughts, and I parked behind Phillips' Seed and Supply Store in Taylor County. While sitting there, I noticed my car was gently rocking from side to side. I knew that I was parked close enough to the building to be sheltered from the wind. I sat up and happened to look in the rear view mirror and saw an image behind my car. I was so scared that I began screaming. I tried to start my car but it began to rock harder and faster. I finally got the car started, and, boy, did I ever take off to get away from there! I don't think it was a person that I saw because of the crouching position it held behind my car.

Later that same month, I was out there at the same place again, and a similar incident occurred while I was with this friend. A loud, screeching noise was heard that sounded as if someone ran their finger along the length of the car. We quickly turned the lights on and looked all over for a prankster, but no human was in sight.

5. "Ghosts of Lovers on Keno Bridge"

Back in 1956, this young dating couple were going to a high school prom here in Pulaski County. On their way to the prom, they got into an argument, an argument that eventually led to a fight between them.

The girl orders him to stop and let her out of the car, that she's had enough of this nonsense. Well, he pulls over, slows down, and she hops out of the car and takes off down the hill toward this bridge over the railroad track. We're talking about the Keno Bridge, located not far from Somerset. The bridge is 200 feet, or thereabouts, above the railroad tracks.

The girl runs at breakneck speed on down to the bridge where she is preparing to jump to her death. Just before she leaped off, the fellow runs up and tries to grab her. Well, he does take hold of her, but not soon enough. Unfortunately, she had already lost her balance and, as she fell, he tumbles off the bridge with her. Both of them died when they hit the tracks below.

It is said that if you go to Keno Bridge each year on the anniversary of their death, you can see them walking together, hand in hand, along the railroad tracks below the bridge.

6. "Ghost of Murdered Girl Seen on Bridge"

Over on the big old bridge close to here, these guys raped this girl and then killed her. Her ghost is still seen there. The girl is standing on the right front corner of this bridge. She is wearing a long, white gown and is staring off into space, looking for these guys that did that to her.

You can't see her except at night, and then only when you first round the bend in the road and your headlights flash on the bridge. I've seen the girl's spirit there myself, and I'll tell you right now, I don't ever want to go back to that bridge again. No, sir!

7. "Ghost of Eyeball Bridge"

This place that we used to go to when we were still in high school was haunted. Truly it was. The story behind it is that this girl was on her prom date when their car broke down. Her boyfriend started walking away to go get help, and she stayed there with the car.

What happened is, a crazy guy comes to the car and killed the girl. And if that wasn't enough, he then pulled the girl's eyes out of her head. Some people say that he ate her eyes, but others think he just threw them off the bridge, and that's why it's called Eyeball Bridge. Anyway, this girl supposedly came back to life, or maybe it was her ghost, and tried to kill the man who murdered her. But since she didn't have any eyes, she mistakenly killed her boyfriend who was coming back with help.

Some people claim that her eyes glow, and that she and her boyfriend can still be seen there at Eyeball Bridge trying to find her killer. I was there once sitting on the bridge, and when I looked over my shoulder I saw those glowing eyes. She was looking right at me. That was the last time I ever went to that place.

8. "Headless Woman's Rock"

Headless Woman's Rock is located about nine miles southwest of Leitchfield, here in Grayson County. This legendary rock is situated a short distance off Highway 1133, which branches off Highway 187.

Generally speaking, the rock is in an isolated area that has steep rolling hills, high cliffs, caves, eroded land, and is heavily wooded. The population is spread out thinly across the land, and all of the families out there are farmers.

For many years, I heard stories told by my parents and others in the area. I was always interested in the one told about the woman who lived in this area by herself back in Indian times. One night, either some Indians or some outlaws came and killed this woman, then cut off her head. Her body was found the next day, but her head was never located. Most of the stories about this woman revolve around the body's exploits to find its missing head. The body has been seen several times by a lot of people around here. You can see it day or night. But most people are afraid to go over there to that rock at night, because they say that they can hear the body looking for the head. When the night is warm and clear, you can hear a screaming sound coming from that rock. My mother always told me that if I would not be good, the headless woman would get me. Even today, most all of the children around here are afraid of the headless woman.

Charlie Taylor, who has been dead several years, always told that when he was out hunting with a double-barrel shotgun one day, he saw the body of the woman out by the rock. It scared him so bad that he turned around and ran all the way home. And Tommy Meredith's girl saw the headless woman once while hunting for holly at Christmas. As far as I know, they are the only two to have actually seen her. However, Stoy Downs, who lives here in Blowtown, claimed that Tom Willis's father was riding a horse by the rock one day. He said that a woman crawled up on his horse behind him and rode for a while, then jumped off. He didn't see her, but knew it was her.

Now, it just may be that the headless woman is just in the minds of the people here. Stoy Downs also told that when he was a small boy, he was out hunting wild animals over there by that rock. He heard a noise in the bushes and thought it was the headless woman. He had never seen her, so he thought he would look for her. Said he took just a step or two and suddenly a big bear jumped out of the bushes and chased him for almost a mile.

It just might be that the headless woman never existed. But, believe me, people around here still talk about her.

9. "The Haunted Rock"

I have heard many stories about a rock where everyone says a ghost or some type of spirit lives. The rock is here in Leslie County, where everybody rode mules and horses in the days before cars were introduced.

A young girl and her husband lived about ten miles above this rock. The girl was pregnant, and in those days there weren't many doctors. Even where they were found, they were so busy that they didn't have time to help deliver babies. So there was an old woman who lived in Hyden who was a midwife. She did most of the birthing around here. So when it came time for the young girl to have her baby, her husband was away from home and this neighbor woman had to ride a mule into town and bring back the midwife.

When the woman got to the rock, she felt something get on the mule behind her, but when she turned around she couldn't see a thing. The mule slowed down so much that it seemed that whatever it was, was so heavy that the mule could barely carry it. The woman became terribly frightened, but there was nothing that she could do. As she rode into town, she felt whatever it was get off, and the mule began to pick up speed.

She went to the midwife's house, but she didn't tell her what had happened because she was afraid that the midwife wouldn't go with her. The two ladies started on their way, but when they passed the spot where the creature had gotten off, it got back on the mule with them again. The mule began to slow down again. Finally, it seemed to be so tired that it couldn't take another step. The midwife asked the woman what was wrong with the mule, but the woman wouldn't answer her.

When finally they got back to the rock, they felt the creature get off. This same thing happened to many people in the community, but no one was ever able to solve the mystery of the big rock that had this ghost.

10. "The Ghost of Gravity Hill"

A friend of mine from Princeton told me about a place in Caldwell County where a girl was raped and killed under an underpass at the bottom of the hill. He said that if you park your car under this bridge, turn off the engine, put the transmission in neutral, then get out of the car, the car will roll up the hill for about 150 yards under its own power.

My friend said that those who have been there and experienced this, feel that the ghost of the murdered girl is pushing her offender out or away from her, thus is pushing their car. This friend of mine later took me to this place, and sure enough, after we got out of our car, it did roll uphill of its own accord a few feet. And there were handprints in the dust there on the trunk of the car. The girl's ghost, or whatever it was, had pushed the car!

Now, I'm a believer.

[In 1998, two school teachers went in separate cars but at the same time to see what would happen while they were at this "haunted spot." When they vacated their cars, with the transmissions in neutral, both vehicles rolled uphill for a short distance.]

11. "The Ghost of Middle Bridge"

There's a story about this little girl that fell out of the back door of a car as it was crossing this bridge on the Old Middle Bridge Road here in Warren County. This little girl died there on the bridge, and her ghost is still seen or felt there by lots of people, myself included.

I worked for a farmer at one time who owned a field on the Old

Middle Bridge Road. This old road has been closed for a long time. Anyway, I was driving a tractor late one night, but the farmer had told me that I didn't have to work past dark if I didn't want to. But I wanted to go ahead and get the job done, so I was out there on the tractor just working away and playing the radio that was hooked up in the cab of the tractor. When you're on a tractor, you can only see just where the headlights are shining.

I turned the tractor around when I got to the end of the row, and the tractor lights shined over where the old bridge was located. There's trees and stuff all around it now. And the tree limbs and branches were really blowing; I mean real bad, but I didn't think anything about it until I realized that there wasn't any wind blowing any place else. Just to prove it, I shined the tractor lights on some other trees and saw that they weren't even moving. So I got real scared and picked up the farm disk with the tractor lift, then drove the tractor up this little dirt road just as far as I could.

I mean the trees were hitting me, hitting the tractor. I was scared spitless. The ghost of that little girl was causing all this to happen. I knew I had to do something, so I got out of the tractor, ran to my truck and drove home. I never went back to work over there again after dark.

12. "Middle Bridge Ghost"

It is said that a girl was abducted by some boys out by a bridge here in Warren County, and either she jumped or was thrown over a cliff by this bridge to get away from them. Anyway, they say that any time a couple parks out there by this old bridge, the girl will come down onto the hood of the car to see if the boy that's got the girl with him is the one who attacked and killed her. There's been several times that I know of when a couple has run into this ghost girl out there on the bridge.

Fred Fenimore, President of the IFC, was out there with some boys one night and they were sitting. They had to sit there several nights in a row. Anyway, on this particular night, they were sitting there at about two o'clock in the morning, and they saw a light coming down the hill. When it got a little more than half way down the hill, they decided it was time for them to leave.

There were these two other couples that were double-dating one night. They decided to go out to the old bridge and park. They said that this light got all the way down the hill before they saw it. The light settled on the hood of the car, and the car started vibrating. They got scared and tried to start the car, but it wouldn't start.

The ghostly light just kinda disappeared, but it was still five minutes before they could get the car started.

Fred also told me that there were three professors here at Western Kentucky University, three men, a philosopher and two psychologists, that decided to go out there just to see what this was all about. One of the three men had a Chihuahua dog that rode up on the back of the car seat.

These three men did this every night for about a week. And then one night, late at night, the dog started shivering and whining. They looked up at the cliff, and here comes a light down the cliff. It came on down and settled on the hood of the car, as the couples had said that it did when they were doubling, and the car started vibrating, shaking. They couldn't get the motor started. Said they watched the light as it moved over onto the bridge and, when it got there, it took the shape of a girl. Fred told me that these three professors will swear to anyone right now that this really happened.

13. "The Haunted Bridge"

There is a ghost story about a young woman who was drowned one night while going across this bridge. This woman had her baby with her. They had an accident there on the bridge, and their car ran off the bridge and into the water underneath it. Both were drowned. There's a legend that says that if you go up to this bridge at midnight, and if you blink your lights three times, then honk your horn once, there on the bridge you'll see the young lady and her baby all dressed in white.

I wasn't with them, but cousins went there to this bridge several years ago, and they blinked their lights and blew the horn. They didn't see anything, but they did hear the baby crying. They took off as soon as they heard it.

14. "The Phantom Workman in Spurlington Tunnel"

For two straight Saturday nights in 1873, the eerie sound of a banging sledgehammer echoed from the Spurlington Tunnel.

Nobody was supposed to be inside the pitch-dark shaft, 160 feet of which had been burrowed through Muldrow's Hill for a new branch of the Louisville and Nashville Railroad. It was midnight; work had halted for the Sabbath.

Warily, workers lit lanterns and crept inside the blue limestone hole where the banging grew louder. The men froze in terror when a ghost worker and his mule flew past them, then disappeared.

The workers "speak of it with bated breath, and the stoutest-hearted of them will not be easily persuaded to again molest the Phantom Work-man and his mule," according to an article in the *Lebanon Weekly Standard*, February 19, 1873.

Trains no longer travel the 1,800-foot Spurlington Tunnel, which straddles the Marion-Taylor County line in central Kentucky. Dug between 1872 and 1874, the man-made cavern is named for nearby Spurlington, a tiny Taylor County community.

"As far as we know, neither ghost was ever seen again," said Betty Gorin, a Campbellsville historian.

The *Standard* reported that construction crewmen "heard very strange and unearthly sounds" coming from the unfinished tunnel. "The noise seemed to resemble that which would resound from the regular but heavy blows from a sledgehammer." When workers heard the sound the next Saturday night, "they resolved, if possible, to solve the mystery."

In their dim and flickering lantern light, the workers spied the ghostly mule charging at them. "One of the men fired at it, and the mark of the ball can now be seen on a timber," according to the *Standard* feature story.

Silently and swiftly, the specter "passed among them, emerging from the mouth of the tunnel and vanishing into the air. Next and instantly came the Phantom Workman, with a dozen heavy hammers swinging to his body in a strange and unaccountable manner. Like his mule, he rushed from the cavern and vanished into the air," according to the *Standard*, which added that "the workers fled to ponder on their midnight excursion."

The Spurlington Tunnel line, which wound up as part of the CSX Railroad, was abandoned about ten years ago, Gorin said. The tunnel still gapes, wide-mouthed, under the county-line hill.

15. "Red Hill Ghost"

"The Red Hill Ghost is our ghost." That's how those of us who grew up in the Leonard Oak community of Butler County described it. It was all cen-tered on our community doctor, Dr. Embry. He used to make house calls all the time, day after day. He said that every time he rode his horse to Red Hill, this headless woman's ghost would hop on the horse behind him.

My father-in-law said that he'd seen this ghost woman, too. He was on a horse by himself. When he saw her, he tried to outrun her, but he couldn't.

They all claimed that you could actually see her. But now I don't know what would cause her ghost to run over and jump on their horses behind them, or ride in a buggy in the same seat as the driver.

They said that Dr. Embry said that he never went over to Red Hill but what he didn't see her. If he was in a buggy, he'd see her. Said the first thing he knew, she'd be right there in the buggy beside him. And she also got on his horse with him, would sit there on the horse just behind him and ride down the road. Sometimes, he could feel her arms around him.

To get to Red Hill, go out to Leonard Oak Church and then proceed as if you were on your way to State Highway 70, close to the present-day Fourth District School. On your way to Highway 70, you come to a big long hill. That's where this headless ghost woman was always seen.

Back then, they'd say, "You'd better behave, or this headless woman will get you!"

16. "Now, That Was a Ghost!"

My granddaddy, Dr. Billy Richardson, always rode a big brown horse, the prettiest thing you ever laid your eyes on. I never saw it, but did see pictures of it.

When people back then got sick, they would send someone on a horse to Grandfather's house to ask him to come see their sick family member. Grandfather would get ready to go on a trip; he'd just get on this horse and go. Well, back then, he loaded medicine and personal items, such as his money, in a saddlebag instead of a pill box. He'd load one side of his saddlebag up with pills, and he'd always take some of these "sugar pills" with him. And if this person who thought they was sick didn't really have anything wrong with them, he'd give them some of these sugar pills instead of medicine.

Sometimes, he'd be gone two to three weeks at a time before he ever went back home. People would just stop him at every house. The only communication they had back then was by mouth. So he'd go to this house, and they would tell him that Mr. or Mrs. So-and-So wanted him to come doctor them, too. Well, when he got there, they'd tell him that someone else wanted him. See, the word just spread through the community that the doctor was in the area, and people would send for him to come see them.

Well, when Granddaddy would ride his horse and get up in that area, that's when he would see or hear these ghosts and things would start happening.

As I already said, he'd put medicine in one side of his saddlebag, and he'd put his money in the other side. He did this because if people were going to pay him, they'd give him cash right then. Everybody in the country knew that he'd go home with that other side of the saddle pocket full of money.

On one of his trips, it was raining. He said it was "raining cats and dogs." I never will forget him saying that! He said that it was thundering and lightning, and that that lightning was striking the ground right there beside him. Well, he knew where this house was that was on this little log road that he was traveling. When he got to it, he went into this building, took his horse in, too. He sat over in the corner on a box. When it would lightening in one corner, he could see something over there. Every time a bolt of lightning would strike, he would see this ghost-like thing, but it never would move. He kept thinking, "Well, it'll shoot me in a minute, whatever it is. And they'll rob me, because they know that I carry money when I travel through here."

He said, "My hair was standing straight up on my head. Then, all at once, the lightning just stopped. And whenever it did, whatever it was there in the other corner just got up and walked away. I never did know what or who it was."

Then, he'd end his story by saying, "Children, now that was a gh-o-o-o-s-t!"

17. "The Ghost Was a Bat!"

One time, my granddaddy, Dr. Billy Richardson, was going on house calls up into Cumberland County. He was going through this wooded area—big trees, little trees, all kinds of underbrush. He said that on this one occasion, he had gone from Monroe County almost all the way through Cumberland County. He said, "I'd ride that big horse of mine up through there, and all at once something would jerk on the left side of my bridle reins. I'd go a little farther and they'd jerk on the reins on the right side of the bridle." Said, "I thought to myself, that's somebody taking hold of my reins to my bridle."

He'd ride a little further. By that time, it would be getting dark back in them woods. Said something would jerk his bridle reins again. He'd try to see whoever or whatever it was, but he couldn't see a thing. Then it would jerk the reins again.

He had to go several miles down through those dark woods. Said, "Every little bit, it would jerk my bridle nearly out of my hands." Said, "The horse would sort of jerk back every time it'd jerk the bridle." Said, "I knew

Numerous ghosts, especially of the hitchhiking variety, were reputedly experienced temporarily by many local residents in north-central Monroe County as they rode horseback by this cemetery that was established in the early 1800s. (Photograph by the author)

that it was somebody. I just knew that." Said, "There I was with my saddle pockets full of money." Said, "I just kept going, for if it's going to hurt me, I can't get out of here. So I kept going. When I got back into Monroe County, it had begun to get a little bit light and I could begin to see, and whatever that was started to leave." Said, "I just raised up on my toes in my saddle stirrups and looked, and believe it or not, it was a bat! It was just flying back and forth jerking the bridle reins."

Now, wasn't that a ghost-and-a-half! Granddaddy believed in ghosts, and he was scared of all of them.

18. "The Ghost of Clara Morrow Field"

My family, including my husband Earl, our teenage son Fred, and daughter Margaret, moved to Somerset back in 1978. It was good to be in Somerset, the home of Senator John Sherman Cooper and Governor Edwin Morrow. I began teaching at Meece Middle School, and Margaret enrolled there as a student. Within a few weeks we were involved in local sports and community events.

Our involvement within the Somerset schools and community intensified when Margaret entered Somerset High and became a cheerleader. Thursday nights brought all of us to Clara Morrow Field. The school band led the football players, cheerleaders, and fans from Clara Morrow, around the town square, and back to Clara Morrow for a spirited pep rally in preparation for the big game on Friday night. When I asked the locals how the football field happened to be named for a woman, their responses revealed a most interesting story.

The Sam Morrow family lived on College Street next to Somerset High School. Clara's mother, Jean Fox Curd, was in Somerset High's first graduating class, and her father, Scott Morrow, served as a major during the Spanish American War. He was a brother of Governor Morrow.

Clara was born June 21, 1896. Her long curls, beautiful smile, and winning ways made her a favorite of all who knew her. Tragedy struck this happy Morrow family when Clara, an outgoing ten-year-old, died of meningitis on January 25, 1907. Some stories say she was roller-skating on the sidewalk when she fell, injuring her knee. Other versions have Clara falling into icy water while skating on a pond in her back yard. The entire town of Somerset mourned with her grief-stricken parents. Hearts were heavy as the community struggled to help the parents cope with life's greatest heartbreak—the loss of a child. Clara's parents focused on how they could preserve the memory of their departed daughter.

In 1923, when additional land was required to meet standard requirements for a football field, Major and Mrs. Morrow gave the necessary footage, plus a driveway, from College Street to the new field. In appreciation of the gift, the Somerset Board of Education named the field "Clara Morrow Field." Major and Mrs. Morrow erected a most impressive entrance as a tribute to Clara. The dedication of Clara Morrow Field was a major event in the town of Somerset. However, nothing could erase the fact that one of the town's most beautiful and promising young girls had been denied her teenage years. During those years, Clara would have attended games at the football field and studied with her classmates at Somerset High School. The contributions she could have made to the community would never be fulfilled.

After the death of Clara's father, the heirs sold his home and nine acres of land to the Somerset Board of Education. The Board later bought the land containing the house where Clara died. Then the Morrow home, with its sad memories, was torn down. Along about that time, the ghost of Clara Morrow began to be seen or felt on numerous occasions.

According to local legend, Clara's spirit was restless. It had roamed through her old home there on College Street trying to capture her idyllic childhood. After all, Clara had spent ten years of her life living next door to the high school. People said that she just loved watching the teenagers carry their books to class or cheering at the football games.

Her spirit was not to be denied. When her home was sold, her ghost moved over to the football field which bore her name. Countless sightings have been made of the white, misty apparition that floats up from the fifty-yard line during homecoming week each fall. In years past, the brave-hearted youngsters camped out until the stroke of midnight to wait for Clara's ghost. One of the school's night watchmen witnessed Clara's ghost-like figure and verified their stories. She is only visible at midnight, but her spirit is felt during countless activities on the football field and in the school building as well. Some say that Clara's ghost is in search of the homecoming dance. Others say that when they see her, she is searching for her parents.

The restless spirit of Clara cannot diminish the many uses which have been made of Clara Morrow Field. The football team has moved on to Clark Field, a much larger stadium. The elaborate entrance donated by Clara's parents is no longer in existence. However, the field dedicated to Clara's memory is now home to Somerset's soccer teams, band practice, and crazy games during homecoming week. All these activities are over before the stroke of midnight. I can't help but wonder what would happen if a soccer game should go into more than one overtime, thus extending the game beyond the stroke of midnight into the witching hour. Might Clara be seen running down the field or maybe giving Somerset's goalie a little extra help in blocking the opponents' goal. Or perhaps if the band practiced late, I mean really late, Clara would be seen in the woodwind section. She would be far too fragile to be a percussionist. Are you willing to come with me during homecoming week this fall to wait for Clara?

19. "Ghosts at Mammoth Cave"

Curiosity and wonder are among the many urges that draw people into the depths of Mammoth Cave. I know these urges very well, as I grew up in Park City, which is about one mile from this great cave system.

Along with Mammoth Cave's lustrous wonders there is a dark side, a dark, unknown side to the cave that many persons have witnessed. I never knew any of the ghost stories of Mammoth Cave until my sister got a job there three years ago. It is customary for the seasoned rangers to tell new employees about all of the unexplainable phenomena that occur in the caverns.

A natural opening was "rediscovered" by a hunter named John Houchins about 1809 while he was tracking a bear. I say rediscovered because it is known now that he was not the first inhabitant of the cave. Four thousand years ago an Indian culture known as the Adena explored the cave to a depth of two miles. They left behind many artifacts, most importantly dead bodies. The Adena people mined gypsum, which is believed to have been used for ceremonial purposes.

Many of the rangers at Mammoth Cave believe that the Adena are responsible for some of the ghostly happenings that continue to occur there. Some of these happenings can be considered friendly, while some are considered anything but.

Moving now to historical times, about seventy black slaves are known to have mined saltpeter that is found in the soil in the floor of the cave. . . . One story of the saltpeter mining facility told by the rangers is the warning signals sent by the slaves to the visitors and employees at the cave. About three years ago the guides came in to find the largest boulder in the room had crashed into the exact spot where the guides stand to give their speech about the saltpeter mining. The guides think this was a message from the slaves to stay away, that they don't want anyone in the cave. It is felt that the slaves view the guides as intruders.

In 1838 Mammoth Cave had a new owner who brought many slaves to work there. A good number of these slaves came to be known as both guides and explorers. The most widely known of these slaves is Stephen Bishop. He is the one who discovered one of the rivers inside the cave, and also found its great mammoth dome, along with other important rooms and passageways.

Bishop is the main focus of many of the ghost stories told about Mammoth Cave. All of the stories involving Bishop speak of him as helping the people with whom he comes into contact. One park ranger speaks of a strange occurrence that happened three years ago. It is said that a visitor to the cave system had injured himself inside the cave, so a few other rangers were sent in to help get him out. Each ranger always carries along three sources of light when they go inside the cave, a flashlight, a backup flashlight, and a lighter. One of the rangers that went in to help get the visitor out decided to take a shortcut to get to him more quickly. Almost immediately, he found himself lost when his flashlight went out. He retrieved his second light, but it, too, was not working. As a last resort, he got the lighter out of his pocket, but it would not work either. Alone in the horrible pitch-black world of the underground, he quickly became panic-stricken.

He saw a faint light in the far distance and thought it was his party, so he started walking toward the light. As he moved closer to the light, he noticed it was not that of a flashlight; rather it had the shape of an old-fashioned oil lantern. But since it was a light, he kept walking toward it anyway. He still didn't hear any voices. Suddenly, as he got closer to the light, it dashed sharply to the right, then disappeared. At that point in time, he heard voices to his left, and saw the light of a modern flashlight. His companions were not far away. He didn't say anything until they exited the cave. Once on the outside, he checked his lighter and found out that it had plenty of lighter fluid in it.

The ranger and many others will tell you that the light belonged to Stephen Bishop. He is always the ghost who is thought to help people who are lost or in trouble there in the cave because he himself thought the cave to be very frightening at times. Bishop was once quoted as saying, "Mammoth is a grand, gloomy and peculiar place—a place not soon to give up its last, deepest secret."

Another guide there in Mammoth Cave once spoke of actually seeing Bishop. At the Giant's Coffin one ranger was speaking to the visitors and another was trailing the tour, turning off the lights as the tour progressed. Up to the left of the Giant's Coffin is a very steep ledge. The ranger claims that on this ledge he saw an old black man with a stick cane in one hand and a lantern in the other. He was wearing old slave-type clothes and a railroad hat. Stunned, the ranger grabbed his flashlight and shined it up to the ledge and could see the old man staring right down at him. In a flash, whoever it was, was gone. The ranger still believes it was Bishop that he saw that day.

After being used as a saltpeter mine, Mammoth Cave was used as a church and as a tuberculosis hospital run by Dr. Croghan. He had thought that the constant temperature inside the cave would cure the disease. Less than a year later, five people had died, and Dr. Croghan himself died a short time later.

This cave has seen its number of horrid deaths. Some people view this as the reason for the many ghosts that seem troubled or angry. By way of illustration, one time one of the tour guides was at the chute site and was reaching to turn off the lights as the tour progressed. As he bent over he felt a very strong force grab him from behind and actually throw him to the ground. He first thought one of his coworkers had done it as a joke, but upon looking around he found no one there. After the tour was over, he even asked who had thrown him down, but everyone swore that they had nothing to do with it.

Most of the regular tour guides report random pecks on the shoulder, being pushed down, tripped, and even hearing footsteps behind them when no one was supposed to be there.

Approximately five years ago, a renowned psychic came to Mammoth Cave because of all the talk about the ghosts and spirits that were haunting the cave. She specialized in actually being able to "see" the dead who haven't crossed over yet. At first everyone was joking about her seeing Stephen Bishop and some other usual ghosts once you got inside the cave.

When entering the cave one has to go down a series of steps before actually going through the main entrance. As soon as this woman cleared the stairs and started into the cave, she began screaming at the top of her lungs. She was asking the other people there if they could see what she saw; then she began screaming for them to get her out of there. One of the guides had to actually escort her back to the outside, as she refused to go any farther into the cave. Once outside, she was visibly shaking, stating that she literally saw hundreds of people all around the walls of the cave. She screamed out, "They do not want us here."

As stated earlier, it is indeed splendid to explore Mammoth Cave inside and out, but keep an eye out for Stephen Bishop and some of his friends while touring the cave. You never know what you might see.

20. "Jim Rabbit's Woods"

In 1965 our family moved from Murray, Kentucky, to the Rich Pond community here in Warren County. Soon, my brother and I began wandering around and soon learned about some of the stories concerning our new surroundings. One of the stories that comes to mind is about Jim Rabbit's Woods. "The woods is haunted," says one man who is now in his eighty-ninth year, "and I just never go near that place. It's scary."

My question was, "Who is Jim Rabbit?"

Being curious, as most boys are, we visited the woods quite frequently. It became a part of our young lives. I'll never forget the summer when our cousin was visiting from California. We decided to camp in the woods one weekend, trying to arouse some spirits, but to no avail. We made sure that a campfire was kept burning to ward off any wandering animals. Not because we were afraid, of course. If we had been afraid, we would not have been there to begin with. I suppose that we still couldn't help but wonder about the situation we could be putting ourselves in.

We finally drifted off to sleep, after staying awake over half the night. Something seemed not to be quite right about the whole affair. My dog, Brownie, would not go near the woods. She would stop, hold her nose in the air, sniffing and whining as if she could sense something that we couldn't. Still, we never saw anything.

The remains of an old two-room house was still present, although it had been destroyed by fire several years earlier. An old iron bedstead was still standing, covered with a thick overgrowth of weeds. Many other reminders of Jim Rabbit, the one-time inhabitant, were still present. I'm talking about bottles, jars, rusty pots and pans, and the remains of an old potbelly stove near a cellar covered with blackberry briars.

I have always been drawn to that place, going and sitting there time and time again, thinking about the man who once occupied the house. I was also drawn to another place nearby. It was an old overgrown cemetery. I used to ride my bike to this old, neglected churchyard cemetery to read the inscriptions on the stones. At that time I did not know that the old house and the old graveyard were connected. Some thirty years later, I discovered that Jim Rabbit was buried there in an unmarked grave. After searching for information about this mysterious man, I found out that he was a black man and that his real name was James Arthur Moore. He was born in 1887 there in Rich Pond to George W. Moore and Fanny Foster.

It was said that Jim Rabbit sold bootleg moonshine whiskey and was often seen sitting at the L & N railroad crossing at night, peddling his whiskey during Prohibition [1920–1933]. One local resident stated, "He would always be sitting at the railroad crossing and would warn us of his presence, because he didn't want to frighten us as we walked by. He would say, 'It's just me.' He also did handy work in the community for extra money."

Trains often stopped near the Jim Rabbit Woods. The tracks ran alongside Jim's place and made it convenient to board there. Jim would go to Bowling Green in the morning hours, then would be seen coming back on the afternoon freight train. It is said that he paid the engineer with a bottle of his finest.

I eventually learned that Jim had been committed to an insane asylum by a group of men there in the community in the mid to late 1940s. "It was so sad when he was sent away," stated another local resident. "The men did not want an old black man wandering about the neighborhood, although Jim was actually harmless. Really, the rest of the community folk didn't really appreciate these men's actions."

James Arthur Moore, or Jim Rabbit as he was called, died May 9, 1953, and was buried in this old local church cemetery. It has been reported that his spirit has been seen walking the railroad tracks near Rich Pond, usually around dusk or at night, carrying a burlap bag that makes a rattling noise, as if he had it full of glass bottles. According to an elderly woman, "From time to time, you can hear bottles rattling in the dark down near the railroad tracks. It's an odd, lonely sound, fading as if someone is walking away."

Jim Rabbit is gone, but I suppose that he'll always be close by with his whiskey bottles in hand.

21. "The Ghost Rider"

Over the hill from Dewey Lake in Van Lear there was an old tale of a ghost that liked to scare people. This was supposed to have happened on the Johns Creek Hill. It seems that between the mountains, the road got very narrow. People who went that way on horseback were likely to have a ghost jump up behind them and ride over the hill to a certain little cove and then get off. You couldn't see him, only his shadow, and the feeling that he was really there. The horse would go very slowly, and no matter how much the rider tried to hurry him along, he would hardly go at all.

Many years ago, my grandfather told this to my mother. The story must be one hundred years old, for it was told to my grandfather by his father who was in the Civil War. Before my grandfather was born, my great-grandfather was going across the mountain before daylight to get a doctor who lived on the other side. This ghost jumped on the back of the horse and rode over the hill with him, then disappeared.

When this incident was mentioned, the people said that this happened all the time. It makes one wonder if people really believed this, or if they only told it as a tale.

22. "Haint Holler"

The story I'm about to tell happened just below Crockett here in Morgan County.

One night about midnight, sometime around 1900, French Ferguson was walking down the road when all at once he heard a noise coming from the hollow beside the road. He stopped and looked and listened. While he was standing there, he saw a white figure coming out of the holler. When the figure got up closer to him, he saw that it looked like a man without a head. As it came closer, it began to fade away and finally completely disappeared.

For years afterward, people saw lights moving around in the holler at any time of the night. My parents started to build a house where I was born at the mouth of this holler, and people tried their best to keep them from building it because they said a booger lived up in the rock cliff just above the house.

After the house was built no more lights were seen in or around the holler. The booger must have been scared away. I have heard this all my life as the reason this place was called "Haint Holler."

23. "Haunted Rock Cliffs"

This was heard from George Parker, Sam Pike, Clyde Estup, and Joe McKnight. One night they were walking the girls home there at Shields, going up the Ridgeway Hill. There by Trace Gap and through there by the old cave was where the cliffs were located that all the Indians used to camp in. This is the place it is said where the lone wolf dog howls. People have sworn to have seen fireballs there. George Parker does not believe this, as he was a brave man.

As McKnight walked through there, him and his girl and the other three couples—one of the girls, Maggie, pointed to the rock cliffs that were behind them and was scared. To show his bravery and courage, Parker picked a rock up and throwed it against the rock cliffs. The rock cliffs commenced thundering and lightning and pouring down, and fireballs ensued from out of the rock cliffs about a foot in diameter, and red and gold in color, and went right around and around and around in circles. It looked like there was people in there with black hair and headdresses on, a-dancing.

This scared them all and two of the girls fainted. The other one got sick, but it didn't seem to bother none of them too much. All were scared stiff except George Parker. He swore up and down that he wasn't afraid of nothing. He went down and went up to the cliff. They were still dancing around, but the fireballs were slowing down.

He up with another rock and throwed it. This time the fireballs come out two or three times as fast as they had before. On the rocks just beside him there was a skeleton of a young man about twelve or thirteen years old with a Spanish sword in his hand.

Parker stood there frozen in his tracks. He wanted to hit the boy. And he wanted to run but something just held him. When he reached out and touched the boy, the whole earth trembled and thundered and lightened like they had never seen before. And to this day, if you ask Parker what happened, he just shudders in his tracks. And, still, if you go by there at night when the moon is up, you can hear the lone wolf call.

24. "Two Ghosts Fighting at Mill Site"

One evening, two of the Butler boys in Kenton County rode their horses to town and stopped by our house on the way home. They stopped at our house to play with the children, and they enjoyed playing so much that it was just about dark when they got on their horses on their way home.

They rode about a mile to the site of an old mill that had been burned down, when their horses stopped and would not go on in spite of the fellows urging them. On looking down, they saw two men fighting with knives in the dust of the road. They were rolling over and slashing each other with the knives, but they were not making a sound. Both horses had stopped and would not go on. Both boys saw the men fighting.

The two boys turned their horses around and headed back to our house as fast as they could go. When they returned to the spot with some older fellows, there was not a trace of the two men.

25. "The Haunted Mine"

When Brown Logsdon was a young man, he moved to a new farm. On exploration of this farm, he came upon an old abandoned mineshaft. He was curious about this shaft because he had not known that his new property contained it. He went to several neighbors in this little community and was surprised to find that the people were hesitant to discuss it. But on further questioning, he found out that this was a mine which once had a very rich vein.

The vein was also believed to still be there. But the trouble lay in the fact that everyone in the community believed the mine to be haunted. They said that many years ago several men had been killed in a cave-in. When rescuers tried to get to them, there was another cave-in, trapping several of them.

No bodies were ever recovered. To this day, the old mine is believed to be haunted, and it is not a very thickly inhabited place after dark.

26. "The Haunted Cliff"

There is a scary story about a cliff in Upper Maulberry. This cliff is said to be haunted. Dad says that back when he was younger, he and some of his friends went camping down towards Upper Maulberry. There were six men camping above them under that big cliff. Late that night it started misting rain. These six men came running out from under that cliff, shaking, scared, and refused to go stay under that cliff any longer. They said that they heard something like horses pulling a wagon.

There's a story that says there used to be an old logging road around there that log wagons used to travel on. These wagons would go around the top edge of the cliff. Well, one night a wagon was going across the cliff and the horses ran away with the wagon and went over the top of the cliff.

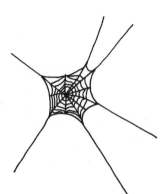

Chapter 12

The Vanishing Hitchhiker

1. "Early Vanishing Hitchhiker"

My grandmother never did say what she'd consider right-down lies. They're either stories that she's heard or things that actually happened to her, I'm just not sure. This story is one that her uncle had told her that happened back in the late 1800s. And there'd been some talk of haunted woods. The woods are still there. They're along Kino Road in Barren County.

What happened was that, even years before my grandmother's uncle had lived in this area, a young doctor and his wife had moved there. The doctor caught her with another man, so the doctor took her out one night and chopped her head off. And there were stories told about people going through these woods and they would hear a bunch of noises, like a bunch of horses coming through. Well, they'd get off the road out of the way, but nothing but a gust of wind would come through.

It so happened that one night my grandmother's uncle was going through these woods to somebody else's house. He heard this noise that sounded like a bunch of horses running by. And so he pulled his horse and buggy off the road. Well, nothing but a gust of wind went by. He got ready to start the horse up again, but the horse wouldn't go. He tried and tried but the horse just wouldn't budge. All of a sudden he heard this lady's voice beside him say, "Can I have a ride?"

He turned around, and there was this young lady standing on the other side of the carriage. He responded, "Sure, hop in."

So the young woman hopped in, and the horse started up by itself. They were just traveling along, and grandmother's uncle asked her, "Where do you want to go?"

She said, "Well, when I get to the place I want to go, I'll hop out."

He said, "Well, I'll have to know where you're going so I can stop when I get there."

And she said, "Don't worry about it."

So they went on and on, and he started to think there was something odd and strange about this woman, because she just seemed weird and eerie. Finally, he decided to try to strike up a conversation with her, but when he turned toward her she had her head sitting in her lap. She was just sitting there with her head in her lap. As they approached this old graveyard my grandmother's uncle was just scared spitless, didn't know what to do. When they got to the graveyard, the horse just stopped by itself; just as if it knew what to do. The lady got out of the carriage, thanked my great uncle, then walked into the graveyard and disappeared. Then the horse just took off running! Even that horse was scared.

2. "Ghost Rides Horse behind Rider"

Back in 1955, I was riding horseback in the dark, up through a holler here in Hardin County. I was going home after being at a friend's house for a visit. I guess it was about 11:00 p.m. As I was passing between two cliffs, something pounced on the back of my horse. I turned around to look see what it was, but nothing was there. I got scared, so I kicked the horse into a fast gallop.

As the horse was running down the road, I suddenly felt two arms wrapped around me, and some hands gripping my chest. I could feel the pressure of each finger as it made an indention into my chest. I looked around again when the moon was shining, but could still not see anything there on the horse with me.

When I finally reached my house and got off the horse, this thing—this hitchhiker—also got off, because the pressure was no longer there. I was very scared but never knew what that thing was that hitchhiked up behind me on my horse.

3. "The Girl Who Keeps Vanishing"

We have a little restaurant in town that all the teenagers refer to as the Greasy Spoon, or Ptomaine Palace. But a long time ago, it was referred to as the Sturgis Cafe. We get a lot of traveling salesmen in here. My dad and I were up there when this guy came in and sat down at the table with us and started talking to my dad. He told about this eerie incident that happened to him on this route that he makes.

He comes through Union County, then goes down through Murray, goes down into Tennessee, cuts back up through Bowling Green, and comes back up through this way.

Anyway, I was a little bitty kid when he and my dad were sitting there talking. He told about the time that he was right outside a little town close to Nashville, and he saw this beautiful blonde woman standing alongside the road. She had on a long, beautiful dress. They were about a half mile outside this town, and he stops and asks her if he can give her a ride into this town.

She said, "Yes, I'd appreciate it."

She got into the car, so he took her into town and asked her where she wanted to go.

She said, "Just take me down this street and turn there by the big church sitting there on the corner. You can just let me out there."

So he pulled up in front of the church. It was very dark. There was nobody in the church, and no lights were on. He asked her, "Are you sure that this is the church you want to go to?"

She said, "Yes, it is."

Well, he let her out and he went on, made his route.

About three months later, he approached this town at practically the same time as it was when he was through here the last time. Well, so help me, the woman was standing along the side of the road again, long beautiful blue dress, pretty blonde hair. He stopped, said, "Hi, do you remember me?"

She responded, "No, I don't."

He said, "Well, I gave you a ride the last time I came through. Can I offer you a ride to town again?"

She said, "Yes, you can."

She gets into the car. He asks her, "Where do you want to go this time?"

She said, "The same place."

He said, "Do you mean the big church?"

She told him, "Yeah."

So he takes her to the church, pulls up, and again it's pitch dark. There's nobody there. She gets out and goes in.

Three months later, the same thing happens again. He picked up the lady, took her to the church. But it upset him so much that there was no-body there that he decided to stop to make sure that everything was all right. So he stopped at this little diner, got out, went in, and talked to this guy at the bar. Told him about the strange thing that had happened to him the last three times he had come through here.

A funny look came over this guy behind the counter. He turns real white. He says, "Charlie, I don't want to upset you, but that woman has been dead for three or four years. And there's been two or three people that have seen her out on that road just like you did. I'd advise you the next time that you come through, just don't stop. Keep right on going."

4. "The Vanishing Girl"

Some college guys were going to a dance when they saw this girl in a laven-der dress on the side of the road hitchhiking. They picked her up and took her to the dance with them. On the way, she complained of being cold, so one of the fellows gave her his jacket to wear. After the dance, they took her home and dropped her off out front of her house.

The fellow later remembered that he had left his jacket with her, so they went back to her house to get it. A man answered the door, and looked funny at the guy when he explained what had happened. The man told him that it couldn't have been his daughter, because she had died a year ago, and that if he didn't believe him, he could go and look at her grave out in the backyard.

The guy went and looked because he was sure he had the right house. Well, there on the girl's grave was his jacket, and in the jacket pocket was her photograph that she had given him earlier that evening.

5. "Sweater Found Hanging across Girl's Gravestone"

One time this boy was going out at night, but he didn't have a date. So when he was driving down the road, he saw a beautiful young girl walking alone along the side of the road. He wondered why she was by herself when it was almost night. He thought that maybe she might be in some sort of trouble, so he stopped to ask her if she'd like a ride somewhere. The girl said, "Yes," and got in the car but she didn't say where she was going.

They talked for a while, and this guy really was liking her, so he asked her if she'd go out with him that night.

She did, and they had a real good time. Later, when they were driving home, it was almost midnight. The girl told him that she had to be home by twelve.

It was a real cold night, so the guy gave her his sweater to keep her warm. When they got to the front door, the girl told him goodbye and went in the house.

Well, when the guy got a few miles down the road, he realized that she still had his sweater, so he decided just to wait until the next day, then go back and get it.

The next day, he went back to the girl's house, and a man answered his knock at the door. When the boy asked the man if he could see his daughter, the man got real mad and told the guy to get out and get lost.

Finally, the guy convinced the girl's father that he didn't mean any harm. The man then told this guy the truth—that his daughter had died a year ago last night. This guy just couldn't believe that he'd been out with the girl's ghost. He asked the father to take him to see the girl's grave. When they got there, the sweater he had lent her to take away the chill was hanging across the girl's grave marker. And, sure enough, the date of her death was exactly one year ago from last night.

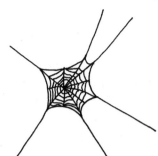

Chapter 13

Felt Presences of Ghostly Beings

1. "Mother's Presence in Room Felt by Her Daughters"

My grandmother died in February 1988. She and my aunt lived together in a house that was extremely large for two older women. After my grandmother died, my aunt insisted on remaining in the house, even though it meant living alone.

In May of that year, my mother moved in with my aunt due to some family problems. When I returned from school at the end of the spring semester, I lived with my mother and aunt for about two weeks, until our family problems were ultimately resolved. Following this, I moved back into my original home.

One day late last summer, my mother asked me if anything strange had happened to me in my aunt's house. Naturally, I knew something was going on, so I asked my mother to tell me exactly what had happened.

She told me that one night just after she had gone to bed, she was thinking about our family crisis and what she needed to do to help resolve it. About this time, the door to her room, which had previously been my grandmother's room, opened of its own accord. However, she said that she instinctively felt that it was my grandmother. Every hair on her body stood straight up, but she said that she wasn't at all scared. She kept her eyes closed because she had the sensation that if she opened them, she would see an almost blinding light. The felt presence there in the room was comforting, as though her mother had returned to help her through her time of trouble. After a few minutes, the felt presence of her mother was gone; the feeling had passed.

My mother never told her sister about this incident, because she was afraid that it would scare the sister. In addition, she didn't tell any of us until some time later for fear that we would not believe her.

In late July, my aunt called my mother at work to inform her of some strange incidents that had been taking place there in the house. Every night after she went to bed, my aunt heard the "kick up" noise made by the arm-chair, the chair that my grandmother, her mother, used to sit in at night. My aunt just knew that it was her mother sitting there, reclining in the chair. That was rather strange to her, as she knew that there was no one there to operate the chair. Besides, the chair was no longer there in the room, for after my grandmother's death my aunt had given the armchair to another one of our relatives. The chair was not even in the house any more.

My mother and my aunt both feel that the spirit of their mother did indeed come back to visit with them after her death.

2. "Something Sat Down beside Me"

I was at my friend Lisa's house a few months back. She had told me on different occasions about ghost-like presences that she had encountered in this house. Needless to say, the house is considered to be haunted.

Anyway, when I was there, a tornado watch was announced and was to be in effect for the entire night. Well, about an hour later, all the lights went out. The house was in total darkness, except for the light of the moon still shining through the window. I could see Lisa's mother and her friend standing by the window. Lisa had also been there, but she had just left to go to the restroom.

I sat down on the couch, still afraid of what might happen that night. While I was sitting there on the couch, I felt the cushion go down as if someone were sitting next to me. But I could see that there was no one on the couch but me. I was all alone. It didn't really scare me, but I truly felt uneasy about the possibility that something just might be there. So I got up off the couch and walked over and stood by Lisa's mother and friend until the lights came back on a few minutes later.

3. "Unexplained Presence"

One night my boyfriend and I were out riding around in this rural area with lots of woods, fields, and dark gravel roads. Riding around is what most people in this area do for entertainment.

The fellow that I was with and I had been out for about three hours. It was around 11:30 p.m. He had been drinking a few beers. I hadn't. Anyway, when we got to Zion Church, he got out of the car to relieve himself.

Zion Brick is an old frame church building that has been bricked over. It is in a fairly secluded area, surrounded by trees and a graveyard. It is where many local teenagers go to drink beer and park.

That night, no one was there when we pulled into the drive leading to the church. My boyfriend circled the church and then stopped the car. Before getting out, he leaned over to kiss me. Suddenly, the car moved. At first, it felt as if the car were out of gear and rolling backwards. Then it began to shake violently.

I told him, "Stop shaking the car," thinking he was playing some kind of trick.

"I'm not shaking it; honest I'm not."

The shaking stopped just as suddenly as it had started. It was then that I began to be aware of a coldness, not in the air but within myself. It gradually grew stronger.

"I'll bet it's some of them boys doing something to us," my boyfriend suggested.

Then he opened the door of the car and stepped outside. "I'll bet that rascal Keenan is out here someplace behind a tombstone laughing at us," he commented.

I was becoming terrified at the coldness that I was feeling. It was very strong and very oppressive. I felt as if I were being watched. As soon as he got back in the car, I insisted that we leave there. He laughed at my fear and said that even a ghost couldn't hurt us.

I wasn't afraid of the shaking of the car, but of the strong presence that I felt. However, as soon as we drove away from the church, the sense of an unexplained presence vanished.

4. "The Cheerleader Who Felt Her Dead Father's Presence"

I was a sixteen-year-old cheerleader at the time this happened. We were playing Caverna High School in a football game there in Hart County. It was a very peculiar night. Everything was so calm that you could even refer to it as eerie. The sky was a solemn blend of blue, red, and black; the air was still, not a trace of a breeze in the air.

There were sixteen cheerleaders on the field at that time, and all of us commented about the strange presence that seemed to be hovering around us. We all felt just as if something bad, or at least strange, was about to happen. When we began discussing the different feelings that we were experiencing, one of our cheerleaders—I'll refer to her as Cam—became somewhat hysterical and started crying. It wasn't long until she commenced screaming. She then told us that she felt the presence of her father there on the football field, just as if he were standing there looking at her.

Her father had committed suicide three years earlier.

5. "Felt Presence of Suicidal Male Student"

An incident took place in 1980 in a basement apartment on Kentucky Street, here in Bowling Green. It happened to my friend, Pam. Her boyfriend Calvin had just committed suicide, and, of course, Pam was devastated.

For weeks after this, Pam's roommate, Kela, slept with her. One night while they were in bed, they felt a cold wind sweep through the room, just like the door had been opened. Then, all of a sudden, Pam's shadow box blew across the room. After that happened, they both felt a presence crawl into bed with them and lie there between them. They both screamed, "Calvin," as they just knew that it was Calvin. He had always hated Pam's shadow box while he was still alive.

While Calvin lay there between them, Pam tried to talk with him, but he would not respond. He then sat up and scooted down to the edge of the bed, as if he were alive. They felt him get up from the bed and heard steps leaving the room. They lay there freaking out, and the last thing they heard was the front door slam.

Calvin would come back to that room to visit them from time to time. Finally, they could take no more, so they moved out of the apartment. Other people later told them that Calvin had stayed on in that same apartment, the one he had known and liked when he was alive.

6. "Ghostly Presence, or Realistic Dream?"

During a lot of nights, I have felt that there was someone else in my room with me. Well, one night the feeling was very strong. I got very scared. I wanted to know if there was indeed something there, and just what it was.

I didn't see anything, so I finally dropped off to sleep. Not long afterwards, I woke up and there were many things in my room. I can't describe them all, but I recall that they held a book and wanted me to sign it. I refused to sign it, and this made them really mad. Well, I ran out of that room, for I was scared to death of what they might do to me. I finally went back in and went back to bed, as I didn't see anything there in the room at that time.

Well, the next morning I thought about it a lot while I was getting ready to go to school. All the time that I was getting ready, I felt that whatever or whoever it was that I had witnessed last night was mad at me and would do something to get even.

I got ready to leave and was looking for my keys. They were almost always on the table, so I looked there. But when I did, they were nowhere to be seen. I even brought in the trash from the night before, thinking that they might be in there.

I began to feel as if the thing I had felt last night was there in my room again. After looking through the trash, something told me to look back at the table. Sure enough, it was there, or truly it felt as if something were sitting there. I never knew what it was, and I have never experienced anything like that since then.

Chapter 14
Civil War Ghosts

1. "Haunted Home Near Ft. Boonesboro"

There's an old haunted house near Ft. Boonesboro that has been the home of five generations of the same family since the Civil War era. The house is situated on a very tall hill. It has tall windows reaching from the floor to the ceiling, and doors with paneling that gives the impression of a cross.

A family that moved there in 1956 reported numerous supernatural occurrences. That family felt that all the repair and renovation work they did to the structure caused a spirit, or spirits, to resist their structural activities. Numerous felt presences were reported, and some sightings of ghostly beings have occurred.

When this family moved away, a tenant family moved in. They didn't stay long, however, and are known to have left due to ghostly occurrences. In 1979, original family members moved back into the house.

They, too, did repair work on the house, most of which was done by hired help—hired help that didn't stick around too long due to ghostly movements, sounds, and lights. They left, refusing to come back and finish their work.

The family now thinks that the ghostly occurrences may have been caused by a Yankee soldier who was buried outside. A bayonet from Civil War times was found in the walls during the renovation work on the house.

The ghosts are no longer seen, perhaps due to the removal of the soldier's bayonet.

2. "Ghostly Civil War Rider"

Jonathan Buck was a Civil War soldier, and he was the first person ever buried on Buck Mountain here in Wayne County. He was in the Union Army and his family lived up there on that mountain.

He came home on a furlough and took sick, or something happened to him, and he died before he ever went back. But he brought a fine horse home with him, likely a stolen horse.

When he died, his family sold this horse to an old man that lived in Denney Hollow, down below the mountain. His name was Matt Denney. He was riding this horse coming home one night. When he got over in a field close to where Jonathan was buried, Jonathan jumped onto the horse behind him. Well, that scared this fellow and that horse so bad that, when they come to the gate, that horse just jumped over it. They said that Denney was just thrown up into the air, screaming something awful.

This fellow Denney wouldn't even unsaddle his horse that night. Left it out there in the yard. He said that it snorted all night.

Well, up there where Buck is buried, foxhunters have heard things up there. My husband, Hershel, never did believe that anything ghost-like could be heard there on Buck Mountain. At least, not until he and four other fellows were up there one night, sitting right close to that cemetery. Something commenced making such a noise that Larry Howard spoke up and said, "These old bones are gonna rise again."

The noise just kept on and on. It came on up there right by these men, but they never could see anything. Finally, they went to shooting at the noise. They still didn't see anything, but my husband now believes that there was a ghost-thing up there.

Then, there's two other men, Bart Piercy and German Kennedy, that went hunting up there. And there's a little spring of water that comes out of the ground right below the cemetery. They got down to get them a drink of that water, but when they did they could hear music coming out of the water.

Of course, that scared the daylights out of them, but they never did see what was making that music.

3. "Ghostly Noises of Civil War Skirmish"

Back up here in Denney Hollow is where the noise of the skirmish between these two guerrillas, Champ Ferguson and Tinker Dave Beatty, was heard. I've heard that myself. It's just screams and groans, all kinds of noises. If you hear it, you'll never forget it.

I just heard it that one time. I was here in the house and heard that noise right back up here in the field. That was where I guess they were camping during the Civil War. Of course, some of them were also camping down in the bottom here.

I can remember that when I was just a small girl, they were hearing the noise at that time. At first, they thought it was just hogs or something making that noise. When they'd go out to try to figure what it was, that noise would just go away. They never could catch up with it.

Well, one night I heard it. And I don't want to hear it no more. That was back in 1942. My folks were here in the house. I was on the outside, alone. It just sounded like a lot of people and they were screaming, and groaning, and struggling. It was so awful that you couldn't tell just exactly what it was. I was so scared that if there were gunshots, I didn't hear them. I guess that I just heard the men a-dying in that battle. There were some graves found up there later on.

Two or three years ago, my son-in-law Roby Rednour was up here at the church house, sitting there listening to his hounds run a fox. All of a sudden, he heard the sounds of these men a-dying in that battle. He's not from here, so he had never heard about those ghostly cries and screams. But he heard them that day, and he came to the house as soon as he could, asking what in the world those noises were all about.

I guess Roby was the last to hear the noises. You don't hear anything like that anymore. These days, people are in their houses with their television on. Even if they're out on the road, they're in a car and they don't hear it. You've got to be out and everything be quiet enough for you to hear things.

4. "Deathly Screams of Slaves"

There are numerous stories told about people that come back to earth as spirits or ghosts to seek revenge for their deaths. The way that some of the old black slaves died would be a good example of what I'm talking about. Take for example this big old colonial house located here in southwestern Pulaski County on the corner of Garland Road and Highway U.S. 27. It is said that this used to be an old plantation house, whose owner had many slaves. They said that he often beat and abused his slaves; just did it over and over again.

People say that you can sometimes still hear the slaves screaming in pain and, at other times, you can see their misty-like forms floating out there in the field.

Hershel Edwards of Powersburg, Wayne County, preparing to go fox hunting in 1958 on the hillside and wooded area behind him, where the mournful cries and sounds of Civil War soldiers killed in a local skirmish had been heard many times by the local residents. (Photograph provided by Hattie Edwards)

5. "Woman Hanged during Civil War"

My uncle Dink Freeman came home from this date he had back in 1961. When he got home, he went into the kitchen and got a drink of something before he went to bed.

He went back into the living room, and would you believe it, there was a ghost-like figure of a woman walking slowly down the stairway. She had on a white dress. Uncle Dink went over and turned on a light, but the woman was gone. He never did see her again and could never figure out why he had seen what he did.

About fifteen years later, in the mid 1970s, Uncle Dink was visiting Mrs. Witt, the elderly lady who owned the house that his family occupied at that time. For some reason, Uncle Dink was looking through one of her old closets and he found a photograph of the woman in white whom he had seen on the stairway fifteen years earlier. Mrs. Witt identified the person in the photograph as her great-great-aunt Jackie Witt, then told him that Jackie Witt was hanged on her wedding night back during the Civil War.

6. "Ghosts of Girls Raped and Killed by Soldiers during the Civil War"

Back in the 1860s, during the Civil War, a very wealthy family, the Feeses, lived in a remote mansion in or near Columbia, Kentucky. This old mansion is still there today and is located on top of a big hill. Right behind the mansion is a steep drop-off overlooking a cliff. At the bottom of this cliff is an old mill that the Feese family owned and operated.

At that time, all the men who lived in this house were away from home fighting in the Civil War. The women were living alone in the old mansion. One night, a group of Union soldiers came to the mansion and took all the woman down to the base of the cliff. Then they raped them, dragged them into the old mill building, where they killed every one of them.

Well, one night some of my friends and I went up there. We just wanted to see what we'd been told, and to check it out for ourselves. We were standing there on the edge of the cliff looking down at the mill. All of a sudden we heard cries and screams coming from the old mill, probably those of the women who were raped and murdered. Since then, I've gone up there several times, and have always heard the same sounds. Truly, I heard these ghostly noises; I'm not just making this up.

The man who owns the house now is afraid to tear down the old mill house. He believes that the ghosts we keep hearing will move into this house he lives in and stay there forever.

7. "Soldiers' Moans Heard"

Just south of Somerset is a place called Ferguson. There is an old abandoned house there in Ferguson which is said to have been used during the

Civil War as a sanitarium. The people who owned the house doctored soldiers in the basement, on a dirt floor.

There is a bricked tunnel that leads out of the basement to only God
knows where. Nobody knows where it went to because that old tunnel was
bricked and blocked off since then.

It is said that if you stand on the outside over where that old tunnel is
said to have run, you can sometimes hear the soldiers moaning and groaning in agony and pain.

8. "Union Soldier's Ghost in Livia"

"You may think I'm crazy but there are strange things going on in this
house," confided a Livia woman. "We've all heard strange noises, but my
husband says, 'It's rats.' Well, rats don't walk like people."

The mother of two college-age daughters doesn't like to talk about
the strange-looking man she saw watching her in one of their upstairs bedrooms, because she knows most people don't believe in ghosts. And those
that do are suspect.

She was skeptical until they unsuspectingly moved into the old two-
story home three years ago.

"People in Livermore and Island say they knew the house was haunted.
I only wish they had bothered to tell us before we bought it," she declares.

However, she accepts it philosophically. She's never afraid in the daytime, but she doesn't like to be alone at night.

The apparition she saw just as plain as day was a short, stocky man
with a hat, little pointed beard, a collarless shirt, and bib overalls. A big
watch chain hung on the front of his overalls. "He just stood and looked at
me," she stated.

One of the girls has felt a cold draft on the stairs. Both have heard the
footsteps.

There is a door in the girls' bedroom upstairs that leads to a long hall.
If they don't put a piece of furniture in front of it before they go to bed, the
next morning it is always open.

One night one of them felt something on the bed, but couldn't see
anything.

One night a guest spent the night on the couch in the living room.
The next morning he reported that he saw a woman with long hair floating
across the living room.

At other times the mother has been aware of a presence close by.
"Have you ever felt like someone was breathing on you?" she asks.

In trying to fathom the mystery of the old house, one of the daughters and a friend decided to ask the Ouija board who it was doing the haunting.

They came up with a scrambled story of Civil War times. A Union sympathizer had a sixteen-year-old son who favored the South. To prevent him from joining the Confederacy, he placed his son in a cellar under the stairs where the boy died when the cellar accidentally caved in. "Jimmy wants out," the Ouija board spelled out. It also said the man walking up and down the stairs was a Union soldier.

9. "Ghost Sews at Night"

I've heard my mother tell about going to Aunt Rachel Kelly's. I don't know, but I think she was Uncle Jimmy Kelly's wife. Tim Lee Carter would know; he'd know just exactly. There's a place called the Red House. Its back up here in the edge of Metcalfe County.

And she stayed all night there that night. She said that they was like pistols would fire in the fireplace. She said there was something that would just whisper, whip across the floor just like somebody a-walking all night. She said along about one o'clock that night the sewing machine went to sewing. Said she thinks to herself, "Well, what in the world is Aunt Rachel sewing for this time of night? Why it's nearly daylight!"

And said she could hear the cloth, hear them rip it, and hear the scissors a-snapping. Said the next morning, said Aunt Rachel come and set down on the side of her bed. Said, "Sara Bell, did you sleep good last night?"

"No," she says, "there is some kind of racket here. I want to know what you was a-doing sewing on the sewing machine?"

"Why," she says, "Child, I didn't use the sewing machine last night."

"Well," she says, "I thought, why would you be sewing at twelve o'clock in the night?"

Rachel says, "I'm going to tell you, none of my boys won't sleep in this room." She says, "They say that this room is haunted. I don't know. Now, in the basement here under this room, there were some people killed in the time of the Civil War. The blood stains are still on the side of the walls down there now."

10. "The Civil War in the 1970s"

In the mid 1970s my family and I moved into a very old house in Wolfe County, in the community of Helechawa. The house had been built before the Civil War and was a large, two-story home with high ceilings and spacious rooms as was common during that era. A wide hallway ran the length of the building, with a stairway leading to the second floor.

We lived in the house for more than a year before anything strange became evident. It began after our eleven-year-old son decided to move from his downstairs bedroom to a larger one upstairs. Shortly thereafter, Bobby began telling us of vivid dreams—at least he thought they were dreams, in which a young man lying on a bed opposite my son's bed (in the room now occupied by Bobby) would beseech, "No, no! Don't hurt my mother! Just take me and leave her alone. I'm the one you want." Then shots would ring out and Bobby would awaken from his "dream."

One morning after Bobby reported having the dream again, I was walking past the stairway when I became aware of an odor much like that from a gun which had just been fired—and it seemed to be wafting down from the upstairs. The wiring in the house was very old; thus, my first thought was of an electrical fire. I searched frantically but could find nothing to indicate a fire. Finally, I gave up although the smell lingered for nearly an hour.

This sequence of events happened several times. First, Bobby would have his "dream," and soon, usually around ten o'clock, I would again smell the odor of gunsmoke.

On a bright, sunny morning in late spring, I was in my bed when I heard what sounded like a gunshot in the living room, which was directly under Bobby's room. I ran to the scene but could find nothing—except a broken ash tray.

The large, heavy ash tray lay in three perfect pie-shaped pieces. There were no slivers of glass, as one would expect from broken glass, just an ash tray laying in three perfectly intact pieces, all of identical size. It was as if the ash tray had simply exploded apart of its own accord.

We asked an elderly neighbor, who had ties with the original owners through his grandfather, of the history of the house. That was when we learned about the incident which had occurred in the room where Bobby slept.

It seems that when the hostilities between the states broke out, the older sons marched off to fight with the Union, but the youngest son (then only in his teens) ran away to join the Confederate Army.

A year later he was wounded and brought home to recuperate. Within a week, on a fine spring morning, a band of outlaws and bushwhackers, under guise of Union affiliation, came to the home and demanded that the injured boy be turned over to them. The young man's mother knew their intent was to murder her son, and being there alone, ran up the stairs and threw her body upon that of her son's, in order to protect him.

The murderous thugs charged up the stairs after her, and as mother pleaded for her son's life, and son begged for his mother's life, the outlaws dragged the woman off the bed and shot the boy before her very eyes. The bandits then ransacked the house and stole much of value then rode away toward Hazel Green to continue their rampage and thieving.

Later, a bullet hole was discovered in the ceiling of the parlor, with the bullet itself embedded in the floor—just where my end table (with the beautiful blue ash tray) sat more than one hundred years later!

We lived there for another year, but the incident with the ash tray was the last of our encounters with the house's troubled past, and Bobby's disturbing dreams, or ghostly visitations, finally came to an end.

11. "The Ghost at Brammer Gap"

The Civil War also took place here in eastern Kentucky as well as in other parts of the South. And ever since then, horses' hoofs, screams, and the noises of battle have been heard at Brammer Gap. Mr. Brammer was killed during the War and ever since then, the doors of his home there will not stay closed. The doors to that old house continue to open and close throughout the night.

12. "Confederate Soldier's Ghost"

When I was about ten or twelve, I had this little friend who was a Humfleet. Her mother was crippled in both feet, but she was a very jolly person. We visited the Humfleets in July. . . . When we got there, Mrs. Humfleet sent Flossy and I on an errand. We went up this little road. On one side was a grove of trees, and on the other side the ground sloped down hill. . . . There were young sassafras trees and blackberry briar vines thick all over this field.

As we walked along, Flossy said to me, "Who in the world is that man riding through all that brush?"

"I don't know him. He's going right through those briars, and not making a noise, or moving the bushes," I said.

"He has on a uniform like Grandpaw Sparkles' [when he was in the war]," Flossy said.

Then the man disappeared into the deeper brush. The whole thing was a mystery to us because we knew everybody in this end of the mountains. When we got back from the errand, we told Flossy's folks. They were surprised and couldn't imagine who in his right mind would be riding through rough brush in an old Confederate uniform.

The incident was forgotten for a while. It wasn't until I was visiting Mrs. Stansbury that the thing came up again. She was very curious about the whole thing and made me tell her exactly where it happened. Then she told me her story that really made me wonder.

When she was a little girl she lived with her aunt. They had heard a wagon load of salt was coming in from Virginia. That was a rare occasion, so they went to meet it and get some salt. They traveled over the same road where they saw this mysterious rider. She and her aunt, when they were on the exact spot where we saw the rider, heard something moaning. This startled them, but they got off their horse and went down into the field and found an old Confederate soldier lying there wounded.

They loosened his clothing, got him some water from a nearby stream, and promised him that they would send a man after him. Then they rode on to meet the salt wagon. They told some men about the soldier, and they went and got him and were taking him to a house, but he died on the way.

This really makes me wonder if this wasn't something really strange. I wouldn't have believed it if Flossy and I hadn't both seen him, but we did. And then Mrs. Stansbury's tale—it really makes you wonder if we didn't see a ghost.

13. "The Blue-Gray Hants of Bishop's Hill"

The term "hant" and "ghost" both refer to the same sort of supernatural or spiritual being, and here in this part of Pulaski County people still talk about the blue hants of Bishop's Hill. The majority of long-time Pulaski residents are definitely aware of the legend about these blue hants.

The setting for a blue hant discussion is usually after a large family meal, about dusk, when the kids are anxious to explore the woods and the old graveyard on Bishop's Hill. They never go after dark, however.

My family has lived for generations in a small, rural area called Possum Trot, which is where Bishop's Hill is located. The graveyard is on the side of the hill and at the bottom of the hill is Jessie's Spring, also notorious for blue hants. People stay away from these places after the sun goes down. The blue hants are extremely territorial. The only thing to do when a blue hant confronts you is to run away and hope that it doesn't follow you.

The best I can tell, explanation for the blue hants comes from Civil War times. There was a Union soldier who got shot during the war, and he barely escaped from the Battle of Dutton's Hill. He was taken in by one of my ancestors. My people back then were from the South and didn't want to be accused of being Northern sympathizers. They put the Union soldier in their basement. He was there for about three days, and on the third day when my ancestors went to check on him, they thought he was dead. They buried this Union soldier on Bishop's Hill. He was the first person to be buried there, so this started the graveyard.

After the dirt was put over the grave, they paid their respects, but about that time the dirt started moving. The soldier hadn't died at all. They decided that he would die anyway because he was in such bad condition, so they left him there. Not long after that, a Confederate soldier was buried there right next to the Union soldier. That was when it was decided to make a community cemetery out of it. A lot of my family ancestors have been buried there. I strongly believe that the blue hants legend comes from the story of these two soldiers. I think that the "blue" part of the blue hants comes from the death of the Union soldier who was buried in his blue uniform. And the color of the Southern soldier's uniform was blue-gray, thus helping to explain the term "blue hants."

14. "Murdered Soldier's Ghost"

Last summer while taking an outing with a friend through the eastern portion of Nelson County, night overtook us while on the road to Louisville. No habitation was to be seen. Riding on for some distance we espied a large frame house a little ways from the highway, and here we concluded to seek shelter for the night. Riding up to the door we dismounted from our bicycles and knocked for admittance. Receiving no answer, we opened the door and discovered that the house was unoccupied. Not knowing how much farther we might have to travel before finding shelter, we decided to spend the night where we were.

The apartment we entered was large and roomy, as we could see by the bright moonlight that streamed through the windows. Finding some dry sticks in a corner we made a fire, as the night was chilly. We then lay down on the floor and were soon sleeping soundly.

About midnight I awoke without any seeming cause. The moon had gone down and the room was in total darkness. Looking up I saw a bluish light dancing on the ceiling; then suddenly a bright light appeared at all the windows and the room was brilliantly illuminated for a few minutes. Turning to arouse my companion I found him awake, and he told me that he had observed all from the beginning. From the adjoining room came sounds like glasses being broken, chairs and tables overturned, mingled with loud quarreling and cursing. Then came the sound of a revolver being rapidly discharged. The light then disappeared as suddenly as it came, and all sounds ceased.

We were badly frightened and did not know what to make of the noises we had just heard, as we had observed all the rooms before retiring, and all were destitute of furniture of any kind. We collected ourselves enough to stir our fire, as it had burned almost out, and looking at our watches we found it near morning, so we decided to remain no longer, and mounting our wheels rode rapidly away from the uncanny house.

We rode four miles to the small town of Mt. Washington, where we stopped at a boarding house for breakfast. We told the landlord our experience of the night before. When we finished our recital, he informed us that the house at which we had spent the night was known as "The Haunted House," that no one would live there for any length of time. Then he related to us the following story of the house:

During the Civil War a family resided there who kept an inn. One night some half-dozen Federal soldiers stopped there. Soon after supper they engaged in a game of cards. They were all drinking and were very noisy, and one, a young soldier named McCorkhill, was very abusive and accused one of his comrades of cheating him. Finally the men clenched and a general fight followed. The table was overturned and the glasses shattered and the chairs thrown across the room and broken. McCorkhill pulled his revolver to shoot, but his adversary wrestled the weapon from him and fired several shots at McCorkhill. During the melee the lights were extinguished, and when quiet was restored it was found that McCorkhill was dead, having been shot through the heart. His comrades and murderer carried the body out and buried it in a corner of the garden, and the grave is still to be seen.

"The owner of the property sold it shortly after the war and went West. The present owner can never get a tenant to occupy the house for any length of time."

Louisville, Ky. J.G.C.

Chapter 15

Haunted Dorms, Fraternities, and Sororities

1. "Strange Noises behind Dorm Door"

I went to this Lindsey-Wilson College in 1975. They had one girls' dormitory and its kinda built in a square. It's a large, two-story building, but the second story of the building had remained unfinished for several years. It was just a shell up there: just the walls, but no finish.

I didn't realize that no one lived upstairs at the time I moved into the dorm. I recall that as I was unpacking and getting all settled in, I heard a loud noise right above my room. I heard somebody dragging something across the floor up there. I didn't think much about it at that time. I just thought that somebody who lived upstairs was awfully noisy. Later on when my roommate, a second year student there, came back I told her about it. And she told me that no one lived upstairs, but that strange things happened up there.

She also told me the old story about how the dorm was haunted upstairs in one of the rooms. Supposedly, years ago one of the girls had gotten pregnant and hanged herself in the room. That room has been haunted ever since that happened.

Now, that's just a story told on campus, but there really were some strange things that happened. I remember my roommate telling me that she had heard a loud noise upstairs. And said that she was president of the girls' dorm. She and the dorm mother went upstairs, and you need to understand that all the doors were locked. Only the dorm mother had a key to the doors, and she doesn't even want anybody to walk up the stairs.

Well, they went up this one night, and they kept hearing this loud noise. They went right to this one room where so many strange things happened. She said that she and the dorm mother kept hearing this loud noise, and when they went to open up the door, the door was stuck, not as if it were locked, but as if someone were standing there holding the door from the other side.

She got down on the floor and looked underneath the door. Said that she saw this green mist, which other people claimed that they had seen. It was a green mist that kinda hovered over the floor. But she couldn't see anybody's feet on the floor on the other side of the door.

The two of them kept on and on trying to get in the room, but whatever it was wouldn't release the door on the other side. Finally, the dorm mother told them that she was going to shoot, that she had a gun. She shot through the door and the door came open, but there was no one there, and there was no sign that anyone had been in the room. There was no green mist on the floor anymore. They really thought that was strange.

2. "Ghostly Footsteps in the Hallway"

Several times here in this dorm, girls would hear something late at night, like 2:00 a.m. or 3:00 a.m., walking up and down the halls. They'd hear the footsteps right outside of their door, thus would think that it was somebody coming to their room. But when they'd open up the door, nobody would be there. Half the girls were too scared to get up and go to the bathroom by themselves at night.

3. "The Dorm Ghost"

When I was there in this college dorm back in the early 1980s, I remember the night that we heard this loud noise. Ms. Chumbley, the dorm director at the time, had asked me to go with her. And I recall that we kept hearing this loud noise, like someone was banging on the walls upstairs.

We tiptoed up the stairs just as quietly as we could. We heard this loud noise that sounded like it was coming from right on the other side of the door. She unlocked the door, and the second that the door came open the noise stopped. We searched through the whole upstairs, went to that back room and searched it. While in that room, for the first time we noticed that some sawdust had been lightly sprinkled over some wood. This wood had been cut from where they had been building and just stopped. There were footprints in the sawdust. At that time we didn't know whether they were fresh prints or whether we just hadn't noticed them before.

We began sprinkling powder down all over that room, and all up and down the hall, and at the exits. We went back downstairs, locking all the doors behind us. The next day, we went back up to check things out, and there were fresh footprints all up and down the halls, and all over that room by the exits. But all the doors were still bolted shut, and nothing looked as if it had been touched.

This room that we're talking about overlooks the campus. You can see it from just about everywhere you stand on campus. Several times people would come and talk about how they had seen a figure of a person sitting up there in that room looking out the window; just looking out over campus.

One night in particular that I remember, I was coming back from the student union building and I looked up and saw a light on in that room, and I saw the figure of a person sitting there at the window looking out.

Most generally, guys were not allowed in the dorm. But for some reason that night they were allowed in the girls' lounge. So we came in and I told them that there was somebody upstairs looking out that window. Ms. Chumbley had all the guys surround the dorm on the outside. They had some of the guys to climb up on the roof, had them to stand in all the exits. They let every one in the dorm, the girls and the guys that were there. They went upstairs through all the exits, and Ms. Chumbley unlocked the doors and we all went through different doors and met in the middle of the upstairs dorm. You could hear these sounds upstairs, like someone was there banging on the walls. But when we met in the middle, no one had seen anyone or anything, and we couldn't find any signs of anybody being up there.

But the sounds stopped. There is no way that anyone could have gotten out, because there was someone standing by every exit, and there was someone standing on the roof. No one could have gotten on the roof, because there were people up there watching out for strange things.

We went through the dorm that night with a fine-tooth comb, but we found nothing or anybody standing around. That really gave us more concern than anything else, I guess.

What scared me more than anything, I remember one weekend something that happened to me personally. I don't remember if this weekend was a holiday or what, but it seems like it was a long weekend, because most of the people in the dorm went home that weekend. There were only about six of us who stayed. We were the ones who lived a little bit farther from campus, and for some reason or another couldn't have gotten home that weekend.

We were all kind of scared, because so many strange things had been taking place in the dorm—noises, things misplaced, just a lot of strange things. So we decided that we were all going to stay in this one room together. That way we could comfort each other; not be scared.

Well, all six of us piled into this room. About one or two in the morning, someone unlocked the door. I was closest to the door, and I remember waking up, looking up, and seeing the silhouette of a person standing there, just looking at us all. I remember just thinking that it was Ms. Chumbley checking on us, making sure that everyone was there in the dorm. She was kinda strict.

I didn't think much about it that night. And they just closed the door very lightly; I could hear them walking away. The next morning, one of the other girls asked if anybody else had seen this ghost-like figure the night before.

I told them that I had. So we went to Ms. Chumbley's room and knocked on the door. She had not yet been awake when we woke her up. We asked her about it, and she told us that she had not been up all night long. She said that she had gone to bed early last night with a headache, and that she had not been awake all night long.

We again searched the dorm and didn't find anything or anyone, but nevertheless the next night we did not get much sleep until all the other girls had come back.

4. "The Ghost of Van Meter"

Van Meter Auditorium was built on the campus of what is now Western Kentucky University in 1910, and it was dedicated in 1911. This historic building, named for Captain C.J. Van Meter, a major contributor to Western in the early years of the twentieth century, housed the administrative offices of the college for fifty years. But for what it is worth, Van Meter Hall is haunted!

Most explanations for the ghost of Van Meter claim that the ghost is that of a man who fell to his death while helping to construct the building. He was standing on a high scaffold and accidentally killed himself when he fell many feet to the ground below.

After Van Meter Auditorium was completed, students who were in the building, even now, and especially at night, would hear a person's footsteps or hear doors slam shut. Yet, they were the only people in the building at the time.

In about 1981, a Mark Twain look-alike came to the campus to give a lecture. So that the impersonator would know exactly when to go on stage, he asked the faculty member in charge of the program to come to him one minute before he was to go on stage. While preparing for the lecture, the faculty member thought that he saw the Twain look-alike standing in the doorway of the entrance to the stage. Thus, he didn't go to the dressing room to get the fellow. After a few minutes of waiting for the Twain look-alike, the faculty member finally went to the dressing room to get him. The actor asked him, "Why didn't you come to get me like I asked you to?"

The faculty member stated, "Because I thought I saw you standing there in the door."

5. "Ghostly Light in the Ceiling"

When I had this ghost-like experience, my roommate was gone for the time being. I was lying on the floor of my dorm room here at Western when this happened. I remember that this strange feeling just took control of me. I felt all tingly. Something was happening to me over which I had no control, and which I had never experienced before. After a few minutes, I saw this strange light hovering over me. I just laid there, frozen, staring at the light. But I wasn't really afraid. Actually, I had a very calm, warm feeling as the light hovered over me.

The light seemed to stay in one place and appeared as though it was just trying to be nice, or to let me know that it was there and would not bother me. I felt like it was an apparition of some kind, but I wasn't scared.

After that escapade, I sat up, very calm and relaxed. My roommate, Mary Ann, returned and I told her what had happened. I think it made her very nervous because we started thinking about past experiences that had happened to us during that semester.

During that time, when something weird happened, we always put the blame on something else. For example, when we would come back to the room, sometimes there would be a strange or eerie feeling there in the room. Often, the clocks would be blinking, or turned off, as if the electricity had gone off, but it hadn't. Objects in the room would be moved from where we left them. For whatever reasons these things occurred, I don't know.

During the spring semester, 1986, I was having many problems, so I moved out of [this particular dorm] to [another.] Some of these things happened only to me, but Mary Anne was going through a very troubled time, too, and was depending on me for support. She and her boyfriend were wanting to get married after only a few dates, and I knew that things wouldn't work out for them.

After I moved out of this dorm that year at Christmas, I felt better. My life took a 360—degree turn for the better.

I can't say that that was the end of everything peculiar happening to me or to her. She had a strange occurrence one evening. She told me that she was in her bathroom when this strange feeling came over her. She was at the sink brushing her teeth when she looked up and saw this girl's figure in the mirror, and a ghostly light beaming over her head. Yet, when she turned around, no one was there.

To this day, I can't go over to that dorm without getting strange feelings when I get to the sixth floor, the floor that she was on when she saw this ghostly figure and the strange light in the background. I can never seem to understand the strange feeling that comes over me, even now, when I think about that.

6. "Ghost Haunts Alpha Gamma Rho Fraternity House"

The brothers of Alpha Gamma Rho tell haunting tales of the ghost of Mr. Elmus Jackson Beale.

Fraternity president Justin Downs, senior from Dover, Tennessee said Mr. Beale built their house during the Depression, and his funeral was held in what is now the fraternity's chapter room. Originally, the room was Beale's bedroom.

"They lowered his coffin outside through the double windows because they couldn't get it down the stairs, and buried him in the yard," Downs said.

"Tulips grow over his grave," said J. Scott McIntyre, senior from Bardwell, pointing to the spot beside the house. "We've tried to dig them up, but they keep coming back."

Footsteps roam the house and lights that were turned off are mysteriously turned back on while attic windows that were securely shut have been reopened by an unseen hand.

Todd Tyler, junior from Arlington, believes he has had a firsthand

experience with Mr. Beale. "I was alone upstairs and heard someone running up the steps," Tyler said, "but no one was there. I had B.R. Coursey
and Chris Kivett get a baseball bat, but we never found anyone."

A couple of brothers claim to have seen or felt Mr. Beale. Downs
recalled a story from several summers ago. He said Stacy Williams, an
alumni, was alone in the house watching television. He heard someone
walk by and then stop in the doorway to ask how he was doing. Williams
did not recognize the voice, and when he looked up he saw only the shadow
of a man.

McIntyre said he had a physical experience with the ghost. "I awoke
one night and couldn't move," he said. "It was like someone was holding
me down."

Marvin Zwahlen, junior from Evansville, has heard footsteps and doors
slamming, and McIntyre backs up his story. "I've heard footsteps come to
my door and then stop," McIntyre said. "No one ever comes in."

7. "Halloween Resurrects Old Stories of Spooks"

Halloween is a time for haunting. . . . Murray State has had its share of
ghost stories. Ghosts have supposedly been found in more than one fraternity house and have been seen silently visiting some of the buildings on
campus.

An article printed in the October 26, 1884, issue of the *Murray State
News* tells of a "friendly ghost" haunting the Delta Sigma Phi house. . . .
Then-president Mike Olson said the ghost would turn on water faucets,
stereos, and televisions when there was no one in the vicinity.

James Thompson, the current Delta Sigma Phi treasurer, confirms
the story. He said that he and his fraternity big brother, Lloyd Taylor, witnessed the happenings. "It happened during Christmas break of 1980,"
James Thompson said. "We were staying here at Christmas and had the
house shut off, due to the cold. When we came downstairs, we found the
water running. There were also lights on in some of the rooms we weren't
using," he said.

Thompson said that he and Taylor were using only one room in the
big house at the time. "One night we went out to eat dinner, so we locked
the room," he said. "When we came back from dinner we found the light
on and the stereo playing." He went on to say that he and Taylor knew that
they had not left them on.

"It's kind of weird," Thompson said. "This is a good-sized old house,
and it makes you wonder who's around the corner."

Thompson stated that he had no clue as to what caused the strange occurrences. "No one claims they were pulling a practical joke," he said. . . .

Thompson said that the apparition is supposedly the ghost of the son of the man who built the house approximately fifty years ago. He said the story says that the child was playing on the roof, fell off, and died. "That's the history as I've heard it," Thompson said, adding that it may be just "a rumor."

Notes

1. Graveyard Ghosts

1. Told by Cindy Morris, Bowling Green, Mar. 28, 1999.

2. Told by Joan Bennett Brockman, Russell Springs, Apr. 22, 1997, to Mary Ann Brockman.

3. Told by Jeffrey Lynn Jessup, Butler County, Apr. 26, 1988.

4. Told by Ronnie Bryant, Tompkinsville, to Mitzi Robertson, Apr. 1974.

5. Told by Julie Elkins, Paducah, to Sherrie Mallicoat, Mar. 29, 1989.

6. Told by Mrs. Prentice Head, Lewisburg, to Mary Kirk Deshazer, Russellville, Jan. 4, 1970. Folklife Archive, Kentucky Library, Western Kentucky University, 1970–60. Hereafter all documents obtained from this archival source are cited as WKU Folklife Archive, plus manuscript number.

7. Told by Vern Louise Baldridge, as learned from her aunt who died in Bonanza in 1949 at age 80. Recorded by William Hugh Jansen, Lexington, 1953. Provided by Robert Rennick, 1999.

8. Told by Doris Breeding, Adair County, to Jeddy Price, 1957. Provided by Robert Rennick.

9. Told by Lois Tackett, Amba, Floyd County. Provided by Robert Rennick.

10. Told by Elizabeth Hall, Monroe County native, Feb. 25, 1999.

11. Told by Jane Smith, Tompkinsville, Mar. 25, 1999, who learned the story from her husband, Sam.

12. Told by Jeremy Ray Logsdon, Munfordville, Apr. 1999.

13. Told by an unidentified man to Cornelius Allen, date unspecified. Leonard Roberts Collection, Southern Appalachian Archives, Berea College. Further references to this archival source are cited as L. Roberts Collection, Berea College.

14. Told as a true story by Taylor Tedders, Knox County, to Mary Ellen Cobb, 1956. L. Roberts Collection, Berea College.

15. Told by Mrs. E.C. Threlked, Warsaw, to Jeanette Rider Sallee, May 1955. L. Roberts Collection, Berea College.

16. Told by Vernon Noffsinger, ca. 1988, and Ruby Noffsinger, July 2, 1999, to their daughter-in-law Judy Noffsinger.

17. Told by Henrietta Morgan Ross, Barlow, Ballard County; published in the *Paducah Sun,* Oct. 27, 1985, sec. D. Provided by Special Collections, Murray State University Library, hereafter referred to as MSU Library.

18. Written by Jeannie Brandstetter and published in the *Paducah Sun,* Oct. 21, 1990, 1D, 7D. Provided by Special Collections, MSU Library.

19. Ibid.

20. Information and story provided by Betty H. Seay, Bloomfield, Aug. 16, 1999.

21. Told by Mary Ann Gentry, Carrollton, Sept. 6, 1999.

22. Told by Nancy Gray, Madisonville, to Jim Francis, 1956(?). WKU Folklife Archive.

2. Disappearing Ghosts

1. Told by Kristina Watt, Chalybeate Springs, Nov. 19, 1998.

2. This apparitional visitation was experienced and later written about by Susan M. Clay, Lexington, as an entry in a ghost story contest sponsored by the *Louisville Evening Post,* date unspecified. She won the second prize for this entry. Copies of the newspaper story and a letter from Mrs. Clay, dated Mar. 8, 1876, describing the strange visit, were provided by Claire McCann, manuscript librarian, Margaret I. King Library North, University of Kentucky, Lexington.

3. Told by Sena Smithhart, Henderson, to Jim L. Clark, Feb. 21, 1969. WKU Folklife Archive, 1971–8.

4. Told by Dennis Elzey, Louisville, to Donna Sue Smith, Oct. 28, 1972. WKU Folklife Archive, 1972–509.

5. Told by Kelly Hazelrigg, Louisville, 1989.

6. Told by Dan Townsend, Elizabethtown, to Aaron C. Clark, Lexington, Mar. 30, 1989.

7. Told by Donna Mitchell, Mayfield, 1989.

8. Told by Connie Vaughn, Glasgow, to Terri Vaughn, 1989.

9. Told by Stan Lemaster, Daviess County, to journalist Jim L. Clark, Feb. 7, 1969. The account was later published in Lemaster, *Authentic Kentucky Ghost Stories* (Owensboro, Ky.: privately published, 1970).

10. Told by Etta Wade, Russell Springs, to Denishia Miller, Sept. 16, 1972. WKU Folklife Archive, 1972–388.

11. Told by Jerome Sparks, Nashville, Tennessee, to Tim Nichols, Apr. 11, 1989.

12. Told by Ada Mae Cromwell, Frankfort. Bayless Hardin Collection, Kentucky State Library, Frankfort.

13. Told by Elbert Cundiff, Irvington, Nov. 2, 1997.

14. Story told initially by Opless Walker, Cookeville, Tennessee, Oct. 1992; revised by the author.

15. Told by Delinda Wilcoxson, Greensburg, to Todd Hagemeyer, Toledo, Ohio, Mar. 23, 1989.

16. Told by David Baker, Louisville, to Amanda Davis, Apr. 9, 1989.

17. Told by Hugh Williams, Tompkinsville, to Ruth Montell, 1959.

18. Told by Fannie Anders, Burkesville, 1960.

19. Told by James Pearson to Linda Crafton, Lewisburg, Apr. 1999.

20. Ibid.

21. Told by Jerry Goodnight, Bowling Green, to Anne Zoellner, Bowling Green, Apr. 8, 1989.

22. Told by Paula W. Atkins, Greenville, June 20, 1999.

23. Told by Gertrude Laing, Frankfort, to James W. Stephens Jr. Initially published in the *Kentucky Folklore Record* 9, no. 1 (Jan.–Mar. 1963): 10.

24. Told by Della Mae Allen, Magoffin County, to Tolbert Montgomery, 1960. L. Roberts Collection, Berea College.

25. Told to Elbert Douglas by Robert Tye; the tale was told to Tye about 1937. L. Roberts Collection, Berea College.

26. Told by Rena Evans, Middlesboro, to Chesney Busseni, 1957. L. Roberts Collection, Berea College.

27. Told by Jerry Goodnight to Anne Zoellner, Apr. 8, 1989.

28. Told by Tammy Taylor, McCreary County; included in Sara McNulty, *If These Hills Could Talk* (Ky.: privately published, 1996), 9.

29. Written by Berry Craig and published in the *Paducah Sun*, Nov. 21, 1980, page number unavailable. Provided by Special Collections, MSU Library.

30. Told by Obie Van Cleave, Logan County, to Angela Van Cleave, Aug. 10, 1999.

31. Told by Mary Ann Gentry, Carrollton, Sept. 6, 1999.

3. Ghostly, Unnatural Sounds

1. Told by Elbert Cundiff, Irvington, Nov. 7, 1997.

2. Told by Dona Dubree, age 82, Persimmon community, to Robert Curtis, May 1970. WKU Folklife Archive, 1970–64.

3. Told by Greg Evans, Paducah, to Kevin Reynolds, Apr. 6, 1989.

4. Told by Sally Cambron, Henderson, Apr. 4, 1989.

5. Told by Shirley Smith, Glasgow, to Michael J. Smith, 1972.

6. The original version of this story was published in James A. Shope, "Ghost Tales and Legends, Mainly from Eastern Kentucky" *Kentucky Folklore Record* 12, no. 2 (1966): 55.

7. Told by Golda Swain, Paintsville, May 21, 1971. Provided by Robert Rennick.

8. The account of her brother's death, as told by Golda Swain, Paintsville, May 21, 1971, and submitted by Robert Rennick, was revised in some instances by the author in order to shorten the account.

9. This account was provided by Melissa Hammers, Bowling Green, Jan. 1999.

10. Recorded from an unidentified person in the 1930s by Mary E. O'Malley,

member of the Federal Writers Project (hereafter cited as FWP). Archives, Kentucky State Library, Frankfort.

11. This story is one in the series of ghost stories collected by Stan Lemaster, Frankie Hager, and Ralph Dorris, and published in the *Owensboro Messenger-Inquirer*, Oct. 24, 1968. Lemaster later published the story in *Authentic Kentucky Ghost Stories*, 11.

12. Told by Leonard F. Cole, Rothwell, Menifee County, early 1960s. Copy provided by Robert Rennick, Jan. 1999.

13. Told by Thomas "Bud" Montgomery, Auxier native, Floyd County, 1971. Copy provided by Robert Rennick.

14. Told by Mrs. Leslie Adkins, Boyd County, to Irene Howard, 1959. L. Roberts Collection, Berea College.

15. Told by Angeletta Adams Fields, Letcher County, 1969. L. Roberts Collection, Berea College.

16. Told/collected by Faye Brawner, Bardstown, May 1955. L. Roberts Collection, Berea College.

17. Told by Arnold Taylor to Tammy Taylor, May 1996, then published in McNulty, *If These Hills Could Talk,* 6.

18. Told by John Holder, Allen County, to Pat McGuffey, fall 1969. WKU Folklife Archive, 1970–10.

19. Told by Muriel M. Scott, West Paducah; published in the *Paducah Sun,* Oct. 27, 1985, sec. D. Provided by Special Collections, MSU Library.

20. Told by Obie Van Cleave, Logan County, to Angela Van Cleave, Aug. 10, 1999.

21. Told by Mary Ann Gentry, Carrollton, Sept. 6, 1999.

4. Headless Ghosts

1. Told by Ronnie Bryant, Tompkinsville, to Mitzi Robertson, Apr. 1974. WKU Folklife Archive, 974.

2. Told by Elvin Byrd, Clinton County, to M.B. Byrd, Sept. 1974. WKU Folklife Archive, 1974–88.

3. Told by Watson Dubre to his daughter, Misty Dubre, Metcalfe County, date unspecified.

4. Told by Cordell Dishman, Sunnybrook, Wayne County, Dec. 1978.

5. Told by his Grandfather Bunch to Michael W. Bunch, Glasgow, Nov. 1998.

6. Told by Willie Bunch, 1992, to his daughter and grandson, Juanita Anderson and Mark Anderson, who submitted the account in writing, Mar. 1992.

7. Told by Thomas "Bud" Montgomery, Auxier, Floyd County, Apr. 18, 1971. Provided by Robert Rennick.

8. Told by Thomas "Bud" Montgomery, Auxier, Floyd County, Apr. 18, 1971. Provided by Robert Rennick, Jan. 1999.

9. Told by Della Hammond, Hardwick, Wayne County, Aug. 26, 1973. Provided by Robert Rennick.

10. Told by Jeremy Ray Logsdon, Munfordville, Apr. 1999.

11. Told by Mrs. Hall to Iva Lewis, 1959. L. Roberts Collection, Berea College.

12. Told by Shirley Nelson, Alva, to Betty Rae Reynolds, 1957. L. Roberts Collection, Berea College.

13. Recorded by Lilliam Palmer Moore, Bath County, 1959. L. Roberts Collection, Berea College.

14. Told by Jean Hurd to Tina Roberts, McCreary County, May 1996; published in McNulty, *If These Hills Could Talk*, 15.

15. Told by Obie Van Cleave, Logan County, to Angela Van Cleave, Aug. 10, 1999.

5. Animal Ghosts

1. Written account by James Pleasant, Madisonville, Apr. 1988.

2. Written account provided by Jennifer Hansel, fourth-grade student, Wallins Creek Elementary School, Harlan County, 1997.

3. Written account provided by Judy Hensley Bryson, teacher, Wallins Creek Elementary School, Harlan County, 1997.

4. Written account provided by Sean Payne, Nov. 18, 1998.

5. Told by Karl Brown to Terrence Cecil, Owensboro, Apr. 4, 1989.

6. Told by Rusty Young, Shepherdsville, to Sherrie Mallicoat, date unspecified.

7. Told and written by Amy Spalding, Bardstown, Apr. 25, 1989.

8. Told by Robert Wilkie to Stan Lemaster, Frankie Hager, and Ralph Dorris, who collectively published the account in the *Owensboro Messenger-Inquirer*, Oct. 1969. Lemaster later published a slightly revised version in *Authentic Kentucky Ghost Stories*, 4.

9. Told and written by Katie Bunch, North Hopkins High School, Madisonville, 1993.

10. This story was first collected by Ralph Dorris and Stan Lemaster, and edited by Frankie Hager for publication in the *Owensboro Messenger Inquirer*, Oct. 24, 1968. In 1970 it was included in Lemaster, *Authentic Kentucky Ghost Stories*, 16.

11. Told by Muriel Wurts, Summitt, Boyd County, to Linda Tufts, Ashland, 1960. WKU Folklife Archive, 1960–132.

12. Told by Malcolm Moore, Louisville, to Robert Morris, Jan. 1954. WKU Folklife Archive, 1954–133.

13. Told by Clay Pearce, Gamaliel, Monroe County, 1954.

14. Told by Elvin Byrd, Clinton County, to M.B. Byrd, 1974. WKU Folklife Archive, 1974–88.

15. Told and written by Elbert Cundiff, Irvington, Nov. 5, 1997.

16. Ibid. For this tale, Cundiff used his grandfather's account.

17. Told by Ronnie Bryant, Tompkinsville, to Mitzi Robertson, Apr. 1974.

18. Written by Melissa Hammers, Bowling Green, Jan. 1999.

19. Told by Lois Tackett, Amba, Floyd County. Provided by Robert Rennick.

20. Told by Lucy Robert Coe, Fountain Run, 1960.

21. Ibid.

22. Written by Mabel Martin, London. Provided by Shirley Caudill, Mar. 1999.

23. Told by Jim Bowles, Rock Bridge, Monroe County, July 1961.

24. Told by Jasper Stapleton, Greenup County, to James E. Porter, 1961. L. Roberts Collection, Berea College.

25. Told by Lawrence Spradlin, McCreary County, to Sebrina Campbell, May 1996, then published in McNulty, *If These Hills Could Talk,* 14.

26. Written by Katie Thomas, staff writer, Murray State University, *Murray State News,* Oct. 26, 1995, 7. Provided by Special Collections, MSU Library.

6. Scary Tales

1. Told by Buddy Walters, Louisville, to Mike Brannik, Oct. 1972. WKU Folklife Archive, 1972-216.

2. Told and recorded by anonymous persons.

3. Told by James Pleasant, Madisonville, Apr. 1988.

4. Told by Tennille Stockdale, Bedford, 1998.

5. Told by Nora Farnon, Louisville, Oct. 1972.

6. Told by April Richardson, place and date unspecified.

7. Told by Penny Flener, Warren County, to Mary Kirk DeShazer, Dec. 11, 1969. WKU Folklife Archive, 1970-60.

8. Told by Susan Price, Louisville, Oct. 1972. WKU Folklife Archive, 1972-509.

9. Told by James Pleasant, Madisonville, Apr. 1988.

10. Told by Linda Reeves, Louisville, Oct. 1972. WKU Folklife Archive, 1972-509.

11. Told by an unidentified person, Oct. 1972. WKU Folklife Archive, 1972-439.

12. Told by Stanford Moore, Tompkinsville, to Sharon Walden, Karen Walden, and Steve Hurt, Dec. 1974.

13. Told by Lettie Durham Moore, Greensburg, to Terry Durham Wells, Oct. 1972. WKU Folklife Archive, 1972-471.

14. Told by Elvin Byrd, Clinton County, to M.B. Byrd, Albany, 1974. WKU Folklife Archive, 1974-88.

15. Told by Stanford Moore, Tompkinsville, to Sharon Walden, Karen Walden, and Steve Hurt, Dec. 1974.

16. Told by Ruth Ann Birge, Temple Hill, 1959.

17. Told by W.E. McCoy of Webster, Breckenridge County, to Lloyd B. Claycomb, Feb. 13, 1956. WKU Folklife Archive, 1991-81.

18. Told by Dennis Elzey, Louisville, to Donna Sue Smith, Oct. 28, 1972. WKU Folklife Archive, 1972-528.

19. Told by Terri Carpenter to Emily Farley in the early 1990s.

20. Told by Billy Luckert, Louisville, Nov. 1970. WKU Folklife Archive, 1970-13.

21. Told by Dwight Adkins, Oct. 1989.

246 Notes to pages 112-136

22. Told by Dawn Freeman, Western Kentucky University, Fall 1998.

23. Ibid., Oct. 1998.

24. Told by John Masters, Louisville, to David Sutherland, 1971. WKU Folklife Archive, 1971–64. A similar version was told by Leslie Calk, Fleming County, to Lee Goodpasture. WKU Folklife Archive, 1972–531.

25. Told by Melissa Hammers, Bowling Green, Jan. 1999.

26. Told by Hazel Montell, Rock Bridge, Monroe County, 1961.

27. Told by Elizabeth Hall, Monroe County native, Feb. 25, 1999.

7. Hanged or Murdered Persons' Ghosts

1. Told by Elbert Cundiff, Irvington, Nov. 7, 1997.

2. Told by Lisa Edwards, Irwin School student, Clinton County, 1993.

3. Told by Betty Powell, Caneyville, to Louise Hellstrom, Apr. 6, 1989.

4. Told by Raymond L. McClure, Grayson County, Oct. 14, 1993.

5. Told by Jerry Goodnight, Bowling Green, to Anne Zoellner, Apr. 8, 1989.

6. Told by Margaret A. Cooper, Sturgis, to Laura Wellington, Jan. 21, 1989.

7. Told by Laura Wellington, Marion, Jan. 28, 1989, as a personal experience.

8. Told by Nancy M. Berley, Columbia, to Ben Gordon Berley, Apr. 26, 1978. This legend was also featured in the *Columbia Daily Statesman*, Oct. 31, 1975. WKU Folklife Archive, 1978–40.

9. Told by Vanessa Ross, Versailles, to Denise Goodrich, Mar. 25, 1989. Bedford is a pseudonym for the real name.

10. Told by Joseph Britt, place unknown, May 1955. A feature story in the *Madisonville Messenger*, date unavailable, by Hall Allen, corroborates much of the above account, as does Susan Hollis's interview with Rev. John Taylor, Madisonville, Oct. 25, 1986. Although no one accuses Mandy's stepson outright of being the person who killed her, the charge is implicit in accounts of the incident. WKU Folklife Archive, 1986.

11. Recorded by Penny Vance, Hodgenville, 1970. WKU Folklife Archive, 1970–13.

12. Told by Cynthia Riley, Louisville, to Margaret Austin, Bowling Green, 1973. WKU Folklife Archive, 1973–19.

13. Told by Hattie Edwards, Powersburg, Wayne County, Dec. 30, 1992.

14. Told by Patti, a fourth-grade student at Wallins Creek Elementary School, Harlan County, 1997.

15. Told by Jennifer Hansel, fourth-grade student, Wallins Creek Elementary School, Harlan County, 1997.

16. Told by Steven Bender, Henderson, date unspecified.

17. Told by Rita Sparks, teacher, Clinton County Elementary School, Albany, 1992.

18. Told by Bobby Runyon, Glasgow, May 1972, to Mike Brannik.

19. Collected by W.T. Beadles, member of Graves County FWP during the 1930s. Provided by Robert Rennick, Jan. 1999.

20. Told by Matty Fry to Pat Satterfield, both of Whitley County, 1958. Copied from Leonard Roberts, "Spirits in the Mountains," *Kentucky Folklore Record* 23, nos. 3–4 (Oct.–Dec.1977): 62.

21. Told by James Leach to Helen E. Mink, both of Rowan County, 1960. Copied from Roberts, "Spirits in the Mountains," 62–63.

22. Told by Herman Adams, Clay County, to Leonard Roberts, 1957. Copied from Roberts, "Spirits in the Mountains," 63–64.

23. Told by B.H. Vanover, Pikeville, June 22, 1999.

24. Ibid.

25. Told by Tabitha Hibbs, Madisonville, Feb. 27, 1989.

26. Told by Nancy Gullette, High Bridge, to Paul K. Lane. Initially published in the *Kentucky Folklore Record* 10, no. 2 (Apr.–June 1964): 26.

27. Copied from Lemaster, *Authentic Kentucky Ghost Stories*, 18.

28. Told by Flavis Wells to Geneva Cox, Morgan County, Aug. 26, 1960. L. Roberts Collection, Berea College.

29. Told by Dicie Hurley, Majestic, Pike County. L. Roberts Collection, Berea College.

30. Told by Mrs. Harry Moran, Hopkinsville, to William Moran, Dec. 26, 1953. L. Roberts Collection, Berea College.

31. Told by R.B. Brooks to Barbara Clay, May 1957. L. Roberts Collection, Berea College.

32. Told by Mrs. E. McClanahan, Freeburn, Pike County. L. Roberts Collection, Berea College.

33. Told by Dorothy Major, Greenup County, 1960. L. Roberts Collection, Berea College.

34. Told by Mrs. Lewis Good, Hopkins County, 1950. L. Roberts Collection, Berea College.

35. This account was abstracted virtually verbatim from two 1871 newspaper reports (Glasgow and Bowling green) and from oral interviews with James Howard Young, July 1999, Clayton Barrett, and Vergie Glass. The latter two were conducted by Kay Harbison, Apr. 1969.

36. Told by an anonymous person to Carolyn Bryant, McCreary County; later published in McNulty, *If These Hills Could Talk,* 16.

37. Told by Mrs. Marshall Murphy, Cumberland County, to Judy Baise, Feb. 13, 1970. WKU Folklife Archive, 1973–15.

38. Copied verbatim from an article published in the *Nelson County Record,* late 1890s. Provided by local historian Dixie Hibbs, Aug. 31, 1999.

8. Ghosts of Persons Killed Accidentally

1. Told by Ann Curtis, resident of central Kentucky, Nov. 5, 1988.

2. Told by an anonymous person, age 18, Bowling Green, to Laura Wellington, Jan. 21, 1989.

3. Told by Veronica Gibbons, Vine Grove, Meade County, Apr. 27, 1989.

4. Told by Cindy Hibbs Rowley, Sturgis, to Laura Cooper, May 1, 1978. WKU Folklife Archive, 1978–201.

5. Told by Elbert Cundiff, Irvington, Nov. 9, 1997.

6. Told by Ethel Merriman, Harrodsburg, to Molly Tuttle, Apr. 13, 1973. WKU Folklife Archive, 1973–48.

7. Told and written by Ronald Lafferty, Munfordville, Dec. 2, 1985.

8. Told by Sandy Martin, Madisonville, date unspecified.

9. Told by a Prestonsburg Community College student, Apr. 1971. Provided by Robert Rennick.

10. Told by Sammy Lawson, Meade County, to Nelson Graham, Jan. 5, 1968. WKU Folklife Archive, 1965.

11. Told by an anonymous person to Tammy Taylor, then published in McNulty, *If These Hills Could Talk*, 6.

9. Ghosts of Suicide Victims

1. Told by Margaret Cooper, Sturgis, to Laura Wellington, Marion, Jan. 21, 1989.

2. Told by Kimberly McConnell, North Hopkins High School, Madisonville, to his teacher, Linda Nance, 1992.

3. Told by Kim Birmingham, student at Western Kentucky University at the time this account was recorded, date unspecified.

4. Told by Steve Breitenstein, Jeffersontown, 1989, with real names changed.

5. Told by Donna B. Stinnett, Oct. 28, 1996.

6. Told by Caroline Kimmule, Anchorage, to Jackie Crouch, Mar. 27, 1989.

7. Told by Jeffrey Lynn Jessup, Apr. 26, 1988.

8. Told by Shanda Hall, student at North Hopkins High School, Madisonville, 1992.

9. Told by Elbert Cundiff, Irvington, Nov. 2, 1997.

10. Told by Tobey Crafton, Lewisburg, to Linda Crafton, Apr. 1999.

10. Weird, Eerie, Ghostly Lights

1. Told by Charles Evans, Somerset, to Don Brake, Oct. 25, 1978. Provided by Pulaski County Library.

2. Told by Evelyn Stephens, Tompkinsville, to Ruth Montell, July 1957.

3. Told by Michael W. McDougal, Sept. 10, 1985.

4. Told by Darcy Smith, Crossville, Tennessee, 1994.

5. Told by James Harrison, Glasgow, to Kim Harrison, Apr. 4, 1989.

6. Told by Thomas S. Brizendine, Greenville, 1996.

7. Told by Elbert Cundiff, Irvington, Nov. 2, 1997.

8. Told by James R. Keltner, born 1893, Adair County, to Glenn Groebli, 1972. WKU Folklife Archive, 1971–82.

9. Told by Rhonda Reynolds, Russellville, to Mary Kirk DeShazer, Dec. 11, 1969. WKU Folklife Archive, 1970–36.

10. Told by Laura Cooper, Sturgis, 1978. WKU Folklife Archive, 1978–201.

11. Told by Willie Montell, Rock Bridge, Monroe County, 1961.

12. Ibid. Montell told the tale to a group of community listeners.

13. Written by Cindy Cassady, niece of Maxie Martin, Edmonton, June 16, 1999.

14. Told by Mrs. Joe Buckley, Hopkinsville, to William Moran. L. Roberts.

15. Told by an anonymous person to Amy Rollins, McCreary County, May 1996; published in McNulty, *If These Hills Could Talk,* 7.

16. Told by Faye Perry, McCreary County, May 1996; published in McNulty, *If These Hills Could Talk,* 9.

17. Told by Ronald Dobler, Morehead, July 13, 1999.

11. Haunted Spots on the Landscape

1. Told by Jason Bergman, Madisonville, to Linda Nance, Sept. 1992.

2. Told by Penny Davis, Edmonson County, to Joseph Metzger, date unspecified.

3. Told by Alice Baird, Williamsburg, date unspecified.

4. Told by Marnie Dishman, Campbellsville, to Veronica Gibbons, Vine Grove, Meade County, date unspecified.

5. Told by Phillip Paul Walker, Somerset, Mar. 27, 1989.

6. Told by Karen Bartlett to Alice Jackson, Browder, Kentucky, Oct. 1972. WKU Folklife Archive, 1972–100.

7. Told by Claude LeCharite, Lexington, to Aaron C. Clark, date unspecified.

8. Told by Dolly Downs, Blowtown, Grayson County, to Percy Ray Downs Jr., Nov. 7, 1971. WKU Folklife Archive, 1972–73.

9. Told by Haley Cornett, Leslie County, to Virginia Sizemore, Sept. 1972. WKU Folklife Archive, 1972–489.

10. Experienced and told by Emily Farley, Bowling Green, Mar. 1987. The insert about the two school teachers was provided by an anonymous contributor, July 2, 1999.

11. Told by Allen Barber, Bowling Green, to Joseph Metzger, Oct. 1988.

12. Told by Sammy Lawson to Nelson Graham, Jan. 5, 1968.

13. Told by Deborah K. Bunch, Glasgow, Oct. 1979.

14. Copied verbatim from a newspaper Associated Press article "Around Kentucky," written by Berry Craig. Permission to publish granted by Craig and the AP.

15. Told by Nadine West, Morgantown, Feb. 18, 1999.

16. Told by Elizabeth Hall, Feb. 25, 1999.

17. Ibid.

18. Written Mar. 1999, by Marybelle Duff, Somerset, on the basis of numerous oral accounts provided by her students and other local residents.

19. Written by Sheila Crump, Park City, Apr. 16, 1999, based on information provided by Gloria Crump and park rangers Henry Wood and Tim Cash.

20. Told by Stephen L. King, Bowling Green, June 2, 1999.

21. Told by Mrs. John Rice, Sitka, Johnson County, to Helen Belcher, 1961. L. Roberts Collection, Berea College.

22. Told by Leota F. Sherman, 1960. L. Roberts Collection, Berea College.

23. Told by Bill Epperson, place and date not specified. L. Roberts Collection, Berea College.

24. Told by Carol Ann Dickson; initially told by her grandfather. L. Roberts Collection, Berea College.

25. Told by Brown Logsdon, Radcliffe, Hardin County, to Francis Daugherty, June 16, 1959. D.K. Wilgus Collection, Southern. Appalachian Archives, Berea College.

26. Told by Jerry Taylor to Tammy Taylor, May 1996; published in McNulty, *If These Hills Could Talk,* 12.

12. The Vanishing Hitchhiker

1. Told by Deborah K. Bunch, Glasgow, 1976. WKU Folklife Archive, 1979–16.

2. Reconstructed by Veronica Gibbons, Vine Grove, Meade County, from version told to her by Lowell Gibbons, Vine Grove, date unspecified.

3. Told by Peggy Sue Hibbs, Sturgis, to Laura Cooper, 1978. WKU Folklife Archive, 1978–201.

4. Told by Karen Bartlett to Debbie Robinson, Vicki Berry, and Sam Bramlett, 1972. WKU Folklife Archive, 1972–100.

5. Told by Mary Kirk DeShazer, Russellville, 1970. WKU Folklife Archive, 1970–60.

13. Felt Presences of Ghostly Beings

1. Told by Wanda Pyles, Lexington, to Becky Toomey, Mar. 26, 1989.

2. Told by Jackie Reeves, Louisville, to Jennifer Miller, Mar. 21, 1989.

3. Told by Tabitha Hibbs, Madisonville, Apr. 8, 1989.

4. Told by Vickie Birge, 1989.

5. Told by Terri Roberts to Cathy A. Caldwell, Somerset, Apr. 2, 1989.

6. Told by Kenny Stewart, 1988.

14. Civil War Ghosts

1. Based on an account provided by journalist Mayleigh Bucher in the *Richmond Register,* Oct. 25, 1984.

2. Told by Hattie Edwards, Powersburg, Wayne County, Dec. 30, 1992.

3. Ibid.

4. Told by Phillip Henderson, Somerset, to Phillip Walker, Dec. 1987.

5. Told to Larry Freeman, Franklin, on the basis of information provided him by his uncle, Dink Freeman.

6. Told by Lynn Feese, Glasgow, to Kim Harrison, Apr. 4, 1989.

7. Told by Phillip Walker, Somerset, Dec. 1987.

8. Copied from Stan Lemaster, Frankie Hager, and Ralph Dorris, "Civil War Era Ghost Walks through House at Livia," *Owensboro Messenger-Inquirer,* Oct. 24, 1968. Published subsequently in Lemaster, *Authentic Kentucky Ghost Stories,* 13.

9. Told by Jim Bowles, Rock Bridge, Monroe County, 1961.

10. Told by Janice E. Jakeman, Canmer, Hart County, Apr. 26, 1999.

11. Told by C.L. Stewart, Louisa, Kentucky, to Mrs. Dan Carter, 1930s, as part of the FWP.

12. Told by Mrs. Sam Dizney, Wilmore, to Paul K. Lane. Initially published in the *Kentucky Folklore Record* 10, no. 2 (Apr.–June 1964): 27–28.

13. Told by Carrie Neikirk, Somerset, Nov. 3, 1987.

14. Copied verbatim from an article published in the *Kentucky Standard,* Sept. 12, 1901. Provided by local historian Dixie Hibbs, Aug. 31, 1999.

15. Haunted Dorms, Fraternities, and Sororities

1. Told by Debby Szczapinski to Lonnie Bailey, places unknown, Apr. 10, 1983.

2. Ibid.

3. Ibid.

4. Unidentified source.

5. Told and submitted by Elizabeth Courtney, Oct. 1988.

6. Written by staff writer Jennifer Potter, *Murray State News,* Oct. 26, 1995, 7. Provided by Special Collections, MSU Library.

7. Written by staff writer Michael Powell, *Murray State News,* Oct. 28, 1988, 1B, 5B. Provided by Special Collections, MSU Library.

Index to Counties

("Ghosts of Crying Babies"), 221
("Ghostly Civil War Rider"), 221–22
("Ghostly Noises")
Webster, 142 ("Ghost at Zion Brick Church")

Whitley, 40 ("The Disappearing Ghost"),
136–37 ("A Killing")
Wolfe, 226–28 ("The Civil War")
Woodford, 127 ("Lewis Bedford's Ghost")

Index to Cities, Towns, and Other Locations